A CHURCH NOT MADE
WITH HANDS

Also by Michael Roden

Jesus and Ourselves: An Alternative Understanding of Christianity

Songs of the Morning: Meditations for Healing and Self-Knowledge

A CHURCH NOT MADE WITH HANDS

CHRISTIANITY
AS SPIRITUAL EXPERIENCE

MICHAEL RODEN

HAMPTON ROADS
PUBLISHING COMPANY, INC.

Cover design by Tiffany McCord
Cover digital imagery © Photodisc/GettyImages,
icon © Fotosearch. All rights reserved.

Scripture quotations are from the Revised Standard
Version of the Bible (unless otherwise noted), copyright
© 1946, 1957, and 1971, by the Division of Christian
Education of the National Council of Churches of Christ
in the U.S.A. Used by permission.

Hampton Roads Publishing Company, Inc.
1125 Stoney Ridge Road
Charlottesville, VA 22902

434-296-2772
fax: 434-296-5096
e-mail: hrpc@hrpub.com
www.hrpub.com

If you are unable to order this book from your local
bookseller, you may order directly from the publisher.
Call 1-800-766-8009, toll-free.

Library of Congress Cataloging-in-Publication Data

Roden, Michael, M. Ed.
  A church not made with hands: Christianity as spiritual experience /
Michael Roden.
      p. cm.
  Summary: "Uses Jesus' own words to strip away centuries of dogma and reveal the
underlying mysticism of the New Testament and Christian spirituality"--Provided by
publisher.
  Includes bibliographical references (p.   ).
  ISBN 1-57174-448-7 (5-1/2x8-1/2 : alk. paper)
  1. Mysticism--Biblical teaching. 2. Bible. N.T.--Theology. I. Title.
  BS2545.M9R63 2005
  230--dc22

                        2005020048

ISBN 1-57174-448-7
10 9 8 7 6 5 4 3 2 1
Printed on acid-free paper in Canada

Dedicated to my father,
Jerry L. Roden.

Contents

Acknowledgments

Thanks to my editor, Frank DeMarco, and to all at Hampton Roads who helped in the publication and distribution of this book.

The Inner Temple

A voice cries:
"In the wilderness prepare the way of the Lord,
make straight in the desert a highway for our God.
Every valley shall be lifted up,
and every mountain and hill made low;
the uneven ground shall become level,
and the rough places a plain.
And the glory of the Lord shall be revealed,
and all flesh shall see it together,
for the mouth of the Lord has spoken."

—Isa. 40:3–5

The House of God

One of the earliest saints in Christianity, Stephen, said that "the Most High does not dwell in houses made with hands" (Acts 7:48).

The passage is a way of saying that reality is not limited to that which humans can comprehend, and God cannot be limited to the things of the

Earth. Though God is worshiped in temples and churches (actually, it was primarily in houses in earliest Christianity), His Reality exceeds anything in the world, for the world is characterized by limited comprehension. The Apostle Paul spoke similarly in Athens:

> The God who made the world and everything in it, being Lord of heaven and earth, does not live in shrines made by men (Acts 17:24).

Though He is originator and creator of all that lives, God lives beyond the world. Nothing in the limited experience of the human being is sufficiently great or expansive to hold the fullness of God. The body's eyes cannot see it, and the limited conceptual mind cannot get around it. The body's eyes see only bodies, the conceptual mind thinks only of itself, and the self is caught up in a circle closed upon itself. The sense-oriented tend to look for the soul, if they look for it at all, in places it could not possibly be.

And so Paul states emphatically:

> Do you not know that you are God's temple and that God's Spirit dwells in you? (1 Cor. 3:16).

God is Spirit, and so must His House be Spirit. This is why Paul can say in another of his letters that the true Self, like the true dwelling place of God, is "a house not made with hands, eternal in the heavens" (2 Cor. 5:1). No earthly tent—neither the body nor the physical church—is required to worship God in the Spirit, though it might indeed be helpful, for it could serve as a vehicle to the nonsensory understanding of oneself as a Spiritual Being with God.

Paul indicates that this mystical household of God heals the desolate part of the human condition marked by separation, alienation, and estrangement:

> So then you are no longer strangers and sojourners, but you are fellow citizens with the saints and members of the household of God, built upon the foundation of the apostles and prophets,

Christ Jesus himself being the cornerstone, in whom the whole structure is joined together and grows into a holy temple in the Lord; in whom *you are also built into it for a dwelling place of God in the Spirit* (Eph. 2:19–22, my italics).

"No longer strangers and sojourners," no longer estranged from God, and therefore no longer suffering the broken condition, the individual is made holy as "a dwelling place of God in the Spirit." The Christian's belief and the Christian's experience, as we shall see, was that "Christ was faithful over God's house as a son. *And we are his house* if we hold fast our confidence and pride in our hope" (Heb. 3:6, my italics). The soul that has been raised to God is Godlike, and belongs in the house of God.

The phrase "household of God" suggests family and inseparable closeness. Members of this household share everything because they share God through His Spirit. They are family in the truest sense. Their close relationship with God is forever part of them. The resulting state of oneness and relationship reaches out to the holy depths within others to form even on Earth a holy spiritual community created of Spirit and participated in through the Spirit.

Mark 14:58 mentions Jesus saying he would build a temple "not made with hands," and that, in saying this, Jesus is referring to himself as the church, eternal wherever he may be. This is how believers are encouraged to think, not only of Jesus, but also of themselves. They themselves are the House of God. Great holiness (because great inwardness) is presented here as the heart of Christianity. In the Lord, the Christian is a dwelling place of God in the Spirit. "We are his house." Early believers came to know that God lived within them, and they in God, through the supernatural and spiritual presence of Christ.

Mysticism and Religion

Mysticism is not only the study of a religion's spiritual and internal side, but it is also the study of the depth and potential of humanity in general. Mysticism is the deep psychological foundation of religion, the meeting place of mind and soul. It asks: Just what is the fundamental, most essential—and therefore most human—human condition?

To the mystic, that which lives within the soul is infinitely greater than that which seems to surround. There is a void outside if there is a void inside the self, where the House of God should be. The darkness within the self is the closed-in effect of alienation, the state of being broken and unfixable, unable to feel integrated, stranger to God and to everyone—utterly, physically, mentally, and emotionally alone. It is the state, as Paul said, of being "strangers and sojourners." The light, which would be the light of communion and of reunion, lights first the inner person. From initial conviction, experience emerges, so that those who once seemed to live in darkness, meet now in light, all seeing together the glory of the Lord as it is revealed (Isa. 40:5). It is upon seeing the world bathed in light and glory that the soul truly begins to know itself.

Religion has always been for me the most individual of matters. It was significant to me as a matter ultimately between my potentially most authentic conscience and the dynamic Spirit that reveals itself according to how authentic I can be. Though I attended the Catholic Church as a young man, it cannot be said that I am a product of the Church. I have always preferred to stay out of my own way. The Spirit within me brought its subtle light to my attention, revealing what to focus on, revealing the light of inner truth. To this day, I appreciate the church, more for the food it provides the Spirit within than for some of the tangential doctrines it would ascribe to "belief."

Many believers seem to have a need for ritual. Ritual can have its place, but it is not necessary for everyone. Some people crave unpredictability and spontaneity in praise of God. It is good for the soul to experience spiritual presence as often as possible; it would be better to live within it. Whatever charms we might find in ritual can help to evoke such experience of glittering treasure all around, yet the church does not often allow its rituals to transcend themselves. The depth behind the ritual always begins and ends in the individual.

I have drawn from church experiences something that stirred my heart, spoke to my soul from deep within, as if I were transported to a personal significance beyond any particular beliefs, rituals, and theologies. I recall feeling a transcendent sense of the sacred in my earliest church experiences, and I remember carrying these experiences home with me and making them my own.

It is difficult to put into words an experience of the sacred. This experience we have not only *within* ourselves, but more accurately *as* ourselves. It is preverbal and postverbal, just as the Self is. Words cannot shed real light on it. For me, the sacred was not confined to the sacred place, to spiritual stories and words, to ritual mystery, to flickering candlelight and stained glass, to majestic music and incense in the air. It was in *me* and it gave a new sense of who I was.

The images and symbols of Christianity have a way of passing themselves by to emerge within a more universal truth. They will always be significant insofar as they are vehicles to the heights of spiritual knowledge. The paradox of religion is that the more personal and individual our religion, the more cosmic and universal it is bound to be. That which affects a person most deeply is bound to have a deep effect on others as well. In this book, I show that this was the case with Jesus and his followers.

Religion in the West has for many years been becoming more privatistic, that is, more private, more individualized. It is common for individuals to talk of being spiritual rather than religious, and what is meant is that the heart's intuition seeks a deeper connection with Spirit than that cited from law books. What is desired, deeply, is more than rules to follow and rituals to enact, more even than theologies to believe. What is wanted is *experience* of the truth of religion rather than a dance around its surface aspects. To experience this, there may be a need for transformation, from the inside out. The heart wants deeply to invest its trust. Though it has been called a secret and hidden wisdom, Christianity reveals the true inner Self.

The Christian religion is rooted in pure spirituality and mysticism. It is not primarily a legalistic religion; it is a spiritual religion. It leads the soul to God through extraordinary means. In mystical Christianity, there are not so much rules to guide behavior as there are calls to inner spiritual guidance and spiritual experience. As Jesus says in the Gospel of John:

> But the hour is coming, and now is, when the true worshipers will worship the Father in spirit and truth, for such the Father seeks to worship him. God is spirit, and those who worship him must worship in spirit and truth (John 4:23–24).

In this book, I examine, through passages from the early biblical records, what early Christians meant when they said that "God is spirit, and those who worship him must worship in spirit and truth." These words represent the highly personal or individual nature of religious experience that even the most transcendent Christianity is meant to emphasize.

"Religion" is a way of *returning* to God. It originated in life-changing individual experience, that place where individuality loses itself and regains itself in encounter with another and a burgeoning sense of union with the Divine Being. The initial sacred experiences of religion prove themselves to be transformers of life. They fan out from one individual to others, and some of these other individuals organize group experiences. These groups of individuals reinforce one another, not so much in their intellectual beliefs or practices as in their spiritual essence. The transformation occurring within the early Christians was described as eternal treasure and gifts of the Spirit. They found ways to open themselves up so as to be in service to the living, leading Spirit and in service to one another. Experience of the Spirit continued through the centuries to change individuals and their purpose, but this experience has seldom received its due as having lain at the foundation of the religion.

The main teachings of Christianity are intended to convey the experience by which they are given life. As such, they are not so much doctrines to be followed, nor beliefs to be adhered to, but rather portals in the heart of the person to the internal world of Spirit, where God abides. Hidden within and beneath the doctrines and beliefs of the original Christians is their true meaning and significance: God is near, very near, and He can be experienced in Spirit just as one may know oneself.

The teaching, then, must infiltrate the depths of the heart to be effective. It must be entirely of the Spirit, imparted directly through spiritual experience and revelation. Ps. 51:6 says: "Behold, thou desirest truth in the inward being; therefore teach me wisdom in my secret heart."

To *know the Lord,* in the Old Testament as in the New, is to enter into personal and universal communion with Him, to have a personal relationship with the Universal. Early Christians practiced that God manifests Himself directly, through His Being. His light fills the innumerable rooms of His mansion in the soul; joy is the estate of those who live there in togetherness with Him.

Freedom through Joining

If knowledge of God is significant in Christianity, then the mystical, spiritual, and personal element of *direct experience* of Divine Presence is central. Evidence of such direct experience is abundant in the New Testament texts. Historian of mysticism Bernard McGinn states that:

> from the start Christianity contained a mystical element, or at least that central themes in the new religion were capable of a mystical interpretation in the sense that they could be understood and appropriated by later believers in such a way as to lead to special modes of direct awareness of the divine presence of Jesus.[1]

It is precisely this direct awareness of Divine Presence that the individual in connection with Spirit encounters. It is within the believer as much as it is in God. God placed it there in order to live there. If His House is within the individual, whether by His Son, His Spirit, His Love, His Sacred Heart, His Presence, then how pure must the individual be! How holy the sacred inmost heart in which God abides!

And how self-sufficient. Yes, the individual—no longer alone—interacts with others, but now on the basis of forgiveness and right relationship, not on old grounds dictated by self-interest and separation. He interacts with them, not so much as creature to creature, but more as mind interacts with mind and heart with heart. It is the internal Spirit that joins them and leads them in the way of God. And so Saint John tells believers:

> the anointing which you received from him abides in you, and you have no need that any one should teach you; as his anointing teaches you about everything, and is true, and is no lie, just as it has taught you, abide in him (1 John 2:27).

The teaching is to "abide in him," which is an experiential teaching rather than an intellectual one. The anointing is the Spirit. This sense of joining personally and intimately with the sacred Presence is the essence of mysticism.

The self-sufficiency of the Christian was from earliest times experienced as an effect of one Spirit. This Spirit is at once more personal and more universal than the sense of ordinary fragmented consciousness. What psychological terms did the earliest Christians have to describe this? The effect of the Spirit is a sense of Oneness, for which the individual self begins to strive. Yet the self is transformed here. The original Christians spoke of being reborn by Spirit and made aware of a new Self in the light of union with Christ. They spoke of universal love and joy and of "the fullness of God." The terminology of deep psychological transformation is central to Christianity, making Christianity a religion of Spirit more than of laws, rituals, or beliefs.

Intellectual belief can very well remain an act of the conscious ego, but Spirit is a gift that opens to God. True understanding comes "not by earthly wisdom but by the grace of God" (2 Cor. 1:12). One truly understands insofar as one opens to the depths and heights and breadth of the experience of Spirit. One truly possesses righteousness and its peace insofar as one is open to receive the Spirit.

When Paul says that the believer becomes a new creation in Christ, he envisions a complete transformation of the inner world. Paul prays for the individuals to whom he speaks:

> that according to the riches of his glory he may grant you to be strengthened with might through his spirit in the inner man, and that Christ may dwell in your hearts through faith; that you, being rooted and grounded in love, may have power to comprehend with all the saints what is the breadth and length and height and depth, and to know the love of Christ which surpasses knowledge, that you may be filled with all the fullness of God (Eph. 3:16–19).

To "know the love of Christ which surpasses knowledge" is "to be filled with all the fullness of God." It is an experience of spiritual fullness that the seeker is called to, brought to light by the transcendence of spiritual encounter and experience.

This sense of personal transformation that Paul commends to believers underlies and permeates the scriptures of early Christianity. "Do not be conformed to this world but *be transformed by the renewal of your mind,*" Paul says in Rom. 12:2 (my italics). What is more purely psychological than the renewal of the mind? He also speaks of believers' "having the eyes of your hearts enlightened, that you may know what is the hope to which he has called you, what are the riches of his glorious inheritance . . ." (Eph. 1:18). What is more spiritual than having the eye of the heart enlightened? The Scriptures burst like a ripened vine with spiritual experience because that is what waters them and gives them light as it once gave them seed.

Adherence to the status quo of cognitive and emotional equilibrium can work as a defense against spiritual transformation, a way of keeping things on the surface, so as not to enter oneself and so as not to be transformed. Humans are almost instinctively afraid of what they might find, suspicious of the depths of their heart. There seems to be curtain after curtain of dark surface fear holding the mind from entering itself and going deeper, which might spark a change to authentic being. Rituals to practice and doctrines to believe may serve to divert focus from a complex of fear that diminishes not only our relationships, but also ourselves. Not acknowledging the fear makes it more paralyzing still. Philosopher Jacob Needleman writes:

> Down deep, we have been forbidden by fear and vanity to ask the questions of the heart. Thus we grow up settling for the answers of the personality.[2]

A gift of the Spirit, mystical experience can lead one past layers of surface fear, closer to God and to one's authentic Self. Each step of the way can draw one ever closer to the recognition that life is already united with God.

Spiritual experience is entered individually, but in the end it leads to unity and harmony. The depth of the experience makes it universal, part of the greater condition of humanity. It reveals knowledge of another reality, a greater harmony with God and His Creation, a transformed sense of Self and Relationship.

It might be said that this individual yet universal mystical experience found in Christianity represents *freedom*. Certainly, there is a release of mind and of heart that accompanies it. Jesus and Saint Paul both spoke against the tendency of religion to emphasize laws and behavioral rules—that which is *outside* a person—over spirit and spiritual experience—that which is *inside*. That which was within the heart and mind was of ultimate significance; the words of the prophets and scribes were most useful as they pointed beyond themselves to the life-changing experience within.

Spiritual experience is the way toward fully realized understanding of everything—God and Self included. Paul writes:

> For now we see in a mirror dimly, but then face to face. Now I know in part; then I shall understand fully, even as I have been fully understood (1 Cor. 13:12).

One does not know oneself until one knows oneself with God. The relation cannot be fully described or explained in words, but it can be pointed out and partaken in.

1

Internal Experience in Christianity

And the ransomed of the Lord shall return,
and come to Zion with singing;
everlasting joy shall be upon their heads;
they shall obtain joy and gladness,
and sorrow and sighing shall flee away.

—Isa. 35:10

Hidden Christianity

Hidden away in the most interior reaches of Christianity is a powerful means of transformation of mind and heart. The Apostle Paul wrote to the Corinthians that he had not given them the full spiritual teaching of Christ because they had not been ready to receive it:

> But I, brethren, could not address you as spiritual men, but as men of the flesh, as babes in Christ. I fed you with milk, not solid

food; for you were not ready for it; and even yet you are not ready, for you are still of the flesh (1 Cor. 3:1–3).

In this passage, Paul notes the existence of two forms of Christianity: one for the surface world, those "of the flesh," and another for those who are open to full spiritual understanding. In the same letter, he says that, although he had previously come to them preaching the simple creed "Jesus Christ and him crucified" (1 Cor. 2:2):

> Yet among the mature we do impart wisdom, although it is not a wisdom of this age or of the rulers of this age, who are doomed to pass away. But *we impart a secret and hidden wisdom of God,* which God decreed before the ages for our glorification. . . . [A]s it is written,
> "What no eye has seen, nor ear heard,
> Nor the heart of man conceived,
> What God has prepared for those who love him,"
> God has revealed to us through the Spirit. For *the Spirit searches everything, even the depths of God* (1 Cor. 2:6–7, 9–10, my italics).

Paul declares that he and his helpers "*impart a secret and hidden wisdom of God*" among "the mature," or those who are made aware of the depths of God in the Spirit. As you shall see throughout this book, the mystical (literally, "hidden," in the sense of internal and spiritual) element is prevalent in the earliest sources we have of Christianity, the books of the New Testament. Why it has not been more fully accepted by Christians is a matter for debate.

The human being has a dual aspect. Much of what it means to be human, in fact the entire inner world, is hidden beneath the surface. Behavior provides information, but cannot represent everything about a person. Intention rules behavior, and the mind chooses what will be valued before it decides what will be done. Thoughts are as real as the person who thinks them, so that there is a hidden reality within.

Paul says that the secret and hidden wisdom of Christianity is "*revealed to us through the Spirit,*" that is, through spiritual experience. Experience that transforms not only behavior but also intentions, not only intentions but also *will,* and not only desires but also deep-rooted *values* is truly mystical experience. The Christian religion for Saint Paul was no mere guide to behavior; it was in all its aspects a spiritual initiation into "the depths of God," from which point guidance would naturally step in. Jesus, too, indicated that he saw the heart of religion and the soul of humanity as abiding behind and beyond behavior, beyond rules and laws, beyond creeds and beyond religious authorities, as it rose all the way up to God Himself from Whom it came.

Where would such a secret wisdom be hidden? In inner chambers that could be accessed only by the Holy Spirit, in parts of the self known only to God. Where are *"the depths of God"*? No one can say because words cannot convey these depths, the mind cannot think of them from outside them; but one may experience some at least of the depths of God through His Spirit. Jesus is portrayed as informing his disciples that there was a truth they could not yet bear to hear, but he promised them that "when the Spirit of truth comes, he will guide you into all the truth" (John 16:12–13). Early Christians believed in Spirit because they experienced it. They believed in allowing themselves to be led and changed by the Spirit into the all-knowing, all-encompassing truth that they in Spirit shared with God.

There is great experience "hidden" in Christianity, spiritual experience of a kind that can transform lives and heal that which is broken. But it is not hidden well. Though such experience cannot be described fully in words, spiritual experience suffuses the scriptures and earliest teachings of Christianity. In fact, the New Testament's mysticism is so pronounced that it would be difficult *not* to emphasize it.

The Bible is filled with keys to the spiritual and living kingdom of God. The Gospels show Jesus to be charismatic, compassionate, intelligent, prayerful, and miraculous, yes, but, even more, connected with God through a shared Spirit and reaching out to touch the world through this same Spirit. The evidence we have shows that Jesus was led by experience of Spirit. Paul and John and other New Testament writers show his transformative effect to have been as far-reaching as it was deep. These early Christians shared experience of the Spirit and felt connected with Christ and with God in being so directly associated.

Jesus showed himself to be spiritual from the depths of his very being.

It was as if he lived in a different dimension, though he partook of this one, asking others to join him as he walked the countryside, entering tiny villages, speaking out about the experience, healing through it, teaching by it, giving out of his internal abundance of it. The Apostle Paul is so spiritual in his essence that he was seen by first- and second-century Christian Gnostics to be a conduit to the spiritual world. The Evangelist John emphasized in his gospel and letters a transcendent spiritual Knowledge and Love.

The Depths of Mystical Experience

Mysticism is the experiential element of religion. Though it begins in the internal spiritual experience of the individual, the ultimate destination for *mysticism* is the Sacred Presence of God. Mystical Christianity holds that there is a way to experience the Heart of God, for full moments, in the midst of daily existence. It suggests that human beings were *created* to experience the spiritual presence of God, to live within it, to share it and so their joy.

Until such inner sense of joining occurs, according to the psychology inherent in mysticism, the human being will feel incessantly empty and deeply dissatisfied. Underneath thousands of everyday feelings and opinions, there may somehow be sensed access to a lost state of beatific original grace. Mind and heart sense that they have fallen from it because they cannot conceive of such grace, though they are told by religion and sometimes by intuition that it is available. But such grace—the illumination from God—can be more truly known through experience of it than from any exposition.

How does one open to spiritual experience? It involves becoming *more* individual but also *more than* individual. The individual accedes to his or her heart for guidance, for an inner light to shine upon the way. The interior world takes on more importance than the world outside and, with grace, everything inside and out begins to shine with supreme significance. God must be near enough to know. Prayer and meditation become means of communicating with God and reaching Him directly. Simply *being* with Him becomes a way of knowing Him, and knowing Him becomes a way of sharing more deeply in Being.

With habituation to the light found in spiritual experience, the individual's mind and will begin to change. Oceanic love may be experienced: the deep, joyous, and tranquil manifestation of a more universal will. Such emotion filling heart and mind changes them as well, fully and by degrees. Visions may be seen and divine revelation may be given, like a message from out of time. There is in mystical experience a sense of joining and at the same time of transcendence of everything except the Being that is God. Only from Him there is no hiding. He infuses all, for He is the eternal originator and sustainer. Inherent in the holy encounter with Him is a strong sense of fullness that matches the heart-deep hunger for it and a sense of having at last surmounted usual lostness for certainty, certainty in the sacredness of everything because of perfect holiness in God.

Simply to learn of the possibility of internal transformation can bring great benefit to the individual. Mystical experience gravitates to the individual who opens to it even slightly. But to give it its practice is to become prone to experience, to enter it more readily. This need not be done through rituals. The process is to let fear and guardedness fall away as the peace and purpose of being spiritually guided settles in.

The process toward achieving experience of this union is not exactly difficult, but it may be long and intricate. Lex Hixon states that sensitivity to the guidance of spirit is indirectly imparted:

> Becoming sensitive to the guidance of spirit is learned from the genuinely ecstatic members of the community, not by rational instruction but as a child learns its own native language. The learning process is gradual, often imperceptible.[1]

Training in spiritual experience makes use of everything, from direct instruction to indirect example, from ritual to reading to prayer, from the repetition of religious precepts to the practice of forgiveness in the larger world. It uses life itself. It can make use of any moment, of any situation, as it shines its light into the mind. As Jesus said:

> there is nothing hid, except to be made manifest; nor is anything secret, except to come to light (Mark 4:22).

To seek the mystical experience is to respond to "the high calling of God in Christ Jesus" (Phil. 3:14). It is to enter the evidence of something more real than surface appearance, as if there were another world hidden behind this one. To seek the mystical experience is to ask in prayer, with Jesus, for the oneness of God. Any open mind can be a vessel for this experience.

We live in a context of experience always. Even in our ordinary existence we live in a context of psychology and inner experience. Our life and our self are internal, a series of psychological, emotional, and spiritual experiences, states, and conditions. We define ourselves and our relation to our world and to others from within a context of inner experience. All our motivation, intentions, hopes, dreams, plans, and goals are determined by what we value. The mind set free would soar to the highest truth, the heart flow from the deepest value. "For where your treasure is, there will your heart be also," says Jesus in Luke 12:34.

Internal spiritual experience is at least as solid and certain a foundation for truth as anything else. Even though "there is no descriptive term comprehensive enough in meaning to express the entire content of experience as such,"[2] for the Christian who is guided by the Holy Spirit of God, which connects and keeps close, not a question would remain that need be answered. That is because the Spirit "searches everything, even the depths of God." It lives in God, and through this Spirit, so do those in whom it once was hidden.

That which remains when an individual encounters God is pure Being, pure Is-ness, pure experience, pure knowledge, perfect togetherness. One's connection to the other realm lies in such an encounter, one's salvation depends on it, one's being *is* it. The lesser self recedes, and an all-encompassing one replaces it, through an encounter with God through the Spirit.

Laying bare the deep psychological and spiritual elements involved in spiritual experience, Rudolf Otto has commented on "the immediately-felt certainty, the axiomatic quality and universality of religious conviction"[3] that could not be explained in normal human terms. The purpose of religion is not to classify and categorize—and therefore further divide—but rather, to join, to personalize and universalize. The sense of sacred experience is that which makes religion transcendent and therefore gives it its ultimate purpose.

Spiritual and mystical experience lies as much in the domain of psychology as of religion. Sometimes the deep psychological and even spiritual component is missed by theologians and scholars who see religion more along the intellectual lines of philosophy or along the historical lines of human society. Yet internal experience is where religion begins and ends.

As Christianity became institutionalized and organized in hierarchical fashion, its emphasis shifted toward conformity of belief, and away from the open individuality of spiritual experience. Historian Helmut Koester states that the proverbial "keys of the kingdom" were originally intended for an experientially based Christianity of individuals. "The power of the keys was originally designed to bolster offices which became typical of the major heresies: the prophet in Montanism, and the teacher in Gnosticism."[4] The offices of *prophet* and *teacher* were replaced with *priest* and *bishop* as Christianity began to value secular power and bureaucracy rather than individual experience of the sacred.

Spiritual experience is the great equalizer of persons. It ends the illusion of separation from God and from others. It "changes every assumption about the purpose of human existence."[5] It reveals individuals to be the same on the most fundamental psychological level, a rock-solid foundation on which to build a house in eternal creation.

J. G. Davies notes that there is little evidence of gatherings for worship in earliest Christianity other than baptism and the Eucharist or ritual of shared meal.[6] The New Testament indicates that early Christians met mainly to share experience, and this could be done somewhat informally. Baptism was more than a ritual; it was an initiation into spiritual experience and to converted identity, and the Eucharist or Holy Communion was the remembrance and restoration of spiritual presence through union. Origen believed that because of their grounding in spiritual experience, "in the life to come, the direct vision of God will make the eucharist and the Bible, which mediate the vision of God to us on earth, unnecessary."[7] There were great internal processes at work in earliest Christianity, interior processes passed down through tradition and deepened by the readings, but the best way to uncover internal processes is to experience them.

If mysticism lies at the heart of a religion, how could religion become overwhelmingly legalistic, so as to derive nearly all its direction from external sources? Wilfred Cantwell Smith explains it thus:

If one's own "religion" is attacked, by unbelievers who necessarily conceptualize it schematically, or all religion is, by the indifferent, one tends to leap to the defence of what is attacked, so that presently participants of a faith—especially those most involved in argument—are using the term in the same externalist and theoretical sense as are their opponents.[8]

Not that theology is inherently bad, but Smith contends that a religion becomes external to the individual when one is defending it against those perceived to be outside it. Human defensiveness and rationalization concretize religion into a thing among things, outside the self, though it began as an affiliation of mind and heart with soul. But externalized religion becomes schematized, whereupon it begins to tend to personalized interests such as self-perpetuation, rather than the good of all humankind, thus neglecting the heart.

Smith goes on to describe the process of the externalization of the Christian religion, saying that Christian discussion began to center:

not on transcendent realities, and not on faith, man's relation to them, but on the conceptualization of both, and on man's relation to those conceptualizations: on believing.[9]

Dogma—systematized teaching—comes from the conceptualization and *concretization* of constant transcendent realities. The mind limited strictly to intellect can avoid the real subject for what seems like forever. And when the mind seeks to defend itself with intellectual propositions and moral proclamations, it is difficult for the Spirit, pervasive as it is, to break through. The individual becomes ensnared in the thicket of his or her own system. Intellectual assent to beliefs and teachings may come to take the place of the presence inherent in spiritual experience. But intellectual assent to the propositions of the intellect does not tend to the integration of the self both within itself and interpersonally with others as spiritual experience does.

Paul offers spiritual experience as the sine qua non, as *the* essential characteristic of the Christian: "Any one who does not have the Spirit of Christ does not belong to him" (Rom. 8:9).

Experience in the Spirit is the great transformation hidden in the heart of Christianity. Paul tells his spiritual brethren that "you are not in the flesh, you are in the Spirit, if in fact the Spirit of God dwells in you" (Rom. 8:9). In other words, one belongs to another order of Being when the other-worldly Spirit overwhelms heart and mind.

Risking externalization then, how is *mysticism* to be defined? It is the quest for Being. To take refuge in God through Union with God is that which the mystical heart seeks beyond all else. In mysticism, the presence of the Lord abides within the individual, and can therefore be experienced in the surrender of everything else. (It is more precisely true that the experience experiences itself; not even the individual is mediator of this experience.) In mysticism, the Church in all its splendor and the Bible in all its glory are ultimately signposts to the true glory and splendor inherent in union with God.

The highest, deepest mysticism always involves a realization of union with God. Mystics as individuals choose no longer to experience themselves as separate from God; they strive above all else to bridge the sense of distance between themselves and God. Their drive becomes to find the highest state of Being and to remain there. Paul speaks of this universal motivation and its resolution in experience in God:

that they should seek God, in the hope that they might feel after him and find him. Yet he is not far from each one of us, for "In him we live and move and have our being" (Acts 17:27–28).

According to the great Christian mystic Meister Eckhart, the mystic longs to be nearer to God than he is to himself: "My being depends on God's intimate presence."[10] The mystic wants above all else to be with God. How better to do so than to give oneself to Him in communion and find in Him the holiest of homes?

Andrew Louth speaks of the passionate significance of union with God to the mystic:

The mystic is not content to know *about* God, he longs for union with God. "Union with God" can mean different things, from literal identity, where the mystic loses all sense of himself and is absorbed into God, to the union that is experienced as the

9

consummation of love in which the lover and the beloved remain intensely aware both of themselves and of the other.[11]

God reveals Himself through the deepest parts of the soul, mind, and heart to the one who can search only for Him. In the completion of true encounter, the self is for a second erased and for days left changed in the experience of union with God.

Mysticism speaks of a relationship with God that goes beyond self yet remains within oneself. Not only is there a subjective world within, but there is an objective world beneath that, a world of truth and certainty, a world of transcendent knowledge and all-encompassing love. There is, at the very base of the subjective mind, something eternally real and true, spoken of in religious terms as Spirit, as union with God, as the kingdom of God, as eternal life.

Some forms of mysticism emphasize the heart of devotion or of helping service, and some emphasize the intellect put to new use as steward of the spirit. The way of action, or service to others, is important and personally fulfilling; through service to others, we help ourselves. Lofty transcendent ideas are not only interesting for the mind to contemplate, but can also lead to a lofty state of transcendence. Yet what matters most is not the particular emphasis, for in truth all forms work together, so that each contains at least a kernel of the others. What matters most is union with God. The mystical *heart* wants deeply to *feel* this, the mystical *mind,* to *know* it.

Mysticism depends on the evidence of objective internal experience. Systems that may grow from this life-giving clarity cannot replace it, so care must be taken that they do not overgrow it. In mysticism, there is an inner reality that seems more real to the deeper mind and heart than does the external world. Mysticism reveals evidence of the interconnectedness behind the multiplicity of which the world seems made. It is as if multiplicity, for all its ever-sprawling array, is just a surface that hides the core truth of Being. The individual will never be deeply and personally satisfied with even hundreds of thousands of things as long as his or her inner heart, will, and mind crave only one.

Mystical experience is reached through the gradual transcendence of that which hides underlying union. The mystical process generally proceeds from purification (the overcoming of self-interest), through illumination (encounter with God), and finally to union (sharing the Being of God).

Mysticism sees no self separate from God. It is concerned wholly with the more ultimate reality within Self at one with others and God. It arrives with a new concept-free, definition-defying identity and purpose in God.

Therefore, with mystical experience comes a sense of liberation, of having escaped from a transitory, limiting reality. Time no longer seems like bondage, ending in death. Time, in fact, begins to take on the quality of eternity. The world opens to a new Earth illumined by the internal sun of Heaven.

Mystical individuals of all traditions share something, not because they believe the same doctrines (though they do end up with doctrines that point in a similar direction), but because they share and experience the same Spirit. The objectivity within their subjectivity transcends all particular subjectivity and even individuality. They share a longing for reunion with God, and the spiritual means to attain it.

Spiritual experience is the great equalizer, allowing young and old alike to experience the perfect serenity of perfect oneness in innocence. The mystic takes to heart what Joel prophesied (and what Peter repeated in Acts 2:14–18):

> And it shall come to pass afterward, that I will pour my spirit on all flesh; your sons and daughters will prophesy, your old men shall dream dreams, and your young men shall see visions. Even upon the menservants and maidservants in those days, I will pour out my spirit (Joel 2:28–29).

For the mystic, revelation is not entirely of a bygone era. The prophets spoke of this eternal outpouring. The Spirit flows freely, where it wills. The purpose of all revelation is to illuminate the present, transcending time to resume the Self in the present where God is.

Christianity gains richness with a renewed emphasis on spiritual experience. Its roots are deeper and more universal than often thought. It offers a vital experience along with its doctrines, rituals, and systems. Were there no great experience at the heart of Christianity, God would be only a concept or a system of concepts handed down through the generations. Mysticism reveals the life in God and in the holy Self He created. For the mystic, such life is shared through experience: "O taste and see that the Lord is good! Happy is the man who takes refuge in him!" (Ps. 34:8)

Mystical experience offers radical change in the here and now. Heaven is more tangible, Earth more tranquil. What could be more real than moments spent in union with God? Whom God fills, He fills completely, with knowledge of primordial equality. God and world are transposed, so that now God is first, and the world reposed. All that is, rests in God. There is a spontaneous rejoicing. "Happy is the man who takes refuge in him!"

Mysticism places experience of God at the center of the self, and so also at the center of all worship and of every doctrine. Highest mysticism adheres to one fundamental truth, that the experience of God, being possible, should imbue all things with its holy light. Experience should be shined in every corner, like turning on a light. Jesus said:

> Is a lamp brought in to be put under a bushel, or under a bed, and not on a stand? For there is nothing hid, except to be made manifest; nor is anything secret, except to come to light (Mark 4:21–22).

Spiritual experience casts new light on the world, and renders vision otherworldly. The world is saved by being made holy through spiritual vision. It is the same world, now shined through with the light of God. The world shines with God, when His Spirit enlightens the eye of the heart.

Christianity, like mysticism, begins with the inner individual and ends when that individual is returned to Oneness. No one can really mediate this for a person. No particular group can claim exclusiveness on Oneness. It must be an individual and profoundly personal experience, and yet it rises well beyond any sense of separate self.

There is one spiritual reality, given many names. Nothing else approaches the experience of the Oneness of all being in God. All things are gathered within it. To experience God is to experience a new sense of Being in God. The sense of separation is succeeded by the Self at one with all things through God.

Psychology and Spiritual Experience

Mysticism has always played a small but deep part in Christian tradition. In earliest Christianity and its texts, it is indeed plentiful, as we shall see. It has enriched the religion because it has taken hold of individuals who found the Spirit of God within themselves. For such mystical individuals escaping the constraints of dogma and even creaturehood down through the centuries, mystical or spiritual experience was the inspiration behind the highest and deepest traditions of their religion.

Yet mysticism does not stop at tradition. The mystical individual knows that spiritual experience cannot be contained. Tradition might help to evoke it, but tradition is also prone to cover it. Tradition carries the seed, but the full flowering is always "hidden" or inherent within the individual, yet beyond the individual. It is immanent yet transcendent, personal yet universal.

I have mentioned the psychological nature of the spiritual experience. There is more than hope, and more than what generally passes for faith, in the mystical experience. There is a sense of *knowing* when one participates fully in what is known by the unlimited mind. The mind limited to conceptualization finds intellectual aspects of a religion easier to grasp than the experiential, but the experiential aspects restore the entire mind. Mind begins to know itself as more than the intellect, and the Self is again more than the individual.

Spiritual experience is mystical or hidden because it eludes endeavors to grasp it intellectually. It escapes any classification system and category. This is why psychologist William James speaks of it as being ineffable—unspeakable and unknowable in ordinary human conception. Mystical experience is not comprehensible to the ordinary state of mind; a new self or consciousness is needed to comprehend it. James' well-known quote regarding mystical experience stresses its difference from ordinary consciousness:

> Our normal waking consciousness, rational consciousness as we call it, is but one special type of consciousness, whilst all about it, parted from it by the flimsiest of screens, there lie potential forms of consciousness entirely different.[12]

Psychology was not a named field of knowledge until the late 1800s when Freud and William James began their practices. But various psychological states and entirely different states of consciousness were known in the ancient world, as psychologist John A. Sanford states:

The reality of the inner world was also known to the people of the New Testament. The demons and angels, principalities and powers, dreams and visions that throng the pages of the New Testament bear testimony to the conviction of the early Christian that conscious life was immersed in a sea of spiritual reality. This same conviction that there was a realm of nonphysical reality that was experienced in nonsensory ways continued for several hundred years and dominated the early formative centuries of the Christian faith.[13]

So spiritual experience and therefore subjective psychology were part of Christianity's origins, even if they could not be systemized as such. And although strictly speaking the discipline of psychology did not yet exist, the study of the mind has always existed. Something had to account for these experiences, and in the Bible they are often expressed in poetic terms that, in their attempt to symbolize something beyond words, seem to carry their own supreme logic and reason.

Psychologists also speak of mystical experience as a direct way of knowing, often called intuition. Dr. Arthur J. Deikman quotes philosopher Henri Bergson saying that there is:

> a deep distinction between two ways of knowing a thing. The first implies going all around it, the second entering into it. . . . [A]n absolute can only be given in an intuition, while all the rest has to do with analysis.[14]

Deikman points out that intuition for the philosopher Plato was knowing "more than we should" because it bypasses ordinary rationality based on sensory experience.[15] The same was true for Spinoza:

> Spinoza's definition of intuition is closest of all the philosophers' to that of mystical science. . . . This highest knowledge he termed intuition, something that grows out of empirical and scientific knowledge but rises above them. In essence, it is Knowledge of God.[16]

14

The mystic has found a way to know God directly. The mystical experience has as much to do with the psychology of sacred relationship as it does with that of the individual. Mystical experience, being the meeting place between God and Self, is also the meeting place or final destination of psychology, religion, highest philosophy, and even science.

Some philosophers and psychologists wonder whether "the mystical state of consciousness is more basic" than "the waking state."[17] As stated, the mystical state of consciousness seems more basic and fundamental. Philosopher Jacob Needleman expresses the nature of the difference between these two realities:

> In myself and in the whole of nature there is a reality and an appearance. The reality is freedom, mind, the realm of divinity; the appearance is mechanism, materiality, necessary connection without ultimate purpose. Incommensurate realms—that is to say, the realm of freedom and mind exists on a scale incommensurate with all the activities and efforts of my ordinary mind and self.[18]

To experience spiritual experience is to experience a state of mind more *real* than ordinary consciousness, the yardstick of reality being in the experience itself.

Mysticism has always infused fountains of depth psychology and spirit into Christianity.

> The word *mystica* came into Christianity by way of the famous late fifth-century Syrian monk, Pseudo-Dionysius, who wrote the mystical classic, *Mystica Theologia.* For him, mysticism involved the secrecy of the mind or that trans-conceptual state of consciousness which experiences God as a ray of divine Darkness.[19]

The influential Pseudo-Dionysius (whose *Mystical Theology* was written circa 500) as well as the medieval mystical classic *The Cloud of Unknowing* championed the *via negativa,* the negative way in the practice of mysticism. This negative way was the process of the mind rejecting (or negating) as too limited and too human every thought and attribute of God, in order to come to an experience beyond conceptualization. Neither

God nor the soul's experiential relationship with Him can be articulated; God transcends any attribute we have for him. Within this nonconceptual experience, beyond the self, beyond the world, God has been hidden.

Contemporary historian of mysticism Bernard McGinn observes that a strain of Judaism in the centuries immediately preceding Christianity was moving away from seeing God's presence as being confined to the Temple in Jerusalem, "and therefore to possibilities of divine-human encounter outside traditional religious structures."[20] Mystical experience is, at its highest, just such an encounter between individuals and God. John E. Smith states:

> If experience is understood as encounter, there is no difficulty whatever in supposing that a reality can be ingredient in experience while also transcending—in the sense of not being identical with—that experience.[21]

Smith goes on to write that:

> It is sometimes thought that approaching religion through experience means a denial of what has been understood in the Christian tradition as revelation. On the contrary, experience understood as encounter is always disclosure of reality transcending the one who experiences. . . . Experience properly understood requires that some place is made for encounter, for the experiencing self to meet what is other than itself, whatever that "other" may turn out to mean.[22]

Early Christians seized upon these "possibilities of divine-human encounter." They experienced in their transcendence of self a new Self, because even individual experience is revealed at its core to be relational: encounter with another Being.

The basic conflict within the self, say the Christian texts, is between inner and outer, light and darkness, spirit and flesh. A choice is put before the individual as to which is more meaningful, with consequences as to which self will be followed and which world will be seen. It is characterized as an urgent choice because it straddles two opposing *ways of being.*

Human beings are trained to see along the horizontal axis, the world spread out before their physical eyes, and yet real vision takes place along the vertical axis, the Self that rises out of the world in order to find another with whom true communion might occur. Mysticism allows the human being to see what is above and beyond the world and self of the world, even to make this above and beyond one's own reality.

Mysticism is a way of following Saint Paul's proscription to "not be conformed to this world but *be transformed by the renewal of your mind*" (Rom. 12:2, my italics). To be so transformed, he says elsewhere, is to be glorified in the Divine. As such, to be renewed is to be reborn. It is to be liberated in the Spirit from the intrinsic limitations of the world. Paul speaks of his own experience as taking him well beyond any physical limitation, saying he was "caught up to the third heaven—whether in the body or out of the body I do not know, God knows" (2 Cor. 12:2). It was his mystical experiences that helped make Paul what he was, and which led to the loftiest of his transconceptual thinking.

The psychological process of mysticism is a paradoxical one to the poor intellect that remains confined to sensory-based premises. It sometimes takes a long time to get to something so exquisitely simple. Though perhaps our experience is not yet strong and does not soar, simply to acknowledge and to take responsibility for the emptiness within is to stand at the brink of a sense of fullness. It is the increasingly convincing nature of Spirit, through experience, that makes the believer believe. For a few, there are sudden transformative experiences, openings to vision or to revelation. For others, there is a subtle shedding of light through the windows of the soul. One common factor seems to be that each type seeks to maintain singleness of intention and purpose in heart: The mind is set on God, the heart fixed on Him. Sanford states of accepting Jesus' parables of the kingdom of God:

> A person who takes his or her "heart" seriously ultimately arrives at the kingdom, for it is when we consciously accept the inner world that the possibility for wholeness emerges.[23]

First comes simple acknowledgment of the inner world, and then it must be allowed to unfold in the heart or center of one's being. Time is given in order that the heart may increasingly accept guidance from intuition and from timeless Spirit. The depths of being are eventually experienced to glow with God, Who dwells in the heart.

In mysticism and in Christianity, the inner world awaits recognition, calling from within even as the wayward mind directs its sights outward. To allow this inner world to reintegrate the mind is to begin to feel whole. Mysticism seeks only openness to the possibility of highest spiritual experience to learn firsthand what it is. Ultimately, to have a great sense of purpose, some kind of deeply unifying inner experience is required.

I have mentioned that in mysticism there is an active search, but there is also a natural inner unfolding. There is an original intention for unification and then a letting go of the means toward that intention, so that it might find its own way, so that unity might find itself. The intention is kept in mind, while faith stirs the fire of the heart to see us through the dark empty night and into the brilliant light of full experience. Intention becomes fulfillment, as that which was before conceived conceptually and imperfectly becomes more and more that which truly *is.*

To access the psychological capacity of intuition, an individual decides against conscious planning. In a subconscious way, a person learns to follow the inner call rather than the outer. One must, as Jesus advocates, take the second place, humble oneself in regard to the world in order to devote oneself to a higher truth. Much of this work is, by definition, effortless. Jesus also advises that one be willing to lose oneself in order to find oneself. (See chapter 8 for an exposition of how this sense of fullness is found in emptiness.) This exchange of selves is necessary because, as Jung states; "Our present day consciousness is a mere child that is just beginning to say 'I.'"[24]

Prayer for Experience

For the Christian mystic, to know Jesus is to encounter him, and to encounter him involves following him, which involves knowing oneself deep in the Spirit, as he did. Spirit unfolds inside even while the individual is preoccupied with the world at arm's length. The call goes out everywhere, its light piercing preoccupation, because it reveals in everyone the urge for reunion with God.

The intellect, trying to understand what experience already knows, tends to make a legalistic and formulaic system out of the raw material of spirit, while the more whole mind of Being much more easily emphasizes the sense of fullness and freedom found in transcendent experience. The subconscious mind steeped in the reality of such experience gracefully begins to reveal spiritual Being. Loss becomes gain, individual experience becomes encounter. To know it is to value it, and to value it is to allow it to undo what was ineffective before, and to unlearn past, imperfect presuppositions about God and ourselves.

The early Christians prayed from the depth of their soul that God's subtle light might shine upon them, illuminating paths in the wilderness. They prayed that they might have "the eyes of [their] hearts enlightened" (Eph. 1:18). They prayed in ecstasy, out of the body and in the Spirit, to the inscrutable God "who alone has immortality and dwells in unapproachable light, whom no man has ever seen or can see" (1 Tim. 6:16). They prayed for internal transformation so as to find themselves within the "unapproachable light."

Prayer for experience offers a way to evoke this inner light of shared experience and the psychological processes of spiritual transformation. The following psalm, taking into account the psychological and emotional context of religion, prays for the process of opening oneself to find another experience:

> Have mercy on me, O God, according to thy steadfast love;
> According to thy abundant mercy blot out my transgressions
> . . . and cleanse me from my sin! . . .
> Behold, thou desirest truth in the inward being;
> Therefore teach me wisdom in my secret heart. . . .
> Create in me a clean heart, O God,
> And put a new and right spirit within me.
> Cast me not away from thy presence,
> And take not thy holy Spirit from me.
> Restore to me the joy of thy salvation,
> And uphold me with a willing spirit (Pss. 51:1–2, 6, 10–12).

Paul prays for experience when he asks that God:

may give you a spirit of wisdom and of revelation in the knowledge of him, having the eyes of your hearts enlightened, that you may know what is the hope to which he has called you (Eph. 1:17–18).

Jesus tells his disciples, "What I tell you in the dark, utter in the light; and what you hear whispered, proclaim upon the housetops" (Matt. 10:27). The core inner truth is hidden no more. Invoking highest mystical experience, that of union, Jesus prays in John's gospel:

that they may all be one; even as you, Father, are in me, and I in you, that they may also be in us, so that the world may believe that you have sent me. The glory which you have given me I have given to them, that they may be one even as we are one, I in them and you in me, that they may become perfectly one, so that the world may know that you have sent me and have loved them even as you have loved me (John 17: 21–23).[25]

This is a prayer for reality; it is a prayer for unity in the Spirit. Above all else, it is spiritual oneness that causes the heart to rejoice. It is a prayer for highest spiritual experience, mystical because it is hidden within the heart until it is acknowledged as part of oneself, to remain elusive until it is accepted *as* oneself.

The process of attaining mystical or spiritual experience begins quite simply, with the mere acknowledgment of the inner world. Its vastness and its depths need not be initially known. Yet once one begins to "taste and see," it begins to spring up everywhere. The greater part of the unconscious is simply the Self that is denied by ordinary consciousness. When experienced, mystical transcendence becomes valued above all else, to be sought and found in all things, and ultimately in the essential oneness of all that lives.

Sublime mystical experience is not so much the window as the doorway into Heaven. Heaven and the mystical Earth gleam through the opened self with the depths of the living God. Spiritual truth and living wisdom are never really hidden, nor can they ever be entirely out of reach. They are always freely given, freely flowing from an eternal source. In the eternal openness of love, there is no fear. And in the progress toward the experience of certainty, all that was lost and hidden now is found, darkness brought to light, the world returned renewed with the Self, the glory of God, His eternal creation.

Spiritual or mystical religious psychology can evoke the experience of Heaven. Through experience of the Unity of Heaven is revealed the great plan and purpose of God on Earth. All things are joined at the level at which they are true to themselves. In the words of Saint Paul:

> For he has made known to us in all wisdom and insight the mystery of his will, according to his purpose which he has set forth in Christ as a plan for the fullness of time, *to unite all things in him,* things in heaven and things on earth (Eph. 1:9–10, my italics).

Toward this end, says Paul: "He destined us in love to be his sons through Jesus Christ, according to the purpose of his will" (Eph. 1:5).

2
The Spiritual Experience of Jesus

And I will lead the blind
in a way that they know not,
in paths that they have not known
I will guide them.
I will turn the darkness before them into light,
the rough places into level ground.
These are the things I will do
and I will not forsake them.

—Isa. 42:16

Jesus' Background in Experience

Spiritual experience permeates the life and teaching of Jesus. One indication of this we glean from the fact that Jesus' life as presented in the Gospels begins in highly mythological fashion. In the first two chapters of Matthew alone, there is reference to: two dreams of Joseph in which "the angel of the Lord" spoke to him (1:20–21; 2:13); a prophecy about the child to come—"his name shall be called Emmanuel (which means, God with us)" (1:22–23); a reference to wise men from the East (2:1–2) who followed a bright and auspicious star to hail the child king (2:9–10); and the gifts of the magi or wise men (2:11). This context of subconscious imagery of dreams, signs, and angels suggests a deeper meaning behind the story of Jesus than ordinary consciousness can comprehend. It must be something beyond ordinary consciousness to which Jesus himself relates.

Jesus is portrayed as having been born into a context of mystical symbolism. Even as a child Jesus may well have had precocious and prodigious talents in relating to the depth of his religion, as Luke recounts in this glimpse of Jesus at age 12 (2:46–47):

> After three days they found him in the temple, sitting among the teachers, listening to them and asking them questions; and all who heard him were amazed at his understanding and his answers.

This sagacious child already had the pronounced confidence of insight and intuition into the Divine realm. We can surmise from this that the child Jesus had spent some time with God; the implication is that he was spiritually taught.

As a young adult, he went his own way, forsaking even his family to walk the road he walked. His family thought him mad—"beside himself" (Mark 3:21)—because evidently he seemed possessed by *something other than himself* in "casting out demons." He did not seem *himself* even to those who knew him well, when he was in the Spirit. Yet he speaks of this Spirit as the essence of the Sacred; it led him to heal and to teach, it chose him to be his highest reality. It seems that he had learned to enter the Spirit and returned to talk about it at will.

Early in his public life, he seemed to have a great sense of mission in doing what he did:

> And he went all about Galilee, teaching in their synagogues and preaching the gospel of the kingdom and healing every disease and every infirmity among the people (Matt. 4:23).

This is the will of God he was to follow as taught by the Spirit. Large crowds from neighboring states came for something new from this man who seemed led by the Spirit (Matt. 4:24). His teaching and healing were greatly sought out. Jesus has been variously described by historical scholars as charismatic healer, as sage or great teacher, as eschatological prophet, as cosmic redeemer, and as initiator into the divine mysteries of God. But it does not seem that he himself would limit himself to any one of these roles, or to any role at all. Just so, it is that which lies behind all the roles that begins to make him understandable.

He does not seem to have set out to establish a new religion, but he did attract followers, disciples, students, those who wanted to learn from him, for, having been led by the Spirit, he had a new sense of purpose, a new way of life and a way to God. The Gospels portray Jesus as someone who did not follow the most popular and authoritative teachings of his day; he had his own ideas about his relationship to God, and he had the spiritual authority to be believed in. His experience in Spirit allowed him to know something of the depths of God that those who heard him wanted deeply to know.

Jesus did not follow the prevailing religious rules of proper association. He and his followers sat down to eat and drink and talk with "many tax collectors and sinners" (Matt. 9:10), without regard to religious proscriptions against such association. Those who have little to lose can afford to be honest; this goes for worldly identity as well as material goods. Perhaps Jesus saw something of himself in these "real people," and there are instances of his identification with them. Perhaps it can also be said that he saw something of God in the most basic of people.

His teachings tend to esteem those who find themselves in others' estimations to be among the lower social strata, "the lost" and "the least." When the religious authorities questioned him on his forbidden association with sinners, Jesus responded by designating to himself the role of a doctor of soul: "Those who are well have no need of a physician, but those who are sick" (Matt. 9:12). In a sense, simply by sitting with them, he was saving them from religious prohibitions that were based on exclusion. Through the Spirit, he had a purpose, and he felt led by the Spirit to impart his personal and spiritual sense of the goodness of God.

Jesus seems also to have himself known the feeling of being dispossessed. He indicates that he felt he had no home in this world: "Foxes have holes, and birds of the air have nests; but the Son of man has nowhere to lay his head" (Matt. 8:20). He had nothing in an earthly sense, yet he had a vision of the glory of God, granted to him because of his great trust and the closeness of their relationship. Just before his crucifixion, he is portrayed as saying to the high priest, "hereafter you will see the Son of man seated at the right hand of Power, and coming on the clouds of heaven" (Matt. 26:64). Apparently, he felt that his true home was in Heaven as well as among the lost; there, he could truly be himself.

Yet does Jesus seem to be more truly *himself* than human beings generally understand themselves to be? He walked an individual path. One of his early mentors, John the Baptist, lived in the wilderness, outside society, wearing rough camel hair and eating locusts with wild honey. The Baptist proclaimed repentance and forgiveness in a transformative river baptism symbolizing death and rebirth, and in a moment of honesty before God. Jesus did not follow precisely the austere teachings of John, but he did feel led to be baptized by him. Yet despite submitting himself to John to be baptized, Jesus and his followers did not fast ritually as the Baptist's followers and religious authorities of his day fasted (Matt. 9:14). Jesus attended and taught at synagogue at times, but he did not adhere to the regulations and minutiae that he came to refer to as "the traditions of men." He is sometimes portrayed as shunning religious authority and often sharply criticizing it for its adherence to the traditions of men rather than to the Spirit of God and to life. He lived outside the institutions he walked among.

It might be said that, in his individuality, Jesus was himself a religion of one. Even for his growing circle of followers, Jesus counsels a very personal, private, even secretive "practice of piety." He says:

> Beware of practicing your piety before men in order to be seen by them; for then you will have no reward from your Father who is in heaven (Matt. 6:1).

The heavenly reward comes straight to the individual. Jesus tells his followers to pray in secret (Matt. 6:6), to fast in secret (6:17–18), to give alms "in secret; and your Father who sees in secret will reward you" (Matt. 6:2). Jesus therefore advocates a very personal and individual practice of religion. He concentrates upon receiving, not praise from people, but rather eternal treasures (Matt. 6:20) and an eternal kingdom of God, which, when it becomes the individual's focus, provides for every need (Matt. 6:33). Jesus prays often in the Gospels, most often going off by himself for solitude. When he returned to his friends, he spoke of a private, in-depth conversation between God and man within the secret places of his heart.

In his teaching, Jesus did not emphasize existence—everyday decisions on how to survive to the next day: "Therefore I tell you, do not be anxious about your life, what you shall eat, nor about your body, what you shall put on" (Luke 12:22). "For life is more than food," says Jesus (Luke 12:23). He indicates that people should think more of themselves than that; they are of "more value" than they think (12:24). He encourages his followers not to focus whatsoever on their temporary span of existence, but rather to seek "the kingdom" of Being (12:31), whereupon they will be clothed as gloriously as "the lilies" (12:27). For Jesus, it seems, existence is not a proper grounding for life. Its hopes are too small, and easily dashed. Its foundation is not sure, as it marches dolefully through its illusions of living toward a certain death. Jesus lived outside not only the bounds of convention, but also outside existence itself.

For Jesus, God was active not so much in the world as in the human being first, and then in the world. His focus was internal and entirely transformative. Finding, experiencing, and living a truer sense of life was for him the great mission, the great purpose of life. He said: "For what does it profit a man, to gain the whole world and forfeit his life?" (Mark 8:36).

This "life" was a new experience of life and a new identity in Spirit. His parables show that nothing in the world compared in value to the sense of life he had uncovered in the Spirit. Jesus counseled individuals to find and enter the seldom-used "narrow gate . . . that leads to life" (Matt. 7:13–14). The narrow gate is the individual way of being led by Spirit. He spoke of an exchange of selves, or the giving up of one sense of life for another, eternally true.

Jesus' teaching centered upon the individual and the individual's experience. Historical scholar C. H. Dodd says that: "this concentration upon the individual and his experience is a striking feature of the teaching of Jesus."[1] Every relationship is an experience of individuals encountering an opening of each individual. Who needs to be saved except the individual, and from what except from the boundaries that beset him all around? Jesus loved the lost, and the sick, and he cared for those who were excluded. He wanted to convince them of divine forgiveness and of their own great power in belief, in order to help them to experience themselves as eternal inhabitants of the Household of God.

Baptism and Sonship

According to the Gospels, Jesus was transformed at the moment of his baptism. Making the pilgrimage to the Jordan River for John the Baptist's "baptism for the forgiveness of sins" (Mark 1:4), Jesus opened himself to forgiveness and to visions of a pure and powerful world. He was leaving everything behind for something completely new. His baptism occurred at the outset of Jesus' more public life, before his ministry and return to the marketplace. At the instant of his baptism, Jesus is granted an experience of Spirit and of revelation from God, revelation into his eternal identity given by God. He realized then and there that relationship to God was that of Son to his Father.

Something eternal and holy was conferred upon Jesus at the moment of his baptism. Having been granted a revelation as to what he really was, he thereby also would realize the greatness of his purpose on Earth. He realized where he was going, for he realized where he was *from*. For he had an experience as Son of his Father, an unshakable closeness with God.

> And when Jesus was baptized, he went up immediately from the water, and behold, the heavens were opened to him and he saw the Spirit of God descending like a dove, and alighting on him; and lo, a voice from heaven, saying, "This is my beloved Son, with whom I am well pleased" (Matt. 3:16–17).

He was struck by the certainty that can come only from intimate encounter in mystical experience. Heaven opened to him, and spoke to him, and he would always carry its message.

Jesus' experience as "beloved Son" at the moment of baptism is reminiscent of this from the Psalms (2:7):

> I will tell of the decree of the Lord: He said to me, "You are my son, today I have begotten you."

There is a sense in this passage of direct emanation from God, with a brand new sense of Self in that knowledge.

To realize that one is a Son of God is to realize how close to God one must be. This closeness is experienced as total honesty and intimacy, and there is a change of identity in the experience as well. A Son of God is *like* God: sharing the characteristics of God. One not only knows how close to God one is, but also realizes that one shares in the universal being of God. One knows through shared experience. One communes with God in Heaven and one reveals something new on Earth, newness of life, through oneself.

As Son of God, Jesus was not himself, yet more than ever himself. As Son of God, he was transparent to God. He clearly had not only a window but also a doorway into Heaven, for he was not only a messenger but also an example of that other realm. He carried a ray of Heaven's light to pierce the surrounding darkness of mind, a touch of Heaven's divine sense to sort swiftly through worldly and personal confusion. Indeed it was "in and through his own person that he claimed to be mediating God's effect on the world."[2]

As Son of God, Jesus is given much, but he is responsible for much: "Every one to whom much is given, of him will much be required" (Luke 12:48). We can see how this saying applies also to himself and to what he has learned about himself through his relationship with God through the Spirit—hence his strong sense that he was called by God to an infinitely higher purpose. The Gospel of Matthew allows a glimpse into Jesus' reciprocal relationship with his Source:

> All things are delivered unto me of my Father: and no man knoweth the Son, but the Father; neither knoweth any man the Father, save the Son, and he to whomsoever the Son will reveal him (Matt. 11:27).

Once again, we have in this most mystical passage an example of how Jesus' experience of Sonship is fundamental to his sense of certainty and to his purpose. And we have him here revealing a great mystery: a revelation of all things having been given him by God as Son. As Son, he has direct knowledge of the Father, and this experience of certainty is accompanied by a responsibility to reveal this knowledge to others. Sonship therefore conferred on him a higher role than any he could take upon himself, and this role as revealer of knowledge and mystery is behind everything he says and does.

His Sonship was not a mere belief to him; it provided his purpose, and he came to identify with it as his own essential being. As Bible scholar James D. G. Dunn puts it, "He *experienced* a relation of sonship—felt such an intimacy with God, such an approval by God, dependence on God, responsibility to God, that the only words adequate to express it were 'Father' and 'son.'"[3] The best image to express his close relationship with God was an intimate familial term.

He was in fact led by something beyond himself to become something beyond himself. As Dunn again states, "The evidence is not extensive, but it cannot be dismissed. . . . *Jesus' experience of God was of a supernatural power compelling him to speak and to act.*"[4] Jesus tells his disciples not to be anxious about how or what they are to speak, telling them, "the Holy Spirit will teach you in that very hour what you ought to say" (Luke 12:12). In John, he claims that his teaching is not his own, but God's; it comes *through* him: "My teaching is not mine, but his who sent me" (John 7:16). Though he seems more than self-assured in the Gospels, it was in another Self that he lived with certainty.

Jesus in the Spirit was himself yet not himself—not himself in the ordinary sense. His experience of God was all-encompassing, affecting every aspect of his life. His experience was deep and transformative enough to confer on him a new identity and a new (because different) life, for he was allowing Spirit to live through him. Jesus probably did not come to his way of life consciously and rationally. He lived as he did through another Being, the Spirit. As evidence of this, we will see that his teaching was not so much the product of conscious thinking as it was the product of an experience that brought its own logic. He had come to know God's will by coming to know God Himself. In other words, to quote Dunn again, his "wellspring of authority was not the law, the fathers, the tradition or the rabbis, but his own certainty that he knew the will of God."[5] This certainty in spiritual experience gave him a seemingly direct and intuitive knowledge of God, which caused people to wonder how he "has learning, when he has never studied" (John 7:15).

His experience at baptism is essential in coming to know Jesus. The entire message of Jesus is best understood in the context of his relationship with a different order of being. Jesus himself can be understood only in relation to his deep conviction and faith, and his conviction and faith are drawn directly from his experience as Son of God. He came to know what he knew about God by way of mystically direct encounter. At his baptism by John in the Jordan River, he also came to know himself as God knew him, perhaps as God knows all.

After his encounter, Jesus was never again alone, no longer estranged from life because no longer estranged from God. At his baptism, the Holy Spirit revealed not only Itself, but also Jesus himself. Not only was God with him, but Jesus was led to seek followers, helpers, students, people everywhere to serve, in small and in great ways, to share God with them. He went out to seek the sick and the lost, the poor and the marginalized, or he came in close proximity to them so that they could seek him. He touched them, sometimes to heal them, sometimes that they might live again. He had a tremendous power working through him, leading him to teach and to heal, to connect with others deeply, heart to heart, mind to mind, spirit to spirit, being to being.

Perhaps others recognized something of their deepest being in him. Otherwise they would not have followed him so willingly, to the point of leaving jobs, homes, families, worldly security, safety, to be in his presence. They felt in his conviction an eternal reply to their own ever-gnawing doubt. In him, they saw what they could be, if they too could experience God and therefore live as he lived.

Jesus had an earthly family, but he was interested only in his divine origin, his direct emanation from his spiritual God. His family and neighbors did not know what to make of his power in the Spirit (Mark 3:21). He gathered new family around him as he traveled on, going by foot from town to town. "Here are my mother and my brothers!" he said. "Whoever does the will of God is my brother, and sister, and mother" (Mark 3:34–35). His family was everywhere; they needed but to join him in his new sense of "life."

On seeing Simon Peter and Andrew fishing, he said to them, "Follow me, and I will make you fishers of men" (Matt. 4:19). And what was their response to this sudden and strange invitation? "Immediately they left their nets and followed him" (Matt. 4:20). In a sense, it seems they knew him already. Obviously, his great conviction and authority, derived from direct experience, added to his charismatic presence. Spirit spoke through him to the longing for Spirit in those who thus recognized him. Jesus was a man with a mission not his own, which he accepted from God and sought to share with others. We might say that Spirit sought to impart Itself through him.

Some scholars believe that Jesus was possessed of an alternate Identity when he realized he was Son of God. This other entity spoke through him and worked through him. Jesus had to leave himself behind, at least at times, so that the Spirit could speak and work through him. For some Bible scholars, including John E. Smith, Jesus is presented in the Gospels as a "self-negating medium that reveals God in the very act of setting itself aside."[6] Similarly, another scholar writes that "by sacrificing 'Jesus,' the finite medium, the Christ 'becomes completely transparent to the mystery he reveals.' That is to say, another picture, a clearer image, is given apart from the man Jesus."[7]

In other words, Jesus' conscious ego had to decrease in order for Spirit to increase, to fill him up and reveal itself through him. He says one must become like a child to enter the experience of heaven (Matt. 18:3). He had to step back, even dissociate himself from his conscious selfhood, to allow Spirit to have Its Identity through him. It was in this way that he came to identify himself as Son of God. When he took on the Identity of Spirit, It became his own. This is the clear understanding of the Gospel of John in regard to Jesus, and it is implicit in the other gospels as well. Or we might say that the Holy Spirit possessed Jesus so that it was not Jesus the conscious ego who was talking and acting—it was the Spirit of God through Jesus, and Jesus *as* the Spirit of God. Jesus was transparent to God. God lived through him, and therefore revealed him to be something more.

This process of stepping back to step forward is further evidenced early in the Gospel of Luke, wherein Jesus, as if introducing himself to the world, stands up in the synagogue and reads from the book of the prophet Isaiah:

> The Spirit of the Lord is upon me, because he has anointed me to preach good news to the poor. He has sent me to proclaim release to the captives and recovering of sight to the blind, to set at liberty those who are oppressed, to proclaim the acceptable year of the Lord (Luke 4:18–19).

Jesus is here proclaiming himself anointed by God due to the Spirit at work within him. It was in this way that he became Savior of people, a Messiah-type figure, a Christ ("anointed by God"), not politically motivated but rather directly and intimately helpful, due to his experience of being in the internal society of the Spirit. He is led by the Spirit to fulfill the great purpose of God in the world.

Before this point, however, Jesus had to undergo the (mythical but psychologically real) trials of the Temptation in the Wilderness. The texts say that the Spirit led him out into the wilderness for 40 days and 40 nights, during which time he encountered the devil, referred to in the Bible as the lord of this world (see Luke 4:5–6). The devil is portrayed as having tempted him to misuse his newfound power, offering him in return all manner of material goods and exhibitions of personal power to fall down and worship him and the world (Luke 4:1–13 and parallels). Jesus sensed already that the ecstatic (literally "standing out of oneself") experience and the power it brings cannot be used for selfish reasons; how could it when this kind of experience involved relinquishment of the former self?

His purpose as Son of God was like the purpose as Christ or Savior to free those who suffer in the present world, for he experienced in his own liberation their liberation through the infinitely higher world of God revealed by Spirit. Like Moses, he worked for the liberation of people who felt themselves oppressed. He wanted to find those who knew their lostness and carry them to joyous reunion in God, and one accord on Earth. His personal salvation turned out to be universal. For all his teaching about being private and even secretive in the practice of one's religion, Jesus' individual religion and relationship with God turned out to be a universal one.

Jesus in Experience

Other experiences of Jesus include this self-reported one: "I saw Satan fall like lightning from heaven" (Luke 10:18).

Perhaps this experience or vision occurred at the time of his final temptation. His selflessness had overcome the prevailing powers of selfishness, self-interest, and self-obsession. His selflessness was experienced simultaneously with the sudden and growing realization that God was everything to him. With this lightning-quick realization is the end of the reign of evil and death and the struggle to survive, and a growing sense that the eternal creation of God is supremely good.

And of course there is in Jesus' catalogue of experience the mystical Transfiguration:

> And after six days Jesus took with him Peter and James and John, and led them up a high mountain apart by themselves; and he was transfigured before them, and his garments became glistening, intensely white, as no fuller on earth could bleach them. And there appeared to them Elijah and Moses; and they were talking to Jesus (Mark 9:2–4).

On the "high mountain," Jesus "transfigured before them," his garments and no doubt his countenance becoming otherworldly. The world is changed, or seen beyond, suffused with the dazzling white light of truth. The reality he experienced was contingent on nothing but God.

The Transfiguration is as much an experience of the disciples as it is of Jesus. It is an experience of the disciples that was imparted by an experience of Jesus. Nonetheless there is a sudden change here, or a sudden realization of the real, eternal world hidden behind the world of appearances. Jesus became clothed in a glistening world of intense internal light, wherein the great prophets of old meet with him. Past has merged into present; the great prophets are able to be met, to be known.

The Christological titles—whatever their usage may say about the Jesus of history—are most useful in explaining the experiences of the early Christians. In the Gospel of John, which I examine at the end of this chapter, abstract images for Jesus are plentiful: First, he is the Word of God, the *logos* (God's Higher Reason), and the Light of the World. He is variously the Bread and Water of Life, the true Vine, the Good Shepherd. He is the Way, the Life, the Truth itself.

Jesus is identified after the resurrection experiences of the disciples to be the Christ: cosmic, universal, cosmically and universally saving. The representations of the Abstract Jesus reveal him to be the universal yet personal Christ who can inhabit every heart at once, universally yet personally. Within himself and his life, Jesus had transformed for his followers the very idea of Messiah or Christ ("anointed") into Savior not of one nation only, or of one group, but Universal Cosmic Redeemer.

Yet despite these high and Christological terms with which early believers represented Jesus, it seems that most often Jesus viewed himself as an empty vessel for the truth. In consenting to undergo baptism, he was emptying himself of the strained distance from God, of his sin, and he became clean, whole, reunited with his Source. Jesus found a way to forgo and *forget* himself in order that God might be remembered and re-understood. Belief in Jesus was not belief in the self he had forgotten and foregone; belief in Jesus came to be understood as belief in the Reality he let manifest through him, and a sharing of the Self he became.

The following story suggests that Jesus identifies himself symbolically, expansively, and universally with every lost soul in the world:

> Then the King will say to those at his right hand, "Come, O blessed of my Father, inherit the kingdom prepared for you from the foundation of the world; for I was hungry and you gave me food, I was thirsty and you gave me drink, I was a stranger and you welcomed me; I was naked and you clothed me, I was sick and you visited me, I was in prison and you came to me. . . . Truly I say to you, as you did it to one of the least of my brethren, you did it to me" (Matt. 25:34–36, 40).

Jesus suggests here that the Christ in him is in everyone, even and especially the least, the lost, and the lowest. To experience Christ within him is to meld into the whole of the world. The experience is made complete not only by the deep sense of care and compassion, but also by identification with those who feel low. As one unites with God, one unites with all that lives, no matter how individual one might believe oneself.

All those who help to heal the alienation of the world through themselves are Jesus' brothers and sisters, who inhabit together with him the kingdom of God. Jesus' experience convinced him that God's kingdom was inside him, and therefore universal in everyone (Luke 17:20–21). He tries to put into words a sense of the comprehensive awareness he achieved: "If then your whole body is full of light, having no part dark, it will be wholly bright, as when a lamp with its rays gives you light" (Luke

11:36). Again we have a sense of transparency, of clarity, of full awareness of oneself joined with everything from the inside.

Jesus calls his followers to follow him in his self-emptying that they too might be filled with life:

> And he called to him the multitude with his disciples, and said to them, "If any man would come after me, let him deny himself and take up his cross and follow me. For whoever would save his life will lose it; and whoever loses his life . . . will save it. For what does it profit a man, to gain the whole world and forfeit his life? For what can a man give in return for his life?" (Mark 8:34–37)

"If any man would come after me, let him deny himself . . ." These are the words of one who has emptied himself of self. Jesus is calling his disciples to the same self-emptying, so that the universal experience might inhabit a similarly empty vessel as it naturally fills the world. What refills the heart made empty is *life,* a new Identity in Spirit.

And so, in his life as in his death, "by sacrificing 'Jesus,' the finite medium, the Christ 'becomes completely transparent to the mystery he reveals.'"[8] Bible scholar Marcus J. Borg notes that, contrary to popular understanding, Jesus' "message was not about believing in him. Rather the pre-Easter Jesus consistently pointed away from himself to God."[9] Jesus was making himself transparent for the sake of the kingdom of God, and the love and care of his Father for all.

Stevan L. Davies concurs, saying that to "understand Jesus' words is to understand that it was not a human being who spoke but the spirit of God."[10] Davies goes on to conclude (his own emphasis) that *"Jesus' experience of God was of a supernatural power compelling him to speak and to act."*[11] His followers were to keep their sights trained not on the external world but on the eternal world, so that the Spirit of God might live through them, and work and speak through them to the point where they became themselves manifestations of Spirit.

That is what Jesus means when he says: "He who receives you receives me, and he who receives me receives him who sent me" (Matt. 10:40).

He stands transparent to God, holding himself out as a conduit to another world and another sense of reality. He became identified with the

Son of God, with Christ, with God Himself, because he allowed the Spirit of God to fill his unoccupied self. He encourages those who sought to follow him to do the same by becoming equally as transparent.

John has Jesus speak directly of his transparency to God:

> Truly, truly, I say to you, the Son can do nothing of his own accord, but only what he sees the Father doing; for whatever he does, that the Son does likewise. For the Father loves the Son, and shows him all that he himself is doing . . . (John 5:19–20).

Jesus knows the Father from his experience. And knowing himself as Son from knowing his Origin, Jesus can do only what the Father does. The Father is revealed through the clarity and lucidity of Jesus. Thus Jesus tells one of the people he heals, "Go home to your friends, and tell them how much the Lord has done for you, and how he has had mercy on you" (Mark 5:19).

In other words, Jesus is dependent on God for his very being, and therefore all his thoughts, feelings, and actions. This utter dependency on God is highlighted very frequently in John, who has Jesus say, for instance, "I can do nothing on my own authority" (John 5:30) and, "I do nothing on my own authority but speak thus as the Father taught me" (John 8:28). His words, his actions, his purpose in life, are given him by God. Jesus says, "But I have not come on my own accord; he who sent me is true, and him you do not know" (John 7:28). Yes, but God is known through him, who knows himself as God's Son.

The Experiential Teaching of Jesus

Because Jesus' experience of God transcends existence, so also do his words. It is most helpful in understanding the message of Jesus to understand the spiritual context from which he spoke it. Jesus had little interest in worldly affairs; he juxtaposed them with the things of God: "Render to Caesar the things that are Caesar's, and to God the things that are God's" (Mark 12:17). He did not seek to reform his native Judaism, but rather to radically personalize it. He was not a political zealot but a spiritual zealot. He was thought of as a Savior of Souls because not only his message and the gist behind it, but his life, came directly from enthused experience of God.

Jesus uses language to transcend language, as well as the former sense of self. He indicates that his words are founded upon the rocklike certainty of direct experience, and tells his followers that they must be put into practice to be truly understood (see Luke 6:47–48). They point to the habitation of another realm, even within the world. He states, "Heaven and earth will pass away, but my words will not pass away" (Luke 21:33). That is why those who follow his words and take up their Spirit in openness are choosing to experience God for themselves.

There is nothing more reassuring and revealing than the experience of spiritual reality. Doctrine confined to concepts cannot touch it, because concepts and premises can and do shift and change. But spiritual experience is from a deeper foundation, an eternal foundation that does not change. Experience of Being is the grounding force for all religion. One's sense of relationship with God depends on it, one's relationship with others flows from it. As Jesus showed, one's true Self, one's salvation, and one's new life, is revealed through such experience.

Jesus' teaching centers upon an experience of the eternal that he called "the kingdom of God." As I will examine in the next chapter, this kingdom of God is as much itself an experience as it is the result of experience. It was communicated to his disciples through parables: unique stories with everyday images that tended to undercut the prevailing thought systems of existence. Historical text critic John Dominic Crossan writes:

> This is what Jesus' parables seek to do: to help others into their own experience of the Kingdom and to draw from that experience their own way of life.[12]

Jesus spoke of the kingdom of God as being a present internal reality. He tells a group of teachers not to expect it to come from outside themselves: "for behold, *the kingdom of God is within you*" (Luke 17:21, my italics). He speaks of the kingdom of God as an element of the true internal being most have not accessed as yet. Yet he also speaks of it as manifesting itself in the world, coming from a new kind of perception.

In this sense, the kingdom of God was for Jesus a new reality that subsumed the old sense of reality. The external world cries to be seen and believed and even worshiped, but the power of the Spirit working within him showed him another reality altogether. It was Jesus' unique perception of reality that caused him to see the eternal kingdom of God where formerly there seemed to be sickness, poverty, death, and sin.

Jesus taught the kingdom of God in a unique form called the *parable.* Scholars propose that Jesus used this form of teaching to impart or transmit an experience that could not be "gotten across" through ordinary concepts. Crossan writes:

> There is an intrinsic and inalienable bond between Jesus' experience and Jesus' parables. A sensitivity to the metaphorical language of religious and poetic experience and an empathy with the profound and mysterious linkage of such experience and such expression may help us to understand *what is most important about Jesus: his experience of God.*[13]

Parables, then, are instructive not so much in a conceptual sense as in an experiential sense. They might be thought of not so much as pointers as portals to a higher spiritual experience. Apparently, for Jesus, extraordinary experience required extraordinary forms of teaching.

The parables function to draw a person into an experience of the kingdom of God. They are stories that describe, point out, and evoke a different experience and state of being than ordinary consciousness, if one allows. This is what Jesus means when he states that those "without ears to hear" cannot understand his parables: "seeing they do not see, and hearing they do not hear, nor do they understand" (Matt. 13:13). One must be open to the experience to have it: this is what it means to lose oneself and find a new Self.

Jesus says through parables that the kingdom of God, beginning as a seed (Mark 4:26), grows by itself, so that even the subject in whom it grows "knows not how" (Mark 4:27). In other words, the kingdom can be understood only through its growing fulfillment in experience. It must arise in its own good time from the unconscious or superconscious mind where it was eternally implanted by the living God. God longs to give His children His kingdom, but in order for them to experience or receive it, it must first be valued above all else (Mark 12:31, 34).

The experience that Jesus teaches with parables has to do with everyone's root origin: "I will open my mouth in parables, I will utter what has been hidden since the foundation of the world" (Matt. 13:35). In revealing his experience of God and of himself as Son, Jesus is revealing the greatest of mysteries. He is calling upon his hearers not only to get right and honest with God, but also to *be fully present with God*. He is calling for a return to the root origin, the Source from which emanates all life, all trust: the grace of being.

In Jesus' sayings, too, he is calling upon his hearers to be like God. "You, therefore, must be perfect, as your heavenly Father is perfect" (Matt. 5:48), which means, be whole, expansive, and entirely integrative. Or as Luke has it, with Jesus' advice for going through the world: "Be merciful, even as your Father is merciful" (Luke 6:36). Being transparent to the Father, one will include all in highest vision. As he heals a paralyzed man, Jesus tells him, "Take heart, my son; your sins are forgiven" (Matt. 9:2). He knows that there is a great gulf between human existence and Godly Being, and yet he sees this rift as bridgeable and crossable, through the new experience of relationship he is attempting to transfer to individuals.

Jesus was given to psychological truisms as well. For instance, "He who is faithful in a very little is faithful also in much; and he who is dishonest in a very little is dishonest also in much" (Luke 16:10). In this passage also, Jesus refers to "the little" as "unrighteous mammon" (16:11)—the things of the world that are not good or true or alive in and of themselves. Jesus posits a juxtaposition between which the individual will serve: God or mammon (16:13), life or death. We have seen that he has drawn a sharp contrast also between "life" and "the world." God is alive, and so He is the natural choice to follow. He indicates that one life precludes the other, which renders it a difficult decision to those most absorbed in the world.

Jesus' parables and sayings reveal his mission to be of some urgency to reveal, as if something wonderful had been lost for so long that it was forgotten, yet is remembered again by being experienced again (Luke 15:3–10). There is an internal, existential crisis involved in there being so great a gap between existence and Being, between humankind and God. His words are intended to point to an experience of God and Self that spans the gulf between the world of estrangement, alienation, and death, and the kingdom of Heaven.

Jesus was not one to call for the betterment of existence, but rather for its transcending. Existence is not the only reality, nor is it the highest reality. Jesus' teachings pertain to the overcoming of existence and forgiveness of all, in which is involved a reversal of values and a corresponding reversal of perception, now to see with the eyes of God:

> But blessed are your eyes, for they see, and your ears, for they hear. Truly, I say to you, many prophets and righteous men longed to see what you see, and did not see it, and to hear what you hear, and did not hear it (Matt. 13:16–17).

Jesus offers instructions as to how to reach his great, gulf-spanning experience of closeness to God. He presents his hearers with something new, not a doctrinal system but the means for them to do what he asks of them in order that they might come to share in his experience of God. According to Jesus, faith in the experience will produce the experience—faith in God will result in God. Faith in His perfect care will bring a prevailing sense of peace and, within this peace, of power.

> And Jesus answered them, "Have faith in God. Truly, I say to you, whoever says to this mountain, 'Be taken up and cast into the sea,' and does not doubt in his heart, but believes that what he says will come to pass, it will be done for him" (Mark 11:22–23).

"And to the centurion Jesus said, 'Go; be it done for you as you have believed.' And the servant was healed at that very moment" (Matt. 8:13). With the experience of such faith and power in the goodness and mercy of God comes conviction, and with conviction comes healing, salvation, knowledge, and experience to share.

Jesus counsels those who would follow him to submit to an inner emptiness that holds open a space for the urgency of Being. "Take nothing for your journey, no staff, no bag, nor bread, nor money; and do not have two tunics" (Luke 9:3). Jesus is calling on his chosen not only to simplify, but also to live in the reality of Being more so than in existence. Be not anxious about earthly existence (Luke 12:29), says Jesus, and your mind will change, your heart will change, your identity will change. For God will not only provide for worldly needs (Luke 12:31), God will fill and fulfill you with His Being.

Jesus says that the "pure in heart" will see God (Matt. 5:8). What it means to be pure in heart, and what it means to see God, and what it means to be saved, and what it means to have eternal life, all seem to run together into one broad but focused way.

> And behold, a lawyer stood up to put him to the test, saying, "Teacher, what shall I do to inherit eternal life?" He said to him, "What is written in the law? How do you read?" And he answered, "You shall love the Lord your God with all your heart, and with all your soul, and with all your strength, and with all your mind; and your neighbor as yourself." And he said to him, "You have answered right; do this, and you will live" (Luke 10:25–28).

To live, for Jesus, is to love God completely, and to love all others as if they were part of oneself. It is to share the broad view and deep sense that nothing anywhere is separate from this love.

Jesus' teachings liberate a person from the body and bodily concerns because his teaching comes from a different state of mind than that which seeks to perpetuate itself in the world. This is why Jesus minimizes the importance of behavior in favor of the intention in the mind and the inner will:

> You have heard that it was said to the men of old, "You shall not kill; and whoever kills shall be liable to judgment." But I say to you that every one who is angry with his brother shall be liable to judgment . . . You have heard that it was said, "You shall not commit adultery." But I say to you that everyone who looks at a woman lustfully has already committed adultery with her in his heart (Matt. 5:21–22, 27–28).

This is also why John has Jesus tell his followers not to judge by appearances. The surface world is less real and true than the interior world. That which can be seen by the physical eye reveals so little about the person within. Faith draws its power from the mind and heart, from the intention and will of the person who opens to it.

The physical senses and all they see, hear, taste, smell, and touch are fleeting. They are destined to exist a while in struggle and then move on:

> Do not lay up for yourselves treasures on earth, where moth
> and rust consume and where thieves break in and steal, but lay up
> for yourselves treasure in heaven, where neither moth nor rust
> consumes and where thieves do not break in and steal. For where
> your treasure is, there will your heart be also (Matt. 6:19–21).

All things sensed by that which blooms and then fades are destined
themselves to bloom and then fade. But the rock of spiritual experience
is forever. It reveals deeper things than were thought knowable. It can
deliver a sense of another reality just above and behind the physical
world, which will soon be encompassed by that other reality with its sense
of eternity.

There is in God a way to see a world of light, via a world of light within:

> The eye is the lamp of the body. So, if your eye is sound, your
> whole body will be full of light; but if your eye is not sound, your
> body will be full of darkness. If then the light in you is darkness,
> how great is the darkness! (Matt. 6:22–23)

A sound eye is a clear eye, a healed eye. Inside there is a great light,
great enough to light up every corner of mind and world:

> You are the light of the world. A city on a hill cannot be hid.
> Nor do men light a lamp and put it under a bushel, but on a stand,
> and it gives light to all in the house. Let your light so shine before
> men, that they may see your good works and give glory to the
> Father who is in heaven (Matt. 5:14–16).

The experience of which Jesus speaks is uncontainable, much like joy.
Much like the mind is uncontainable, so is the goodness of God.

Jesus extols in his teaching a forgiveness that also has no limits:

> You have heard that it was said, "An eye for an eye and a tooth
> for a tooth." But I say to you, Do not resist one who is evil. But if
> any one strikes you on the right cheek, turn to him the other also;
> and if any one would sue you and take your coat, let him have your

cloak as well; and if any one forces you to go one mile, go with him two miles (Matt. 5:38–41).

Forgiveness for Jesus is given in full or not at all. It is a way of life, born of experience. There is no sense in becoming angry at the disappointments in this world if this world is not one's true and ultimate reality.

He promises a heavenly reward, a sense or experience of Heaven, to those who follow his words:

> Judge not, and you will not be judged; condemn not, and you will not be condemned; forgive, and you will be forgiven; give, and it will be given to you; good measure, pressed down, shaken together, running over, will be put into your lap. For the measure you give will be the measure you get back (Luke 6:37–38).

Overlook the world, and you will be rewarded with an experience of Heaven. (I expound further on this key teaching of forgiveness in the next chapter.) Jesus also speaks a parable counseling not to seek to get repaid for giving freely in existence, that you may feel rewarded in Being ("the resurrection") instead:

> When you give a dinner or a banquet, do not invite your friends, or your brothers, or your kinsmen or rich neighbors, lest they also invite you in return, and you be repaid. But when you give a feast, invite the poor, the maimed, the lame, the blind, and you will be blessed, because they cannot repay you. You will be rewarded at the resurrection of the just (Luke 14:12–14).

We can see here as well a sense of the great Care of God for His Children. There can be no self-interest in self-disavowal, self-emptying, self-forgetting. Joined with God and with the world, one's main concern comes to be universalized.

And so Jesus is calling upon those who hear him to join with God and with each other through forgiveness and through spiritual experience. He provides not only parables and sayings to this effect, but he does works, healings, he raises from the dead, and he forgives sin as a representative of

God. He provides an example for those who choose to follow him in following God, provides a portrayal of what the world can be when a person lives in and with the Spirit.

Relationships are profound in Jesus' teaching. They come from God and they lead back to Him. Any soul that is lost will be found, and any two who share the ultimate purpose of God in faith will be rewarded immediately. Everyone a person meets has the potential to be either stranger or friend, either enemy or loved one. Everyone has the potential to be an essential element of the experience of the kingdom of God, the vast internal universe.

Love is the highest experience of which humankind is capable. It contains the whole of knowledge, contains the whole of goodness, contains the whole of God. Love forges such a deep connection that it is unbreakable. Love is eternal. All that can truly be called love is based on the great love of God for His Children. Having experienced his Sonship, there was then nothing more for Jesus to do but to try to bring others with him. He had found joy, he had found love, and he knew he had to share it to feel it.

This is why Jesus says of his mission and great purpose:

> Come to me, all who labor and are heavy laden, and I will give you rest. Take my yoke upon you, and learn from me; for I am gentle and lowly in heart, and you will find rest for your souls. For my yoke is easy, and my burden is light (Matt. 11:28–30).

He knew that others would want to join him in his heavenly certainty born of the experience of heaven. He had himself had a sense of their pain; now they would have a share in his richness.

The Light of Life

I have spoken about Jesus' sense of Sonship, which came with his experience of God in the vision and revelation at his baptism. I have looked into his words for evidence that he meant to share this experience by means of his parables and sayings as well as by healings and miracles. In John, Jesus seeks to impart experience to Nicodemus, saying: "Truly, truly, I say to you, unless one is born from above, he cannot see the kingdom of God" (John 3:3).

Again, Jesus is holding out a sense of new life, being "born from above," grounded in experience of Spirit. Jesus seeks to persuade the Samaritan woman at the well to worship God "in spirit and truth," (John 4:23), "worship" in this case being to join in the experience. The early Christian communities, such as the one (probably in Syria) in which the Gospel of John was written, valued this sharing of experience above all, and that is what bound them together as his eternal church.

The Gospel of John presents Jesus from the point of view of the transformation Jesus taught. The author seems to be writing from the vantage point of the Spirit that writes through him. It is not that John tried to imagine the mind of Jesus; rather, the author suggests that he shares the mind of Christ. Jesus' selfless transparency to God is that which is shared by John and the community for which he writes, and so union with Jesus is union also with God and with all others. The faith, in a sociological sense, was held together by the Spirit.

It is in the Gospel of John that Jesus most identifies himself with abstract images. It is in John (6:51) that Jesus refers to himself—or the Spirit within him—as the eternal manna from heaven: "I am the living bread which came down from heaven; if any one eats of this bread, he will live for ever . . ." Jesus also identifies himself as "the light of the world" (8:12), and as "the true Vine" (15:1) that connects all of life at the soul. Of Jesus, John the Baptist says in John 1:29: "Behold, the Lamb of God, who takes away the sin of the world!" And we have seen that Jesus expands his sense of self also in identifying with "the least" in our self-limiting social lives.

It is in John that it is most apparent that Jesus is transparent to his Father, as he affectionately called God. Jesus continually points away from himself in John so that others might see the God he knew work within him:

> And Jesus cried out and said, "He who believes in me, believes not in me but in him who sent me. And he who sees me sees him who sent me. I have come as light into the world, that whoever believes in me may not remain in darkness" (John 12:44–46).

Hence is belief in Jesus not so much belief in a man as it is belief in everything that that man reveals about the realm of God. Paul agrees, saying that "even though we once regarded Christ from a human point of view, we regard him thus no longer" (2 Cor. 5:16). Humanity is being converted to Divinity through the working of the Spirit.

It is in John also that Jesus said, "Truly, truly, I say to you, before Abraham was, I am" (John 8:58), riling the conventional crowd by suggesting that he originated with God instead of with human being, that he originated in God rather than in the world. In other words, he thought of himself as eternal, with God his Father. That is why even as the Christ, Redeemer of the World, Jesus could say, "My kingship is not of this world" (John 18:36). This is how he lived in the world but was not of it, and why he left in his wake experience of Spirit for others to share his new sense of "eternal life."

As an eternal being with God, Jesus is convinced he has overcome death. "And whoever lives and believes in me shall never die. Do you believe this?" (John 11:26). This is an invitation to join him in this higher realm of eternal being. That is the essence of the teaching in John, that Jesus is not only expositor but exemplar of being with God. He is both the Revealer and That Which Is Revealed because he is transparent both to the Spirit and to the Father.

In John, Philip asks Jesus: "Lord, show us the Father and we shall be satisfied" (John 14:8). Philip is here speaking to Jesus as revealer of the greatest mystery. Let us see and experience the Being of God! Jesus says further in John that he wanted his hearers to "know and understand that the Father is in me and I am in the Father" (John 10:38). Jesus' purpose, function, and mission are to reveal the Father with Whom he felt such close relationship as to be one. "Do not fear, only believe" (Mark 5:36), says Jesus to the one who would be healed.

Jesus sends out his followers to do the same as he, following his lead. "He who receives you receives me, and he who receives me receives him who sent me" (Matt. 10:40). They are to be examples in this world of individuals who step back within themselves to reveal a being of effective and eternal presence. They are to follow him in living in the oneness of God (John 13:20). They, too, take on something of the identity of this Eternal Being that reveals Itself through them. They, too, begin to take on more than a semblance of God in His perfection, as they begin to participate in a greater, more whole and extraordinary sense of life.

Therefore, those who live in accordance with this world, with the world's laws and its ways of doing things, can be thought of as dead (Luke 9:60) because they *are* dead to all the wondrous and beatific possibilities of living in God. "I am not of this world," says Jesus in John 8:23. For, as Son of God, he is of God and God's eternal creation; this is the message in his resurrection from the dead. The gulf between humanity and God has been spanned in him, just as it will be spanned in each of those who follow him closely.

As the Revealer who spans the skies above the Earth, Jesus can say that he is:

> the light of the world; he who follows me will not walk in darkness, but will have the light of life (John 8:12).

"The light of life" connotes not only realization and higher consciousness, but also happiness. "The light of life" is also a sense of being more truly oneself.

Jesus is presenting in himself and his teaching something new and different.

> No one sews a piece of unshrunk cloth on an old garment; if he does, the patch tears away from it, the new from the old, and a worse tear is made. And no one puts new wine into old wineskins; if he does, the wine will burst the skins, and the wine is lost, and so are the skins; but new wine is for fresh skins (Mark 2:21–22).

The experience of closeness with God that he brings is radically different from the ordinary state of consciousness, the state with which we are most familiar. There is no great mystery in this. The plain fact of the sharing of this experience is everywhere in early Christianity.

3

Early Christian Experiences

Thy dead shall live, their bodies shall rise.
O dwellers in the dust, awake and sing for joy!
For thy dew is a dew of light,
and on the land of the shades thou wilt let it fall.
—Isa. 26:19

Rebirth and Baptism

Jesus' experience is reflected in that of his followers. That Jesus called those who followed him to experience is evident not only from his own words, but also from the experiences his followers reported after his ascension into Heaven. Spiritual experience is the cornerstone, the true foundation, on which the early Church was built. There came to be a sense among early Christians that every soul is capable of transcendent spiritual experience, and not only is it capable, but the soul is also made for this experience.

48

There is an abundance of spiritual experience in early Christianity. It may be that there is but one such experience that goes by different names and is seen in different aspects at different points in, not its development, but its realization in the individual. In this chapter, I point out some of the experiences, or aspects of the experience. Rebirth, the kingdom of God, love, and resurrection are central *experiences* of Christianity, which makes them more than concepts. The following chapters continue to look at aspects of the experience of the early Christians, such as being filled with Spirit and identifying with the Sonship of God. It will become clear that the early Christian community was marked by the new and life-changing nature of their transcendent experience.

We have seen that Jesus' teaching revolved around mystical experience. There is much in his teaching that builds on this most spiritual foundation:

> Every one who comes to me and hears my words and does them, I will show you what he is like: he is like a man building a house, who dug deep, and laid the foundation upon rock; and when a flood arose, the stream broke against that house, and could not shake it, because it had been well built (Luke 6:47–48).

To build an unshakeable house, one must have "dug deep." Jesus says that one who hears his words "and does them" has indeed dug deep. It is the same with knowing oneself in a deeply psychological sense. The foundation on which Jesus says to build is internal spiritual experience and its firsthand certainty. This rock of experience is something more overridingly real and solid than the ordinary self. His experience of Self deeply grounded in God is the source of the strength and certainty that Jesus sought to share, through his teaching and example.

And what does Jesus' saying that "the tree is known by its fruit" (Matt. 12:33) mean if not also that a self is known through its experience? Spirit is known through Spirit, which is at once its Source and its ultimate fulfillment. One's identity is known by what one *experiences* oneself as being. And if experience expands, so does the understanding of self. This is all that Selfhood is—being an aspect of God, one with one's experience, part of life itself.

Jesus brought *life*—a different kind of life, life with a sense of surplus and abundant value: "I came that they may have life, and have it abundantly" (John 10:10). This new life is also described as a new and expanded sense of Self. This new kind of life is called in John "eternal life," as in: "He who believes in the Son has eternal life" (3:36). John uses "eternal life" much as the other Gospels use "the kingdom of God."

It seems that the very fact of human existence was a form of death to Jesus (for example, "Follow me, and leave the dead to bury their own dead," he says in Matt. 8:22). To Paul, who said, "For the wages of sin is death, but the free gift of God is eternal life in Christ Jesus our Lord" (Rom. 6:23), to live as separated existents is to be in a state of death, not truly to live. Thus he said, "to me to live is Christ, and to die is gain" (Phil. 1:21). The new sense of life was so different, so transformed, that one's former existence seemed like a lie and like death.

Mystical experience reveals this new sense of life characterized by a greater sense of Self, a Self indistinguishable from God and united with all that lives. This greater sense of self is evident in the early Christians' experience of *rebirth,* or being born again. In John's Gospel, Jesus answers Nicodemus' question about salvation:

> "Truly, truly, I say to you, unless one is born anew [or from above], he cannot see the kingdom of God."
>
> Nicodemus said to him, "How can a man be born when he is old? Can he enter a second time into his mother's womb and be born?"
>
> Jesus answered, "Truly, truly, I say to you, unless one is born of water and the Spirit, he cannot enter the kingdom of God. That which is born of flesh is flesh, and that which is born of the Spirit is spirit" (John 3:3–6).

Spiritual experience is here described as ultimately effecting a new identity and revealing a new sense of Self. To be born again is, obviously, to experience a new self, a new subjective sense of identity. It is as if one came from another world. Though this would seem to be a great mystery to the conscious ego, it unfolds naturally in God's world of Spirit:

> Do not marvel that I said to you, "You must be born anew."

The wind blows where it wills, and you hear the sound of it, but you do not know whence it comes or whither it goes; so it is with every one who is born of the Spirit (John 3:7–8).

To be "born of the Spirit" is to be "born anew" in the sense that the experience of Spirit brings with it a new sense of life and Self. "So it is with every one who is born of the Spirit," every one who is reintroduced, through the Spirit, to the eternal nature of creation.

The First Letter of Peter speaks likewise of rebirth:

By his great mercy *we have been born anew* to a living hope through the resurrection of Jesus Christ from the dead, and to an inheritance which is imperishable, undefiled, and unfading, kept in heaven for you . . . (1 Pet. 1:3–4, my italics).

To be born of the Spirit is to be raised into a new life; it is to have a new Self—experienced as "imperishable, undefiled, and unfading"—raised to predominance in one's experience. This imperishable Self is inherited as by birthright. It is one's true nature, and it is the state of spiritual creation. The First Letter of Peter goes on to say: "You have been born anew, not of perishable seed but of imperishable, through the living and abiding word of God . . . (1 Pet. 1:23).

The overcoming of the physical terminus—that which seems to die—was to early Christians the means to a new, eternal experience in Spirit. They had begun to speak of eternal experience after their encounter with Jesus; they recalled his words to transcend themselves in favor of eternal living union with God.

Spiritual experience is so essentially different from ordinary human experience that it is spoken of as a new birth: a new birth into a new Self, coming from and awakening anytime into a new world with God. This new Self—an eternal identity born of Spirit—spoken about by early Christians is similar to the new identity as Son of God that Jesus assumed at his baptism. For this reason, early Christians followed the example of Jesus and submitted themselves to baptism: to die with him and be reborn, to assume a new identity as Children of God. They followed Jesus' earthly example in order to attain to a degree of his heavenly experience.

Baptism was a mechanism of rebirth for early Christians. Immersion in the river deeply signified a dying to the former sense of self, while rising again out of the water signified transcendence—being reborn as a new Self. Baptism was no mere ritual to the early Christian community. This rite carried with it a deep spiritual significance because it was a way of initiation into an entirely new life through this dying to self and rising to spiritual experience.

Baptism was a means to spiritual experience, and therefore a rite of initiation into a new Self. Baptism for early Christians was clearly associated with *repentance* (from the Greek word *metanoia*), which means a transformation of mind and heart, the earthshaking self-admission that one was wrong about oneself, had been inauthentic to oneself as well as to others, had gone astray and forgotten the way back. In this spiritual psychological process, repentance is the internal act of leaving oneself open to transformation, being emptied of the interfering, self-defining self, so that baptism might fill one with the newly born Self via spiritual experience.

Repentance is a state of release from the past so that the present spiritual moment can be realized for what it is. Theologian Paul Tillich states:

> We are not inescapably victims of our past. We can make the past remain nothing but *past.* The act in which we do this has been called repentance.[1]

To be forgiven of the past is to release it to the void. Guilt and fear cannot sustain themselves; they need the continual urging of the self that feels them. They demand strict attention to survive, because they are transient feelings having nothing to do with God or reality. The psychology of Christianity transcends human feelings. Repentance is forgiveness of the old self so that a new Self emerging from the water might instead hear the voice from heaven saying, "Thou art my beloved Son; with thee I am well pleased" (Mark 1:11).

In the Old Testament, too, *repentance* signified a total transformation—a turning around and a returning[2]—a sudden realization of turning the other way.

> Let him *return* to the Lord, that he may have mercy on him,

And to our God, for he will abundantly pardon (Isa. 55:7, italics mine).

Come, let us return to the Lord (Hos. 6:1).

God has been left behind by the self-directed self, but the turning back to Him restores the reality of eternal goodness. Self-constructed selves have built up walls to enclose and fortify what they thought they were. They had sought to hide within dark caverns of sin, neither knowing nor caring that a new light dawned all around them, with real hope, and a sense that there exists a glorious, universal beauty of life, outside the dank cellars of guilt and fear.

James D. G. Dunn cites the radical turnaround in Jesus' parable of the Prodigal Son (Luke 15:11–24),[3] wherein the wandering, profligate son "came to himself" and realized he was perishing. And so he returned to his father expressing his sorrow, and is greeted with the joy of a warm embrace and a village celebration. Dunn goes on to say:

> The repentance Jesus called for was a reversion to a more fundamental dependence on God as the source of our being, our meaning, our motivations.[4]

This turnaround, this repentance, was radical in the sense that it was fundamentally life-changing. With repentance, the self-directed self is renewed and reborn into a greater sense of life in the here and now.

Baptism followed repentance, then, as a flood of light follows from flicking on a light switch. Another name for *baptism* is "christening," which word implies that the ritual brings believers to an experience like that of Christ, or that likens them to Christ. To Paul, baptism in Spirit allowed believers to identify with Christ:

> for *in Christ Jesus you are all sons of God*, through faith. For as many of you as were baptized into Christ have put on Christ. There is neither Jew nor Greek, there is neither slave nor free, there is neither male nor female; for you are all one in Christ Jesus (Gal. 3:26–28, my italics).

Baptism enlightens, re-creates, renews the christened in the divine like-ness. It does this by doing away with distinctions based on surface views. Universality upends the cordoned-off world, so that all is shaken together as one. The reborn Sons of God may now hear directly what before was perhaps an echo: "You are my son, today have I begotten you" (Ps. 2:7). A new identity is born. "So if the Son makes you free, you will be free indeed" (John 8:36).

To Paul, to be buried with Jesus in baptism was with him to be "raised from the dead by the glory of the Father" so that "we too might walk in new-ness of life" (Rom. 6:4). This is to enter a new world, and to live within it as a new Self. Baptism also made a soul part of a larger spiritual community-being, identified with Christ. To Paul, the apparent distinctions of the world had no more merit than lies and untruths. The world's distinctions and even identifications had fallen away, and now relationships must be based on something very new. Everything—primarily, the self—was seen anew from this experience of the inner unity of Christ.

Psychologically, baptism can release a flood of emotions or ideas that have been dammed up seemingly forever. Repentance renews by releasing the repressed aspects of the obstructed self, thereby uncovering a greater, more comprehensive Self that contains everything but is confined by noth-ing. Because there is a new Self within the self, the former self, unable to integrate it (because they exist in two different worlds), has instead to fade to open to the expanse of new experience. And so, for early Christians, the self died to self and with Christ rose to live more truly.

Just as Paul psychologized or internalized the significance of the Hebrew rite of circumcision, stating that "real circumcision is a matter of the heart, spiritual and not literal" (Rom. 2:29), so the Gospel of John does likewise with baptism. Jesus tells the woman at the well:

> Whoever drinks of the water that I shall give him will never thirst; the water that I shall give him will become in him a spring of water welling up to eternal life (John 4:14).

Obviously, the great effect of baptism was the effect it was perceived to have internally, within the believer. Because baptism with Spirit effects so much, it is spoken of as "living water" (John 4:10). Its miraculous activ-ity was in the exchange of selves it wrought. Baptism was an experience that provided early Christians with the conviction that they had died to the alienated self and been reborn into a new identity in union with Christ and with God and with all of life, by sharing the same essential nature. Baptism with Spirit had unlimited effects (Mark 1:8), even to the point of changing their essential nature. Surface, self-centered feelings drained off and washed away; what emerged were more universal emotions.

The Eucharist

Jesus shared a last ritual meal with his followers just before his crucifixion and resurrection. Mark states that at this Last Supper:

> And as they were eating, he took bread, and blessed, and broke it, and gave it to them, and said, "Take; this is my body" (Mark 14:22).

From a single loaf, the bread is broken into pieces and shared. Union with God through Christ is the purpose and significance of the Eucharist. It was Jesus' way of calling his followers to oneness with him. The purpose of sharing the broken bread in remembrance is to recall the presence that unites them forever.

Paul says that in sharing the Eucharist, believers share the life of Christ:

> The cup of blessing which we bless, is it not a participation or communion in the blood of Christ? The bread which we break, is it not a participation or communion in the body of Christ? Because there is one bread, we who are many are one body, for we all partake of the one bread (1 Cor. 10:16–17).

Again, union, spiritual oneness, is the significance of the Eucharist. It would not matter that Jesus was no longer there with them in the flesh; in fact, his Spirit would prove even more effective.

Jesus had indicated that the purpose of this breaking of bread was to recollect his words and to recall him. That Jesus said, "Do this in remembrance of me" (1 Cor. 11:24), gives the eucharistic formula a sense of "recalling, of making what is past present again."[5] There is a sense of *reexperiencing* in its very remembrance. There is in this sharing of bread and wine a sense of Jesus' continuing and eternal presence, and of believers' continuing and eternal union in Christ.

The action of eating the bread and drinking the wine is sublime imagery of union in eternal life; there is a sense of taking in something from beyond the self. It is not so much the wine that intoxicates, as it is the lowering of barriers to spiritual oneness that intoxicates.

> He who eats my flesh and drinks my blood abides in me, and
> I in him. As the living Father sent me, and I live because of the
> Father, so he who eats me will live because of me (John 6:56–57).

That is, those who practice this ritual meal continually with Jesus share his expanded sense of life in the Father. Their remembrance is of his Sonship and their own.

The Eucharist is reminiscent of the experience of those who, in the Jewish Exodus, were fed with *manna,* the bread of heaven:

> In the evening quails came up and covered the camp; and in the
> morning dew lay round about the camp. And when the dew had gone
> up, there was on the face of the wilderness a fine, flake-like thing,
> fine as hoarfrost on the ground. . . . Moses said to them, "It is the
> bread which the Lord has given you to eat" (Exod. 16:13–14, 15).

The very fact of, let alone ingestion of, the bread of heaven was a present remembrance of the eternal Being. It nourished the memory of God, as the Eucharist for early Christians provided for the continual presence of the Christ. Jesus had overcome death through life in the Spirit, even prior to his resurrection from the dead, and this new life could be shared by believers in him through this rite of union.

The Kingdom of God as Experienced

It is its experience that makes Jesus' *kingdom of God* what it is. I have mentioned that this spiritual kingdom was one of Jesus' primary teachings. Yet it is never precisely defined, but, rather, evoked in images. This is because the kingdom was known by its experience, and from its experiential effects, just as "a tree is known by its fruit" (Matt. 12:33). Jesus says that although it may start small, it blossoms into greatness:

> And he said, "With what can we compare the kingdom of God, or what parable shall we use for it? It is like a grain of mustard seed, which, when sown upon the ground, is the smallest of all the seeds on earth; yet when it is sown it grows up and becomes the greatest of all shrubs, and puts forth large branches, so that the birds of the air can make nests in its shade" (Mark 4:30–32).

The kingdom of God is first hidden, but again is known by its effects:

> And again he said, "To what shall I compare the kingdom of God? It is like leaven which a woman took and hid in three measures of flour, till it was all leavened" (Luke 13:20–21).

From its former hidden state, the kingdom of God can grow to be a place of peace and comfort for all. After an initial action—planting a seed, adding an expansive ingredient—undeniable effectiveness ensues from what was formerly so small and hidden as to be nearly invisible.

In other parables, the kingdom is seen to have preeminent value:

> Again, the kingdom of heaven is like a merchant in search of fine pearls, who, on finding one pearl of great value, went and sold all he had and bought it (Matt. 13:45).

The transcendent value of this experience of the kingdom of God renders ordinary worldly aims pale by comparison. In effect, the kingdom of God becomes everything to the individual who finds it. It turns one's value system upside down as it changes one's life. The Parable of the Wedding Guest (Luke 14:7–11) points up this reversal of valuation, saying that "every one who exalts himself will be humbled, and he who humbles himself will be exalted." Crossan comments on this parable:

> This example of situational reversal shows how the Kingdom

arrives so that one *experiences* God's rule as that which turns one's world upside down and radically reverses its normalcy.[6]

As with baptism, Jesus associates the kingdom of God with *metanoia* or repentance. From the very beginning of his public ministry, Jesus speaks of the kingdom as involving a transformation of mind and heart. "Repent, for the kingdom of heaven is at hand," Jesus states in Matt. 4:17. It is "at hand"; it is inside the individual. The kingdom of God is also "at hand" in the sense that it is present, it is here and now, as a result of having done away with one's past. Thus did Jesus say about those who would live in the past: "No one who puts his hand to the plow and looks back is fit for the kingdom of God" (Luke 9:62). That this experience of the kingdom of God (or for Matthew, the kingdom of heaven) is radically different from ordinary conscious experience is evident from the first.

Jesus speaks of the kingdom of God or Heaven as being entered (Matt. 7:21, 18:3), and yet it also comes (Matt. 6:10, 12:28), is revealed (Luke 13:20–21), is received (Mark 10:15), and is inherited (Matt. 25:34). It is likened by Jesus to a merchant (Matt. 13:45) and his treasure (Matt. 13:44), to a net (Matt. 13:47), and to ten maidens (Matt. 25:1). It cannot be contained by any single image.

This kingdom of God is declared to be present in Jesus' healings and exorcisms (Luke 11:20), and yet it is spoken of as awaiting in the future (Luke 22:18), and as "not coming with signs to be observed" (Luke 17:20). The kingdom might therefore be thought to contradict itself at first glance, but that is because such a new and different experience is difficult to explain in words of old. It is within but also between all its images and representations.

That the kingdom of God is an experience is further evidenced in this saying of Jesus:

> Being asked by the Pharisees when the kingdom of God was coming, he answered them, "The kingdom of God is not coming with signs to be observed; nor will they say, 'Lo, here it is!' or 'There!' *for behold, the kingdom of God is within you*" (Luke 17:20–21, my italics).

The kingdom of God is *within*—like a spiritual experience is within, like an aspect of the Self that has not yet been accessed is within, like another Self is within. To experience the kingdom of God is to experience another Self within, another Self that inhabits another world, another world where there exist entirely new rules about what or who is great and what or who is "least" (Matt. 11:11). To experience the kingdom of God is, in effect, to be born again.

The kingdom of God has a life of its own, and its life is known to those who allow it to rise from its hiding place in the unconscious. It is spoken of as growing of its own accord, effortlessly, seemingly unconsciously, beyond or below and above the human threshold of awareness.

> And he said, "The kingdom of God is as if a man should scatter seed upon the ground, and should sleep and rise night and day, and the seed should sprout of itself, first the blade, then the ear, then the full grain in the ear. But when the grain is ripe, at once he puts in the sickle, because the harvest has come" (Mark 4:26–29).

This is the hidden process by which the kingdom of God is entered and revealed. It is unfolded from within unconsciously, effortlessly, and its very newness and difference bring one to a new sense of the fullness of time. Jesus likens the kingdom to "good seed" sown in a field (Matt. 13:24) and sown in the heart (13:19).

To contemplate the reality of the kingdom of God is sufficient for this unconscious unfolding to begin. A heart that truly "hears the word of the kingdom" and understands it (Matt. 13:19) will be happy in its harvest (13:23). But to wait for, in the sense of expect, its unfoldment is where Jesus' emphasis on *faith* comes in. When the experience dawns, of its own accord, it will *show itself* for what it is. It will be as close then to a person as is any emotion or idea, as close as one is to oneself.

Its recognition, its experience, and its acquaintance will bring realization of the great value of the rule of God (despite individual perceptions, defenses, and delusions of control) to the believer. Jesus speaks of the kingdom as bringing with it a sense of thorough and perfect satisfaction, relating a parable of a man giving up all he has to keep it:

> The kingdom of heaven is like treasure hidden in a field,

which a man found and covered up; then in his joy he goes and sells all he has and buys that field (Matt. 13:44).

It is also like "finding one pearl of great value" for which one would sell all one has to obtain it (Matt. 13:45). The kingdom of God, then, carries with it a sense of ultimate value, with its ultimate and heavenly reward being itself.

In a sense, then, the world of God cancels out this one, just as formerly it had been vice versa. It would seem that one world excludes the other; they are too entirely opposite in value and in reality. Jesus points up the juxtaposition when he says, "You cannot serve God and mammon" (Matt. 6:24), and when he says of the world of divided loyalties, "Every kingdom divided against itself is laid waste, and no city or house divided against itself will stand . . ." (Matt. 12:25).

Yet the kingdom is seen and experienced even in this world. Theologian Teilhard de Chardin thought that the kingdom "grows in some way as it is more fully perceived, since those who perceive it then become a part of it."[7] It is taken within, but it is never fully contained.

The kingdom comes, according to Jesus, through the relinquishment of the worries and anxieties of daily life (Matt. 6:25), through prayer (Matt. 5:9), and through forgiveness (Matt. 5:14). The experience of the kingdom of God, when it comes, works both despite and through the world. It acts both despite and through the self. When everything is seen, despite initial appearance-related judgments, to work for the good, and everything and everyone are therefore seen in the light of this goodness and so changed, irretrievably, then the kingdom of God and the original creation have come upon one in power.

The fullness of the kingdom comes when it is realized that the kingdom is within not only the believer, but also in all. When it is found everywhere, then the kingdom is restored in all its glory. Much of Jesus' teaching has to do with relationships: his teachings about forgiveness, his Beatitudes, his healings, his desire to dine with and reach persons struggling on the lowest social scales. For Jesus, there was no self outside God, and no world outside the universality of his vision.

Jesus teaches of this universality among other things in his Beatitudes:

Blessed are the poor in spirit, for theirs is the kingdom of heaven.

Blessed are those who mourn, for they shall be comforted.

Blessed are the meek, for they shall inherit the earth.

Blessed are those who hunger and thirst for righteousness, for they shall be satisfied.

Blessed are the merciful, for they shall obtain mercy.

Blessed are the pure in heart, for they shall see God.

Blessed are the peacemakers, for they shall be called sons of God (Matt. 5:3–9).

This teaching goes from one end of the spectrum of experience to another. The experience produces a reversal of fortune by effecting a reversal of value, a reversal of thinking, and an exchange of selves. The process seen in these Beatitudes, taken as a whole, is that of a resignation from the values of the world in order to attain an infinitely higher set of values.

When Jesus pronounces blessing upon the poor and the meek and the pure, he is presenting a new vision of a new world, the kingdom of Heaven. Jesus' Beatitudes present what amounts to a beatific way of seeing. The eyes open to epiphany, the ears to revelation. He has seen something in the lowest of the low that goes well beyond the world's way of seeing and well beyond any conventional dictates of value. It is a sense of mutual relationship that Jesus finds within any other beside him, a higher, more eternal, and more real relationship that not only borders on God, but also exists within Him.

Paul speaks of the kingdom of God as an experience of Spirit that comes with universal states and emotions: "the kingdom of God is . . . righteousness and peace and joy in the Holy Spirit" (Rom. 14:17). Only the greatest and highest (most true and eternal) aspect of Self will enter or inherit the kingdom of God (1 Cor. 6:9–10). The kingdom must be an experience of Spirit because: "flesh and blood cannot inherit the kingdom of God, nor does the perishable inherit the imperishable" (1 Cor. 15:50). And what is the eternal and universal emotion worthy of Spirit?

Love

It is the experience of love that stands as the basis, the ground, for every act of love. Love is a grounding emotion and a grounding act of will (being that it can be "commanded"). Love is as natural as sunshine, yet here on Earth it seems to be a choice that can be made.

Love stands as the centerpiece of Jesus' teaching:

> You have heard that it was said, "You shall love your neighbor and hate your enemy." But I say to you, Love your enemies and pray for those who persecute you, so that you may be sons of your Father who is in heaven; for he makes his sun rise on the evil and on the good, and sends rain on the just and on the unjust (Matt. 5:43–45).

Be like God in your seeing, love everyone, even your enemies, Jesus is saying. Be as indiscriminate or complete in your love as God is complete in His love, and you shall be "sons of your Father who is in heaven"—you will be like God.

It must therefore be possible for a human being to love like God, to love universally and consistently. It is possible therefore to be a Child of God, if one could overcome oneself in order to love like Him. God comes to live within a person through love of others: "No man has ever seen God; if we love one another, God abides in us and his love is perfected in us" (1 John 4:12).

To overrule oneself, to love universally, however, is to value nothing else; it is to overlook all partiality, judgment, and, with it, sin. It is to see the entire world through the eyes of innocence, and to rest in a certain sweetness of heart.

Jesus declares that the experience of love precedes and fulfills all of the commandments of God. It is the greatest commandment, the one that includes them all. A scribe asked him:

> "Which commandment is the first of all?"
>
> Jesus answered, "The first is, 'Hear, O Israel: The Lord our God, the Lord is one; and you shall love your God with all your heart, and with all your soul, and with all your mind, and with all your strength.' And the second is this, 'You shall love your neighbor as yourself.' There is no commandment greater than these" (Mark 12:28–31).

To love God and to love like God is to love all those He created out of love—as if they share one being. Distinctions have dissipated and God is one, so believers must love as one. And when the scribe agreed with him, Jesus said to him: "You are not far from the kingdom of God" (Mark 12:34). To love like God and with God is to be very close to God. It is to share His Being. To experience the ultimacy and overwhelming nature of perfect love is not only to know but also to enter the world and the will of God.

To Jesus, to love like God requires an unyielding state of forgiveness. It is with one's "enemies" that the true meaning of love is perceived. The expansiveness required of universal forgiveness, the overlooking of detailed faults and unjustifiable wrongs, is akin to the expansiveness of God in all His mercy and benevolence. The mind opens and with it the heart. The way to reach this expansiveness is to experience for oneself, by willingness to forgive all as one, therefore to see all as one, ultimately to know all as one.

Love, like the kingdom of God, comes from a new sense of Self. This Self comes complete, interconnected, already whole, connected to others and to God through primordial but stately bonds. For love is self-integrating; it overlooks that which would defy love in its constant impetus to be itself by giving of itself. (In that way, it is like the sun.) Love of God, like the kingdom of God, channels every one of one's interests, directs every one of one's yearnings, and focuses all aspects of one's being on its transcendent object, which in the end becomes its very subject.

Love and the kingdom of God are mystical experiences, which entail a sense of going beyond former self-leanings and self-made self-limitations. To enter into these experiences is to ascend to the Heights of Heaven as if one belonged. The love within the mystical experience of union, unites a soul to its object as it unites the subject to God. Love extends universally; it extends to far-reaching states over the most oceanic of feelings. Though felt within, universal love can reach God.

John and Paul treated love with due majesty. Love is spoken of as effecting identification with God:

> Beloved, let us love one another; for love is of God, and *he who loves is born of God and knows God.* He who does not love does not know God; for God is love (1 John 4:7–8, my italics).

John goes on to expound on Jesus' saying that love is the greatest commandment:

> If any one says, "I love God," and hates his brother, he is a liar; for he who does not love his brother whom he has seen cannot love God whom he has not seen. And this commandment we have from him, that he who loves God should love his brother also (1 John 4:20–21).

Again, to love like God is to love every soul and therefore to rise to the expansive realm of God. As in heaven, so within.

Theologian Denis Edwards writes of the direct and unmediated experience of the Love of God:

> The experience is immediate in that it occurs without any sense of an intermediary between the individual and God who is present by grace. There is a sense of God's closeness which occurs without the mediations of concept, image or word. It is a sense of presence and of union which occurs at a pre-conceptual level. Thomas Aquinas teaches that while our intellects in this life cannot know God as he is in himself, yet we can love him in himself.[8]

This is what Paul means when he advises believers to "know the love of Christ which surpasses knowledge" (Eph. 3:19). Love cannot be fully described nor even fully conceptualized. He urges humans to go beyond themselves, beyond time, beyond distinction, subject, and object, to reach God. To consent to love is to shine like God, giving eternally and fully out of oneself. Love surpasses human knowledge in its capacity to raise awareness to God through the inner intermediary, Spirit. Subject becomes object, which renders it subject again. The Beloved is implicit in love. God is experienced in holy relationship.

In a passage that reads like poetry, Paul exults in the eternal and perfect nature of love:

> Love never ends;
> as for prophecies, they will pass away;

as for tongues, they will cease;
as for knowledge, it will pass away.
For our knowledge is imperfect and our
prophecy is imperfect;
but when the perfect comes, the imperfect will pass away.
When I was a child, I spoke like a child, I thought like a child,
I reasoned like a child;
when I became a man, I gave up childish ways.
For now we see through a mirror dimly,
but then face to face.
Now I know in part;
then I shall understand fully,
even as I have been fully understood.
So faith, hope, love abide, these three;
but the greatest of these is love (1 Cor. 13:8–13).

Love shines clearly, eternally, reflecting God, because it is of God, and it *is* God. There is no spot, no stain upon world or self when God through His sun-ship of love shines. Even great wonders such as spiritual understanding and prophecy and even faith are at once fulfilled and subsumed in the clear light of love. They lack its immediate intensity; they relegate themselves to the future or the past. Paul's famous passage stresses the crucial nature of love:

If I speak in the tongues of men and of angels,
but have not love,
I am a noisy gong or a clanging cymbal.
And if I have prophetic powers,
understand all mysteries and all knowledge,
and if I have all faith, so as to remove mountains,
but have not love,
I am nothing.
If I give away all I have, and if I deliver my body to be burned,
but have not love,
I gain nothing (1 Cor. 13:1–3).

Love is for Paul the nonpareil, the sine qua non, the *ne plus ultra,* the eternal essence of what it means to be called Christian.

Universal or perfect love is spoken of as the opposite of fear: "perfect love casts out fear. For fear has to do with punishment, and who fears is not perfected in love" (1 John 4:18). Love is withheld by fear, and fear upheld by judgment, but it all dissipates like mist in morning sunlight in the presence of love. Punishment does not exist for those who love, so there is no fear in them. In 1 Peter 4:8, it says that "love covers a multitude of sins." Love therefore may be spoken of as the emotion that saves, making holy all that it rests its holy arms around.

Love is the great equalizer. Where humans have misused intellect, making it serve self-interest as opposed to the interest of all, employing it for manipulating power games, and obsession with nothing, love comes to transcend all of this. Love transcends intellect as it transcends self-interest, and so synthesizes reason with unity of heart, and employs it always in the interest of all. Distinctions that formerly divided Being fade away, leaving only Soul itself, and the inner clarity to see everything as it is in God.

Followed to its natural conclusion, "Love your enemies" removes not only group loyalty, but also individual distinction. Classes and distinctions are obsolete, and self-obsession and even self itself are of the past. When all are seen as equal in the sight of God, then, we shall see, the world has effectively ended. A new kingdom has been entered, and with that, a new self, and with that, a new world, and with that is granted a new state of mind and heart and soul no longer broken but united as one in perfect peace.

The only boundaries of the all-inclusive kingdom are conceptual and perceptual ones. The one thing that is *ultimate,* that is necessary, that is greatness itself, the one thing of utmost value, is the will of God, the kingdom itself, which *is* those who live within it. The one thing that is real above all else is that which interconnects all else, surrounding each thing with life, Being in relationship, transcending but uniting everything else in its universality, the experience of love.

Love may seem disorienting when it comes, bringing its new mind and its new Self, alive in a newness of world. It initially detaches one from the old whirlwind of scraps once thought of as self, and the world that self called its own, as it leads one to an altogether new realm where there is no detachment. In the new realm, subject and object are preattached; they were never separate in the first. With no distance between them, there is no possibility of any separation one from the other. They were not made to be distinct, nor to die.

The intensely personal nature of the experience of universal love sends the heart and mind to be with Soul and Spirit in eternal spheres. What does "Love your enemies" ask of believers except that they cross over well-barricaded psychological boundaries, to experience universality? Opinions are as mist in the light of the inner sun. Values are easily reconsidered, perception renewed. For the contours that seemed to divide in appearance did not divide in fact.

Love brings happiness, an abiding sense of joy:

> As the Father has loved me, so have I loved you; abide in my love. . . . These things I have spoken to you, that my joy may be in you, and that your joy may be full (John 15:9, 11).

To experience love is to exult in heavenly joy. True happiness is eternal, expansive, yet a constant state, springing from a new kind of life, a life breathing eternal breaths, a life sustained in constancy for eternity. To love is to find oneself in the Heart of God.

Resurrection

Jesus calls his followers to an experience of deathless eternity. He had told them, "But I tell you truly, there are some standing here who will not taste death before they see the kingdom of God" (Luke 9:27). In John 8:51, he says, "Truly, truly, I say to you, if any one keeps my word, he will never see death." There is an explication in John 5:24:

> Truly, truly, I say to you, he who hears my word and believes him who sent me, has eternal life; he does not come into judgment, but has passed from death to life.

There is an experience so otherworldly that it bestows an eternal and deathless perspective. It stands one firmly on the bedrock of eternity. Jesus states that the sons of the new age "cannot die any more, because they are equal to angels and are sons of God, being sons of the resurrection" (Luke 20:36). They have been raised to life with him, being like him, one in essence, in purpose, and in Being.

Paul gives prominence to an experience of dying with Jesus so as to be raised with Christ. He states that "he who raised the Lord Jesus will raise us also with Jesus and bring us with you into his presence" (2 Cor. 4:14). Paul relates the experience of resurrection to baptism:

> We were buried with him by baptism into death, so that as Christ was raised from the dead by the glory of the Father, we too might walk in newness of life (Rom. 6:4).

Paul speaks of the universality of this resurrection: "For as in Adam all die, so also in Christ shall all be made alive" (1 Cor. 15:22). He speaks of the resurrection as being an entirely spiritual phenomenon: "Thus it is written, 'The first man Adam became a living being'; the last Adam became a life-giving spirit" (1 Cor. 15:45). Paul's emphasis once again transforms the realm of existence into that of Being.

Paul points out that this resurrection experience is effected immediately, here and now. He says, "you were buried with him in baptism, in which you were also raised with him through faith in the working of God, who raised him from the dead" (Col. 2:12). He tells them, *"you have been raised with Christ"* (Col. 3:1, my italics). The resurrection is an eternal experience because it is a timeless experience. For Paul here, the resurrection was an experience of a new life in an eternal now.

In Ephesians also, Paul speaks as if a resurrection has already occurred, as if the believer may already be seated with God and with Jesus in "the heavenly places":

> But God, who is rich in mercy, out of the great love with which he loved us, even when we were dead through our trespasses, made us alive together with Christ (by grace you have been saved), and *raised us up with him,* and made us sit with him in the heavenly places with Christ Jesus . . . (Eph. 2:4–6, my italics).

There is obviously here an immediate, here-and-now experience of res-urrection and of ascension into Heaven, available on Earth. Early church father Clement advises: "Let us contemplate, beloved, the resurrection that is continually made before our eyes."[9] This may be a restatement of Eph. 4:23–24, which urges believers to "be renewed in the spirit of your minds, and put on the new nature, created after the likeness of God in true righteousness and holiness." If all one sees happens to be immortal, then so is the one who sees.

Believers in Christ are promised new life, through deathless experience in Spirit, in a world infinitely more promising, eternal, and real. The new world is superimposed on the old that it may take on the innocence of that spoken of by Jesus in his Beatitudes. The kingdom of God with its bounty of peace is seen to spread itself before their eyes and to anchor in the depth of their hearts. They are now one with God, and bonded firmly to their brothers and sisters through shared holiness and love, having been raised thereby to newness of life. The experiences of early Christianity are eternal because they happen in a moment outside of time, in an eternal present, whenever the believer is caught up in the presence of the Spirit.

4

The Holy Spirit

. . . until the Spirit is poured upon us from on high,
and the wilderness becomes a fruitful field,
and the fruitful field is deemed a forest.

—Isa. 32:15

Transformative Experiences of Spirit

The disciples took part in a great collective experience of the Holy
Spirit just weeks after their experience of the resurrection of Jesus:

When the day of Pentecost had come, they were all together
in one place. And suddenly, a sound came from heaven like the
rush of a mighty wind, and it filled all the house where they were
sitting. And there appeared to them tongues as of fire, distributed
and resting on each one of them. And they were filled with the
Holy Spirit and began to speak in other tongues, as the Spirit gave
them utterance (Acts 2:1–4).

This passage speaks to the dramatically new nature of their experience. To be filled with the Holy Spirit is to experience the power of God. The tongues of fire represent the enlightening, inspiring, and otherworldly nature of this experience. Like a rushing wind, the powerful Spirit descended from Heaven and thus from outside of them (who they thought they were). And yet it resides within them. It seems to come from afar, from beyond the skies, from celestial Heaven, because it is experienced as foreign to their ordinary consciousness and their usual way of thinking, feeling, living. The sense of Being it brings is rarefied among human existence, like wind. Yet it is evoked as an experience inside them. The Holy Spirit is an experience that comes from beyond yet within.

There are other instances of early Christians being "filled with the Holy Spirit," such as in Acts 4:31, 8:17, 10:44, and 19:6. Early Christians were a spiritual community by virtue of their shared experience of the Holy Spirit. Jesus' disciples Peter and John are said in Acts 8:17 to have imparted the Holy Spirit through healing touch—"the laying on of hands." Though rarefied, the Divine Spirit comes through in the human realm. I have spoken of Jesus' experience of the Holy Spirit ("descending like a dove") and simultaneous realization of his Sonship to God at his baptism. When Jesus returned from his baptism, he was "full of the Holy Spirit," and he was "led by the Spirit" (Luke 4:1) to overcome self-limitation and thus go on to great things.

Saint Paul spoke personally of two very transforming spiritual experiences. The experience he had on the road to Damascus was transformative for him. This conversion experience resulted in Paul's spontaneous understanding of spiritual Christianity after having been a fierce adherent of the law, and it quickly convinced him of the eternal reality of the risen Christ, and of his own true feelings within a different realm of Being. Saul (his name before this conversion experience) was on his way to Damascus to arrest "any belonging to the Way" (Acts 9:2), that is, early Christian believers, when: "suddenly a light from heaven flashed about him" (Acts 9:3).

From the light, a rarefied and cosmic Jesus appeared to him in a vision (9:5) and, after being blinded and unable to eat or drink for days, Saul was "filled with the Holy Spirit" (9:17) and began to proclaim the Sonship of Jesus (9:20). So powerful was this experience that his very identity was affected, and more than affected, it was remade, regenerated, reborn;

thereafter he would be known as Paul. His foundations were shaken, his sense of reality was transformed.

Paul had other transforming "visions and revelations of the Lord." He refers to himself, indirectly in the third person (to avoid boasting), in the following passage:

> I will go on to visions and revelations of the Lord. I know a man in Christ who fourteen years ago was caught up to the third heaven—whether in the body or out of the body I do not know, God knows. And I know that this man was caught up into Paradise—whether in the body or out of the body I do not know, God knows—and he heard things that cannot be told, which man may not utter. On behalf of this man I will boast, but on my own behalf I will not boast, except of my weaknesses (2 Cor. 12:1–5).

So Paul was very proud of the man Spirit transformed him into, but as a human being and a teacher he had to remain humble. The experience was so transformative that he did not know whether it was in or out of the body. His spiritual experience was granted him by Spirit, and was *not* of his own doing or making. He had been caught up into a kind of "Paradise" ("the third heaven") of the mind; he reiterates that he did not even know whether he was in or out of his body. And he "heard" some of those secret and hidden things that "cannot be told, which man may not utter." And so he can only provide an indirect glimpse of this "third heaven."

Paul's conversion experience on the road to Damascus transformed him. Almost immediately, he became convinced of the truth of the religious ideas he had just a moment before been seeking to persecute. Psychologically, we might say that the strength of his persecution of them belied an underlying fierce attraction to these ideas. But that is beside the point here, for there are no precise psychological terms for the influx of Spirit he received; there are only metaphors. The blinding light Saul was struck by was open-ended because primarily experiential. And though it might suggest a number of poetic and psychological metaphors for us, it remained for him the turning point in his life, granting him a new and universal purpose, a new and universal understanding of God, and a new and universal identity in Spirit. It changed his life, as it changed the disciples, and it led them to offer this transformation to others.

Functions of the Spirit

To be filled with the Holy Spirit is to know the universal truths very personally. Truth of this kind rises beyond words, beyond concepts, beyond even personal experience. Rising beyond individual perception, the Holy Spirit provides a taste of abstract Being within the world of concrete existence. And as the world falls away, so does the limiting self, and as the new world expands to include everything, so is the Self continually augmented, fed with spiritual bread and the fruits of joining.

To experience the Holy Spirit is to presuppose a greater Self (joined with others) that can experience the infinitely greater heights of Heaven. After all, it is not the concrete mind that can understand it, nor the concrete man who can experience it. For, as Paul says: "no one comprehends the thoughts of God except the Spirit of God" (1 Cor. 2:11).

So what hope is there for the concrete human being? Being in the Spirit is the way to know God, for in the Spirit the individual is raised to a new level of Being—beyond human experience—so that God might truly be known from within the heavenly places.

The Old Testament had also spoken of the Holy Spirit as a way of knowing God ("the spirit of knowledge" of the Lord, in Isa. 11:2). In the Old Testament, the Holy Spirit represents God and is in fact an indication of His presence:

> The Spirit lifted me up, and brought me into the inner court;
> and behold, the glory of the Lord filled the temple (Ezek. 43:5).

To experience the Spirit is to experience the immediacy of the presence of God, and therefore to know and to understand (from "the inner court") an entirely new Realm and its eternal ways. All of this is made known through the Spirit, who by revealing the immediate glory of God within leads to the whole truth.

The Old Testament speaks of the Holy Spirit as both an agent of creation (Gen. 1:2; Ps. 33:6; Ezek. 37:1–10) and as an agent of reconciliation and union (Ezek. 11:15–16). Creation and renewal of creation seem to coincide in this passage:

> When thou sendest forth thy Spirit, they are created; and thou renewest the face of the ground (Ps. 104:30).

Though His children are "scattered" (Ezek. 11:16) and seem to reside far apart in this world, God sends His Holy Spirit to renew them, to bring them close enough to be joined. They must be reconciled to themselves to be reconciled to one another, and they must be reconciled to one another to rise to Him. Or as Jesus taught them, forgiveness of one's brothers and sisters will bring about experience of forgiveness of oneself by God and a renewed Self as one of the eternal Children of God.

There is also in the Old Testament a sense that the person who receives the Spirit of God becomes a new being:

> Then the spirit of the Lord will come mightily upon you, and you shall prophesy with them *and be turned into another man* (1 Sam. 10:6, my italics).

Saul became another man after his experience on the road to Damascus. Jesus became Son of God in his experience of Spirit in the Jordan. And Jesus allowed the Spirit to speak the words and do the works of God through him, so that it was not Jesus himself who spoke and acted, but the Spirit within him. Anyone who is "in the Spirit" becomes "another man," another being, from another order of reality inherent in the Spirit.

In the Gospel of John, the experience of the Holy Spirit (spoken of here as "the Counselor" who teaches and reminds of the heavenly things) sparks a remembering of the eternal truth Jesus gave them:

> These things I have spoken to you, while I am still with you. But the Counselor, the Holy Spirit, whom the Father will send in my name, he will teach you all things, and bring to your remembrance all that I have said to you (John 14:25–26).

The Holy Spirit, remembering God, is itself the instruction given it by

God, a way to the most real and eternal truths that continually renew the mind. In John 16:13, it is said that the Holy Spirit "will guide you into all the Truth." This is no mere intellectual or conceptual truth to which Spirit leads; this is the experience of another realm altogether, the experience of being in another reality, in which Truth is known intimately, and experienced as absolute in a way in which nothing else is absolute.

The Spirit not only remembers, but also further reveals, expounding and also expanding on what Jesus had to teach, in John's Gospel:

> I have yet many things to say to you, but you cannot bear them now. When the Spirit of truth comes, he will guide you into all the truth; for he will not speak on his own authority, but whatever he hears he will speak, and he will declare to you the things that are to come. He will glorify me, for he will take what is mine and declare it to you. All that the Father has is mine; therefore I said that he will take what is mine and declare it to you (John 16:12–15).

The Holy Spirit thus reveals Jesus as he is, in the Spirit, in his Divinely resurrected being. Believers are joined with Jesus when they allow the Spirit to transform them as well. The Holy Spirit personifies for the believer, in or out of the body, the abstractness that allows Jesus as the risen Christ to identify with all souls at once. Jesus' sense of the fullness and completeness of God is therefore transmitted to each individual by way of the Spirit, and this sense of fullness contains the whole of Jesus' teaching and beyond. The Holy Spirit brings with it from Heaven an experience of Truth, a Truth that includes and transcends both past and future by residing fully in the present, the complete and perfect Truth.

The Truth brought about by the Holy Spirit is an internal one from beyond the world:

> And I will pray the Father, and he will give you another Counselor, to be with you for ever, even the Spirit of truth, whom the world cannot receive, because it neither sees him nor knows him; you know him, for he dwells with you, and will be in you (John 14:16–17).

The experience of the Spirit is an experience beyond any of this world, yet it comes from within. To be led by the Spirit is also to be comforted by a certainty of which human knowledge knows not, to be led beyond the mental constraints that hold self and world in darkness. To be led by the Spirit so that one knows Him from within is to know the truth, for "the Spirit is the witness, because the Spirit is the truth" (1 John 5:7). The Spirit is one with God, being the Spirit of Truth, for "God is spirit" (John 4:24). God and His Spirit are of the same essence, one created to create, one Uncreated. Because the Spirit has a creative function with God, it can re-create mind, reestablish it in Truth, and reinstitute within the heart a great singleness of purpose. It can cause believers to believe that they too are part of God and of a new Realm in His Spirit.

The Holy Spirit also grants to believers the authority to forgive sins, an authority formerly reserved only for God:

> Jesus said to them again, "Peace be with you. As the Father has sent me, even so I send you." And when he had said this, he breathed on them, and said to them, "Receive the Holy Spirit. If you forgive the sins of any, they are forgiven . . ." (John 20:21–23).

This authority to forgive sins that is given believers through the Holy Spirit is not an administrative function but rather an *experiential* one. It is the transcendence in the experience of the Holy Spirit that results in its overlooking of sin. Its mere presence transforms the mind and grants a new understanding. Because it is the Spirit's function to reconcile and reunite, no form of judgment will be left to distort its function by emphasizing surface differences rather than oneness in Spirit. Its purpose is to keep the realm of God clean of even the thought of impurity.

Paul speaks of this communing in Spirit as granting believers a new identity in God:

> *For all who are led by the Spirit of God are sons of God.* For you did not receive the spirit of slavery to fall back into fear, but you have received of sonship. When we cry, "Abba! Father!" it is the Spirit himself bearing witness with our spirit that we are children of God, and if children, then heirs, heirs of God and fellow heirs

with Christ, provided we suffer with him in order that we may also be glorified with him (Rom. 8:14–17, my italics).

We have seen that the idea or experience of suffering and dying with Christ was central to Paul's spiritual theology. In this passage, though, we have the Spirit, or experience of the Spirit, as being key to *Sonship,* or closeness to and likeness with God: "all who are led by the Spirit of God are sons of God." (More on this sense of new identity in Sonship is found in chapter 10.) Sonship is simply likeness and closeness to God, and the *experience* of this likeness and closeness is achieved through "Spirit himself bearing witness with our spirit."

As noted previously, Paul writes:

What no eye has seen, nor ear heard, nor the heart of man conceived . . . God has revealed to us through the Spirit. For the Spirit searches everything, even the depths of God (1 Cor. 2:9–10).

God has revealed *Himself* through the Spirit. Though far beyond this world, God is *known* through His Spirit, even to the very depths of His Being. The experience of Spirit reveals that which "no eye has seen, nor ear heard, nor the heart of man conceived," because that is what Spirit is. It leads to all Truth and therefore enlightens every one; the resurrection of universal knowledge is its function.

In the books of both John and Paul, Spirit is sent to individuals (or implanted to grow in them) for the purpose of knowing God. God placed within the depths of the heart a call to remembrance of Him and of His True Creation, and a Guide to return to this Truth. Because the Spirit resides in the temple of the inmost heart, to know God truly through His Spirit is to know as well the true Self, Child of God in eternal relation to Him. With this new individual meaning, the world is granted new meaning as well.

As sons or children of God in faith, believers expect His love. In fact, they rely on it. They know it and they know Him, as eternal. This brings up another function of the experience of Spirit. Paul says:

God's love has been poured into our hearts through the Holy
Spirit which has been given to us (Rom. 5:5).

The Holy Spirit is conduit of the love of Heaven. Such love is the
Truth, simple emotion, but complete in transcendent understanding, to
which the Holy Spirit leads. Jesus "rejoiced in the Holy Spirit" and said:

I thank thee, Father, Lord of heaven and earth, that thou hast hidden these things from the wise and understanding and revealed them
to babes; yea, Father, for such was thy gracious will (Luke 10:21, KJV).

Anyone, primarily the most humble, can experience the loving truth
within yet from beyond themselves.

In any case, in all of the functions of the Holy Spirit, the Spirit acts as
Conduit of Divinity for humankind. It reveals knowledge of God, God as
Spirit, and God as Love. It was created by God and implanted in the heart
as not only an eternal blessing but also an eternal *attribute*. The Spirit not
only interprets but communicates, very directly. Though it surpasses human
understanding, it grants an abstract, more comprehensive understanding.
Only fear of the comprehensiveness of this understanding, that is, of losing self-definition, would keep it hidden.

The Pauline epistles teach that the Holy Spirit functions much the way
the cosmic Christ is said to function. Paul seems to equate believers' condition of being "in Christ" with being "in the Spirit." He states clearly:
"Now the Lord is the Spirit" (2 Cor. 3:17).

Paul sees the Holy Spirit's purpose as being equal to that of the risen
Jesus: as intermediary with God the Father. He identifies Jesus with the
Holy Spirit, because both are revealed through the same universal experience, whether this experience be called baptism, or dying and rising, or the
blinding truth of conversion, or being lifted up into the third heaven.

In another function of being in the Spirit, Paul speaks of the Spirit
helping the believer pray in a deeper language than human:

Likewise the Spirit helps us in our weakness; for we do not
know how to pray as we ought, but the Spirit himself intercedes
for us with sighs too deep for words (Rom. 8:26).

Again, transcending any self-limiting understanding, the Spirit communicates with God and the believer, uttering Heaven's native tongue to the heart that *knows* it. A new understanding is achieved through experience of the Spirit, using the sacred bond of the eternal language spoken eternally between God and Soul.

Paul affirms that the Spirit convinces with the certainty of the Truth it brings (or leads to, or reveals from within), saying that the Spirit within the heart is "a guarantee" of salvation (2 Cor. 1:22). One is convinced of one's righteousness and holy truth from within the Spirit of God. 1 John 2:27 speaks of the self-sufficient authority and certainty of the one who is led by Spirit, saying, "the anointing which you received from him abides in you, and you have no need that any one should teach you."

This is reminiscent of Ps. 16:7: "I bless the Lord who gives me counsel; in the night also my heart instructs me," and Isa. 30:20: "your Teacher will not hide himself any more, but your eyes shall see your Teacher." The Teacher is within; the teaching is a remembrance of the eternal and holy truth.

Paul places the worship of God in spiritual experience as the highest form of worship: "For we are the true circumcision, who worship God in spirit [or, worship by the Spirit of God]" (Phil. 3:3). Paul goes on to say in this passage that those who worship God by the Spirit in this way "put no confidence in the flesh." This means that the experience of the Spirit assumes the place of primary and ultimate reality, a reality recognized as more real than body and world. (One can be within the body yet not *of* it.) Nothing is as real as Spirit is real. "For he who sows to his own flesh will from the flesh reap corruption; but he who sows to the Spirit will from the Spirit reap eternal life" (Gal. 6:8).

Therefore, the Spirit carries with it the guarantee of eternity. And, according to Paul, the Spirit grants eternal life by granting, first, a "beholding" (or "reflecting") of the glory of the Lord, and then, a transformation into His likeness:

> And we all, with unveiled face, beholding the glory of the Lord, are being changed into his likeness from one degree of glory to another; for this comes from the Lord who is the Spirit (2 Cor. 3:18).

This then is the mystery "unveiled." "The glory of the Lord," a phrase also used by Old Testament writers to signify the magnificent and other-worldly nature of the presence of God, is likewise here spoken of as a transforming Spirit that transforms the believer "from one degree of glory to another" "into his likeness." What does God have to do with anything that is not like Him?

To reflect the glory of the Lord is to sit in His eternal presence in the heavenly places. It is to have possession of the Spirit: "Cast me not away from thy presence, and take not thy holy Spirit from me" (Ps. 51:11). Like the presence of God, the Spirit is present everywhere. There is nowhere they are not: "Whither shall I go from thy Spirit? Or whither shall I flee from thy presence?" (Ps. 139:7). And yet, "My soul yearns for thee in the night, my spirit within me earnestly seeks thee" (Isa. 26:9). Because it is universal, the Spirit is sought after (consciously or unconsciously) as personal salvation, and for the personal sense of universal purpose it brings.

The risen Jesus tells his followers: "you shall receive power when the Holy Spirit has come upon you" (Acts 1:8), and that they will in themselves be his witnesses across the land (1:8), witnesses of his fulfillment of "the law of Moses and the prophets and the psalms" (Luke 24:44). At that moment some of those witnessing were frightened because they "supposed that they saw a spirit" (Luke 24:37)—Jesus appearing and speaking as a manifestation of Spirit. He tells them that they will be "baptized with the Holy Spirit" (Acts 1:5) and that they will be "clothed with power from on high" (Luke 24:49). Jesus had previously identified the Holy Spirit as the source of his power through God (Matt. 12:28). In this postresurrection appearance in Acts, he is telling his disciples that they would come to share in this power.

Before this appearance, Jesus taught his disciples to ask to receive the experience of the Holy Spirit. He tells them (highlighting with perhaps humorous juxtaposition) that the Father is practically bursting to give the Holy Spirit to those who ask. "If you then, who are evil, know how to give good gifts to your children, how much more will the Heavenly Father give the Holy Spirit to those who ask him!" (Luke 11:13). He tells them simply to ask, to knock, to open the door. He tells them it is theirs for the depth of their desire.

Jesus states that the Holy Spirit will tell believers what to say whatever their need in this world, such as when they are dragged before judges (Mark 13:11). Here again is the Holy Spirit's communicative function. While it prays in groans and sublinguistic utterances, which only God and the yearning soul can understand, the Holy Spirit also expresses itself to others through the believer. It communicates with God for the believer, and communicates God to others through the believer. Its bonds are not simply words, however; they are the reestablishment of eternal links that lead toward the ultimate goal of reconciliation.

And so, the Holy Spirit holds a number of functions, including also for Paul (in the list in 1 Cor. 12:7–11) that of "the utterance of wisdom" and "the utterance of knowledge according to the same Spirit" (1 Cor. 12:8). This would be the wisdom and knowledge of oneness, for they experience themselves as one "according to the same Spirit." At times, spiritual effects seem like "gifts of healing by the one Spirit" (12:9), at other times like "prophecy" (12:10), at others like "faith" (12:9). But that is somewhat of an illusion, says Paul. He speaks of "varieties of gifts, but the same Spirit" (1 Cor. 12:4). He emphasizes that all of these gifts come from the same Spirit: "To each is given the manifestation of the Spirit for the common good" (1 Cor. 12:7). The Spirit therefore synthesizes and orchestrates, harmonizing chaos, effectively re-creating it, giving it a spirit of new life in the one true community: communion of Being.

The Spirit so rejuvenates by searching the depths of the person, psychologically speaking, first for troubled thought and feeling clusters that can block its awareness, and then resting in awareness itself, built into it, inherent in it. Spirit arrives as awareness itself. "The spirit of man is the lamp of the Lord, searching all his innermost parts" (Prov. 20:27). This is part of the Holy Spirit's healing function, but it is also part of its function to remind the human spirit of its original nature, to return an individual or a group to an honestly higher Self-appraisement. In the end, it is the same as its function as revealer of wisdom and of knowledge.

And so, these various functions and gifts of the spiritual church "are inspired by one and the same Spirit, who apportions to each one individually as he wills" (1 Cor. 12:7–11). As part of its communicative function, the eternal Spirit also helps believers to understand the effects of spiritual experience:

> Now we have received not the spirit of the world, but the
> Spirit which is from God, that we might understand the gifts
> bestowed on us by God (1 Cor. 2:12).

The Spirit is an aid in understanding Itself, a Translator of the deeper things of God, through its direct emanation from God. The Spirit strengthens "the inner man" (Eph. 3:16), grounds the soul "in love" (3:17), grants the power of comprehension even of "what is the breadth and length and height and depth" (3:18), and allows the believer in the Spirit "to know the love of Christ which surpasses knowledge" so that s/he might be "filled with all the fulness of God" (3:19).

The Bridge to Being

The Holy Spirit makes of existence a metaphor for Being, the realm inhabited by God, rushing into existence to lead those who share its experience to a higher Truth. In this way, the Spirit also fulfills its function as Organizer of a preexistent chaos or Re-creator. It is also Revealer as it recalls another reality behind this one. As Albert Schweitzer states, "For those who are in Christ and in the Spirit, their being in the flesh is only a matter of outward appearance, not a real state of existence."[1] There are two realities, but only one of them can be true. Once the higher is known through experience, the lower begins to fade.

To experience the Spirit within is to be "in the Spirit." The person who is "in the Spirit" is changed—ushered into a new reality. Paul writes: "But you are not in the flesh, you are in the Spirit, if in fact the Spirit of God dwells in you" (Rom. 8:9–10).

Bible scholar Stevan L. Davies comments on this, saying Paul:

> insists that spirit-possession is the determining factor of membership in the Christian movement. It is the defining Christian experience; without possession, one is outside the movement altogether.[2]

The presence of Spirit is the defining characteristic of the believer. Believers already dwell in Spirit, because Spirit dwells in them. This is *why* they believe; the Spirit within them *knows,* transfers experience of, and *is* the Glory of the Lord. They are, in fact, changed by the fact of its presence. Again, Schweitzer states:

> The possession of the Spirit proves to believers that they are already removed out of the natural state of existence and transferred into the supernatural.[3]

To be in the Spirit is to have passed over fear and death, and judgment, and to have crossed over into Life eternal.

When the Spirit entered early Christians, they became sons of God. This is how they were changed, and this is how they came to know salvation. They were redeemed and reconciled to God by recognizing their right relationship with God, as a direct emanation from Him. Through experience of the Spirit they found themselves in a different reality, infused with God, with a sense of unending union. They had found an eternal sun behind the temporal alternations of day and night. This eternal sun rose upon a new reality in Spirit from within.

Though "Spirit" would seem to be a vague concept, it was not a concept at all to early Christians, but rather a real and present reality. When it came, or was sent, it was more real and so, of course, more valuable than anything else. The Spirit is not consciously learned; it is known, not indirectly through study or through external teaching, but rather directly through experience. It is known even more directly than consciousness, from which we always seem to be a step behind. It fulfills the need for a new grounding through its eternal presence. It even offers to those who have it (or experience it) a new point of Origin in its function as Re-creator, or of calling mind back to remembrance of Creation.

We have seen that the unifying power of Spirit and of spiritual experience is emphasized in the Bible:

> And he came and preached peace to you who were far off and peace to those who were near; for through him we both have access in one Spirit to the Father (Eph. 2:17–18).

Believers are joined with Jesus in his Sonship and with one another through their eternal union in Christ. The Holy Spirit was individualized and personalized when Jesus came to identify with it, and when it came to fill and indwell believers. Spirit became the unifying community for scattered early Christian individuals.

Though it acted upon and within individuals, because it was the same Spirit, it gave these individuals a taste of communion and collectivity in Spirit. Though it manifested differently in each believer, it gave each of them a sense of being part of one spiritual church. After the Spirit has led, the individual is returned to a higher state than before, a state of experience by which one is made aware of one's union with God and one's new identification with Spirit. For: "he who is united to the Lord becomes one spirit with him" (1 Cor. 6:17).

Paul says that believers are united by one Spirit, "For by one Spirit we were all baptized into one body" and "all were made to drink of one Spirit" (1 Cor. 12:13). For the isolated individual existent, cordoned off by walls and by distance within and without, politically, religiously, and existentially, simply by virtue of being an individual, this is salvation, this is togetherness, this is implicit membership in the Community of Being. For the lost soul, this is being sought out and found by the Lord in the most secret of hiding places.

"You are not your own," says Paul, because of "the Holy Spirit within you" (1 Cor. 6:19). If the Spirit is allowed within, the individual becomes, like Paul at his conversion, *someone else,* another order of being. This is how Spirit changes things, how it changes reality by transforming the inner person, delving back into the Origin of that person and that person's being, so that the reborn mind now knows itself to be "born of Spirit." When an individual is thus affected by the Spirit, as we have seen with Jesus, who was "beside himself" when performing his early healings, that person is no longer himself. Paul plays on this characteristic of the early Christian when he says: "For if we are beside ourselves, it is for God; if we are in our right mind, it is for you" (2 Cor. 5:13).

Holy Spirit is the Bridge between aloneness and togetherness, in the way it is shared as one by all. It is also represented as the Bridge between obliqueness and clarity, between the worlds of darkness and of light. It allows for deeper truths to be told: "he utters mysteries in the Spirit" (1 Cor. 14:2), truths deeper than conscious as of yet, truths from the depths of one's inner being. This awareness, this knowledge, this relationship not only includes everything, it *is* everything.

How is this universal Spirit to be obtained, how is its universal nature to be experienced personally? Jesus suggests to his audience that they simply ask for it, open the door behind which it resides, and in faith it will come. Paul suggests: "Make love your aim, and earnestly desire the spiritual gifts" (1 Cor. 14:1). The love of God is revealed in the heart at the same time that the Spirit is made present, for:

> God's love has been poured into our hearts through the Holy Spirit which has been given us (Rom. 5:5).

Spirit is here experienced as God's love in the heart. When the Spirit comes, it reveals the nature of God, and therefore reveals all truth.

As with Love, spiritual truths can be discerned only by Spirit:

> And we impart this in words not taught by human wisdom but taught by the Spirit, interpreting spiritual truths to those who possess the Spirit (1 Cor. 2:13).

Paul states that to "live according to the Spirit," one must set one's "mind on the things of the Spirit" (Rom. 8:5). For, "To set the mind on the flesh is death, but to set the mind on the Spirit is life and peace" (8:6). To be in the Spirit is to be in Christ is to transcend the world.

As such, believers who once were milk-fed may now be addressed as "spiritual men" rather than as "men of the flesh, as babes in Christ" (1 Cor. 3:1). "By this the Holy Spirit indicates that the way into the sanctuary is not yet opened as long as the outer tent is still standing" (Heb. 9:8). The outer tents must be fully opened so that the inner sanctuary may be entered by the community of Being. Whether body or world, identity or perception, if it is outside, it must be brought within. The mind is set instead on the universal Spirit. Now then, "all rejoice together" (1 Cor. 12:26). They have received their commendation from God, their vision and their revelation, for they share experience "in the Spirit." The prophet becomes a poet in it:

And in the Spirit he carried me away to a great, high mountain, and showed me the holy city Jerusalem coming down out of
heaven from God . . . (Rev. 21:10).

The individual in Spirit is taken high so as to see the entire community
from above yet still from within. Each possesses this living experience from
Heaven, so all are equal in it.

5

The Word of God

For as the rain and snow come down from heaven,
and return not thither but water the earth,
making it bring forth and sprout,
giving seed to the sower and bread to the eater,
so shall my word be that goes forth from my mouth;
it shall not return to me empty,
but it shall accomplish that which I purpose,
and prosper in the thing for which I sent it.

—Isa. 55:10–11

The Transformative Interpretation

The Word of God can be defined in many ways, which may indicate either that it is broadly definable or that it is as indefinable as spiritual experience. Its range of meanings suggests that, as it is more deeply and more fully comprehended, it is experienced as a relinquishment of all limiting conceptions and a return to the Spirit from which it came. Like the Spirit, the Word of God is, in the end, not external to the individual. Not only is the Word of God part of God, but it is also part of the hearer and experiencer in union with God.

Scripture is always interpreted according to one's frame of reference. Every interpretation of Scripture will be a dogmatic one, drawn as it is from an individual and therefore narrow belief system, until it is read from a higher context. A legalistic belief system will interpret in behavioral terms, while a mystical one will interpret through transcendence of not only behavior but also thought. Many very different thought systems have claimed strict adherence to the Bible. Yet, as Bible scholar James D. Smart notes, "There will always be a diversity in biblical scholarship because of the high measure of diversity that exists in the Scriptures themselves."[1] Smart points out that theologians have tried for centuries to extract from the Scriptures a completely unified and consistent system of theology, but their attempts were predestined to fall short because of the diversity of material in the Scriptures.[2]

Spiritual experience bursts open the belief system and thereby expands beliefs, thoughts, feelings, and even identities that were once limited to one particular frame of reference. The foreign language of Scripture is meant to evoke something beyond itself, beyond concepts, and beyond theologies it is made to serve. The true function of inspired Scripture, spoken by the Holy Spirit to be interpreted by the Holy Spirit, is to shift the focus of the individual from the finite realm to the ultimate realm of Being, where God resides. Transcendent and transformative Scripture is not intended to encapsulate, but, rather, to liberate. It is meant to expand rather than constrict awareness and understanding.

The purpose of a mystical interpretation of the Bible is to evoke experience. There is an experience to be had simply in hearing the Word with Spirit; doing anything by Spirit is inherently spiritual. When the Spirit within the Bible is read with the Spirit within the individual, experience ensues, an experience born of encounter. Every such encounter leaves the reader transformed, for Spirit pours through and illuminates the dark places within, allowing the belief system and even the self to open to expansiveness beyond self-definition.

The transformative interpretation of Scripture, we might say, seeks to evoke an experience of the immediacy within the passage. It may return to the original moment of inspiration, to meet with the same Spirit that spoke it and sparked it originally. At the same time, it succeeds to the moment of culmination, across the ancient bridge to Being, predestined resting place of soul in union with God. It includes and transcends both past and future because it is always fully present.

Early church father Origen championed a transformative way of interpreting Scripture. Historian Andrew Louth says that for Origen, "The meaning found in Scripture is received from the Word, and the experience of *discovering* the meaning of Scripture is often expressed in "mystical" language; he speaks of a "sudden awakening," of inspiration, and of "illumination."[3] Origen saw the interpretation of Scripture as a religious experience rather than an academic or legalistic exercise.[4] Such an interpretation would be unique to each individual, and yet universal by virtue of the Spirit that sparks it.

The interpretation of Scripture may unfold in meaning over time, growing to encompass the unfolding, deepening, and broadening experience of the individual. Literature professor Northrop Frye speaks of "the traditional but still neglected theory of 'polysemous' meaning. One of the commonest experiences in reading is the sense of further discoveries to be made within the same structure of words"[5] so that "every time we read it we get something new out of it."[6] This view of the unfolding meaning of Scripture presupposes a great and sometimes-hidden depth in the Scripture itself; as the reader unfolds or develops in depth and breadth of understanding, so does what is read. Though the archetypal symbols of Christianity remain "permanent markers of soul,"[7] the degree of significance they possess, over time and with greater experience, reflects the heightened understanding and burgeoning mastery of the individual.

The depth of one's interpretation will depend on the depth of one's experience. Only the Spirit searches the deep things of God. Again, according to Paul, this process goes well beyond any mere human wisdom:

> And we impart this in words not taught by human wisdom but taught by the Spirit, interpreting spiritual truths to those who possess the Spirit (1 Cor. 2:13).

Paul urges the Christian to follow the Spirit rather than a written code of laws "for the written code kills, but the Spirit gives life" (2 Cor. 3:6).

This severe dichotomy indicates the drastic departure Paul took from his previous understanding as a follower of the Law. Spirit can speak directly to the Spirit in the inmost individual, "interpreting spiritual truths to those who possess the Spirit." The Spirit in the message is one with the Spirit within the believer.

Prior to his conversion, Saul was a legalist, a follower and advocate of the law. Within the law, he thought he'd found righteousness, but he was compelled by experience of his vision to rethink and unthink his salvation, his relationship to God, even his religious and existential identity. "For the law of the Spirit of life in Christ Jesus has set me free from the law of sin and death," the new man says in Rom. 8:2. Spirit is his new starting point and foundation; he now comes from there. His new Self originated from experience of Spirit. His interpretation of the Scriptures is therefore legalistic no more; for he has been freed by the Spirit from the law that warred with his mind (Rom. 7:23). In chapter 7, I further explore Saint Paul's new views on the law.

When Jesus is said to have spoken in such personal yet abstract metaphor as "I am the Bread of Life. . . . I am the living bread which came down from heaven" (John 6:48, 51) and "I am the True Vine. . . . Abide in me, and I in you" (John 15:1, 4), it is well to keep in mind that these statements are, as Existential scholar John Macquarrie called them:

> Transcendent statements, if you like, which, because we lack categories for the understanding of transcendent being as such, can only be expressed in symbolic or mythical form.[8]

Simply to begin to understand such transcendent statements is to surpass their particular literary form due to exposure to a sense of the possibility and potentiality of mystical transformation, which automatically debunks concretized thought systems and transcends traditional limitations.

Of the long-established four levels of understanding the Bible, including the literal, the allegorical, and the moral, it is only the fourth that might always be called the transformative. The poet Dante calls it the anagogic (or analogical) level of interpretation, and "the anagogic level is at the center of the beatific vision that fulfills faith."[9] This beatific vision stands at the center of spiritual or transformative understanding, evoking formerly hidden and secret spiritual truths that are able to transform a person's sense of salvation, of God, of life itself. And so, for Christian Mystics such as Meister Eckhart and Saint Augustine, the most literal sense of Scripture was indeed "the deepest level of what God has revealed."[10]

It seems that the resurrected Jesus was able to convey such transformative understanding abstractly, as when Luke reports that, walking with some of his disciples, "he opened their minds to understand the scriptures" (Luke 24:45). During his earthly life also, Jesus tended to speak obliquely in parables and sayings that were intended to be transformative. These parables and sayings could be immediately understood, as nothing else is understood. There is an urgency to his words that belies a new and different understanding of everything. Everything seems new, except the outmoded, in his vision. He juxtaposes the will of God with the tradition of men, saying:

> So, for the sake of your tradition, you have made void the word of God. You hypocrites! Well did Isaiah prophesy of you, when he said: "This people honors me with their lips, but their heart is far from me; in vain do they worship me, teaching as doctrines the precepts of men" (Matt. 15:6–9).

Tradition is far from the Word of God if it does not open its doors to the light of deeply personal yet ultimately transcendent experience.

Regarding Jesus' opposition to tradition, one scholar writes that the religious authorities of Jesus' day:

> evidently sought authority in tradition or written documents rather than in the personal encounter, the dialogue, between the living God and man. For guidance, they looked to the precedents of past authority, or to recognized techniques of scriptural exposition, rather than to the divine encounter within the worshipping community. In a word, those with whom Jesus collided were "authoritarian," not "prophetic."[11]

For Jesus, the divine encounter, experience of union with God and therefore transcendence of self, was the key to understanding the purposeful revelation of the Scriptures. He spoke like a prophet; his words necessitate internal transformation to be understood. This is similar to Paul saying that "the gifts of the Spirit of God . . . are spiritually discerned":

> The unspiritual man does not receive the gifts of the Spirit of God, for they are folly to him, and he is not able to understand them because they are spiritually discerned (1 Cor. 2:14).

The unspiritual self is directed outward, while the Self of Spirit is known from within. Macquarrie says, "Theological knowledge must be from the inside, it must be faith interpreting itself."[12] Likewise, the Word of God is the Word interpreting itself.

Jesus' reinterpretation of the ancient Scriptures was radical:

> At every step in his ministry, and even when he spoke most freely he was reinterpreting his people's Scriptures. But to those who were still imprisoned and loved the security of their imprisoning interpretation, he seemed to be destroying the Scriptures.[13]

Were Jesus' example to be followed, the Scriptures would be interpreted as pertaining to our infinitely higher Self. We saw that he did so with Isaiah in the synagogue. Yet we tend to find instead in the Living Scripture evidences of our preestablished philosophies or thought systems. James D. Smart says that historical critics "were haunted and embarrassed by a strange proclivity for finding in the text the very theology that they brought with them to the text. Rationalists discovered a rationalist theology and pietists discovered a pietist theology."[14] So going deeper within the self than either tradition or theology can go, to Spirit itself, allows the open-mindedness needed for Spirit to discover and interpret itself.

How does the Timeless reveal Himself in time? He sends the Word, not for conceptual understanding, as if the original creation might remain self-conceptualized and self-constricted through time, but, rather, He sends the Word to rise above such limitations and to lift the interpreting mind out of time, at least temporarily. This is why Jesus spoke in parables and in apparent "riddle-speech,"[15] and why Paul referred to "hidden" and "secret" levels of understanding. The conceptual mind searches the

Scriptures, thinking it will find life therein, yet all it finds is more of itself. The mind alive with Spirit also looks within and finds itself; it flies to the truer life therein.

As such, the true meaning of Scripture remains hidden until it is met with a deeper stratum of understanding born of deepening experience. To paraphrase Paul, Scripture is best read with Spirit because it was written with Spirit. Again, Spirit transcends "human wisdom," in its function of "interpreting spiritual truths to those who possess the Spirit" (1 Cor. 2:13). To read the Bible for transformation, one accedes to the same ultimate experience and inspiration with its Author. It is only through the transformation engendered in Spirit that one begins to understand the transcendence of the Word.

Jesus read the Scriptures as glorifying his Spirit-led Self. He interpreted the Scriptures as testifying to the eternal Self he knew himself to be in the Spirit. The story in which Jesus accepts the mantle of Savior, the Spirit of Isaiah's Redeemer figure, is illustrative of this:

> And he came to Nazareth, where he had been brought up; and he went to the synagogue, as his custom was, on the sabbath day. And he stood up to read; and there was given to him the book of the prophet Isaiah. He opened the book and found the place where it was written,
>
> "The Spirit of the Lord is upon me, because he has anointed me to preach good news to the poor. He has sent me to proclaim release to the captives and recovering of sight to the blind, to set at liberty those who are oppressed, to proclaim the acceptable year of the Lord."
>
> And he closed the book, and gave it back to the attendant, and sat down; and the eyes of all in the synagogue were fixed on him. And he began to say to them, "Today this scripture has been fulfilled in your hearing" (Luke 4:16–21).

The Spirit grants a lofty function. Jesus interprets the Scriptures here as revealing something about himself. The Spirit's way of relating to the world was now his own.

In Jesus' Parable of the Sower (Mark 4:3–9 and 13–20 and parallels),

"The sower sows the word" (v. 14). That it is sown in the heart is evident in 1 John 2:14: "the word of God abides in you." Jesus' interpretation of this parable reveals that *all* receive the Word, but some let it slip away (Mark 4:15), and some, whose hearts are like "rocky ground," initially "receive it with joy" (v. 16) but lose it during trials in their lives (v. 17). Others let "the cares of the world and the desire for other things, enter in and choke the word, and it proves unfruitful" (v. 19). But, the Parable concludes, those who receive the Word in "good soil" are those who truly "hear the word and accept it and bear fruit, thirtyfold and sixtyfold and a hundredfold" (v. 20). Good soil is aerated, leaving space and room for growth, for fullness, and ultimately for expansion.

Jesus spoke of eternal truths from the realm of God, and he lived and exemplified an eternal Self. That is why he could say, "Heaven and earth will pass away, but my words will not pass away" (Luke 21:33). His words are meant to evoke an experience that is instinctively and intuitively known to be eternal. His words are meant to impart a sense of "eternal life":

> Truly, truly, I say to you, he who hears my word and believes him who sent me, has eternal life; he does not come into judgment, but has passed from death to life (John 5:24).

Death is subsumed by life. The two cannot coexist; only one will be real in experience.

We can perhaps see, then, how the Word of God might be rendered ineffectual by tradition (as in Mark 7:13). The frozenness of tradition needs to thaw so that life might be felt by the immediacy of experience. Otherwise, misunderstandings might calcify and stick themselves in the lower order, paralyzing higher understanding. This is one way "the written code kills." But, on the other hand, "the Spirit gives life," opening the mind to understand the Scriptures and Life itself through the eternal transformation it brings.

The Living Word

The Word of God is referred to as the Living Word. The meaning behind all meanings is always eternal Life. Set within the sky above form, it allows an individual to transcend form. The Word as Scripture is the means of communication and, as the state of life, the Word is also *that which is communicated.* We might say that the Truth is hidden within it because, as noted, the truth cannot be contained by the strictures of language (no more than life itself can). But when language detaches and dissociates itself from its inherent limitations, allowing for internal transcendence, the experience leads to deeper and deeper understanding.

The Living Word is Life Itself. Jesus identifies with the Word of Life, but only after already having said that it is not him but God working through him (John 5:30–32):

> You search the scriptures, because you think that in them you have eternal life; and it is they that bear witness to me; yet you refuse to come to me that you may have life (John 5:39–40).

Eternal life is not in the inscription, but in the Living Word of which it speaks, which truly interprets itself. It is not so much in the things said about Jesus or even in the things Jesus said, as it is in Jesus himself. It is the same in any believer who accedes to be reborn with him within the depths of soul in order to *"have life,"* a life like God's.

It is the Word within that confirms and constitutes humanity's relation to God. The Word is "living and active," working in the individual and in every individual toward this end, to right the mind that joins them, allowing a manifestation of life itself. As Heb. 4:12 has it:

> For the word of God is living and active, sharper than any two-edged sword, piercing to the division of soul and spirit, of joints and marrow, and discerning the thoughts and intentions of the heart.

The Word of God is more than a book. Jesus says that it is "gods to whom the word of God came" (John 10:34). The Word is as alive as are we—no, *more* alive than we are, because we do not think of ourselves as this alive. Its life is eternal, directly from God, forever inclined to live.

James 1:21 exhorts believers to "receive with meekness the implanted word, which is able to save your souls." The saving Word is "implanted": It may at first seem small and insignificant as it abides within, in the mind, in the heart, in the soul, where it was sown by God in the eternal garden. One's word is also one's promise, and it is an active promise, gently reminding by drawing hearts beatifically to its own full transcendent life and understanding. It is this transcendent life and understanding, born of experience of the inner Living Word, which is "able to save your souls."

> You have been born anew, not of perishable seed but of imperishable, through the living and abiding word of God (1 Pet. 1:23).

The Living Word is able to convey a new sense of life, a sense of life that is known as eternal. As such, the Living Word is the inherent and ancient memory of another realm of being, the eternal creation. God's eternal promise was eternal life itself, not temporality and limitation ending in destruction and death. Through "the living and abiding word of God" and its experience comes a new and more true sense of life.

The Gospel of John begins with a treatise on the Word revealing its function as pertains to the original spiritual creation:

> In the beginning was the Word, and the Word was with God, and the Word was God. He was in the beginning with God; all things were made through him, and without him was not anything made that was made. In him was life, and the life was the light of men. The light shines in darkness, and the darkness has not overcome it (John 1:1–5).

"In him was life," John says of the Word, "and the life was the light of men." Again, the Word grants a saving life. From the beginning this Word lived, seedlike, sparklike, within the mind of man—even in embryo fully mature. Originally, Spirit was created in the likeness of the Word, to create like the Word, but the conceptual mind spawns only more concepts.

The Word is spoken of as an agent of creation, as Message and as Meaning, as message of Jesus and Jesus himself, as an eternal promise of God, as a new life in the abiding Spirit within the Creative Mind. What, then, is the commonality in all these things? The presence of the indwelling Spirit of God is what reconciles them. It lives truly and freely in the modern soul as it did in the ancient; it lives in the Scriptures that speak of the Spirit of God and of ourselves. And so words become in the Word more than describers; they are participators and liberators.

The Word of God, being living, indefinable experience, would have little to describe without the experience itself. The Word, like spiritual experience, is living, vital, moving but unchanging, abiding, and eternal. It draws and it moves the inward being, sparking not only actions and words, but also intention and will from deep within. It blends calling and function with will, and discerns the thoughts and movements of the Spirit in everything it sees.

Of course, the Word contains words full of revelatory content, because it is the experience behind the words that the Word truly is. From such experience does the Word grant newness of life, and a newly reborn Self. I will show that the Scriptures point to this new Self and they confirm its appointment; it is in this way that they confirmed the appointment of Jesus. A new sense of mission comes with a new mind and, with that, a new Self.

Proclaims Moses: "Would that all the Lord's people were prophets, that the Lord would put his spirit upon them!" (Num. 11:29).

And so the Spirit is free and enduring. Like the Word, it is vital, dynamic, alive. Like the Word, it is the living Presence of God ("the Word *was* God" [John 1:1]). It stops and restarts the world as it transcends time. It is the Universal Spirit, emanating from within young and old alike, rich and poor, male and female, native-born and alien. It is Spirit, Holy and Divine, luminous through and through, extending forever from within the true creation.

Inspiration grants limitlessness—this is the sense that it gives. Both the words one hears and the individual oneself are granted significance through expansiveness and connection through spiritual sight. Without vision, the words remain sealed: "And the vision of all this has become to you like the words of a book that is sealed" (Isa. 29:11). The Word of God remains hidden except to Spirit. To read the inspired Word with unbounded inspiration is to meet it in the sky in which it lives. The implanted Word ensures that the soul has access to limitless Truth, despite prevailing ground conditions. To all who "received" the Living Word, says John:

he gave power to become children of God; who were born, not of blood nor of the will of the flesh nor of the will of man, but of God (John 1:12–13).

Truly to hear and to abide by the Limitless Word is to have one's very *point of origin* changed. It is to be reborn in Spirit, and, in essence and in deepest reality, to be "born of God."

The Truth is everywhere if it is in the soul; if it is in the soul, it is in every soul, the essence of all that lives. John says of the Word:

The true light that enlightens every man was coming into the world. He was in the world, and the world was made through him, yet the world knew him not (John 1:9–10).

The Word went everywhere with Jesus, and the light of its very Presence and Being reinterpreted the world in an extraordinarily broad range of vision. He heard it in the Scriptures, heard it in the words he experienced at his baptism, heard it directly from God in prayer in solitude, and, upon his return to society, he saw it alive and glowing in every soul he encountered.

2 Tim. 2:9 says: "But the word of God is not fettered." There are no limitations to his "elect" (2:10). "All scripture is inspired by God and profitable for teaching" (3:16), and not only for teaching. Scripture, alive as the Word, interprets itself, and so relates to those for whom it interprets in a new way. No longer conceptual, it has become actual. If the Word is not fettered, neither is the soul that believes. The Word is an elemental and essential aspect of the Self, implanted by God, willed to remain forever in the Garden of Being.

Jesus found in the Holy Scriptures a vision of the universal and the personal lying together. There he found fulfillment for himself, and religion for others, but a religion that contains the notes of fulfillment, blessed joy in everything. As each soul senses the fulfillment of its religion, it is transformed because the soul is transformed.

Jesus portrays the Word as actively purifying and sanctifying: "You are already made clean by the word which I have spoken to you" (John 15:3). Salvation therefore lies within it. It recalls the eternal baptism by Spirit through water and air, wherein is born a new being, clean, unfettered head to foot, joined with real life because joined spiritually to God. The Word spoken by God in His Creation was truly given—without expectation that it would ever be temporary or limited in any way.

The Word lends to existence the state of Being. Without the Word, there is only speculation, and speculative living, a stultifying existence. The experience of God Himself is whispered eternally and transcendentally through the Word, and the Children of God are reborn through the abiding and living Word. Transformative words are accorded value insofar as they lead forever to their ultimate destination and do not detour from their true mission. The Living Word of God experienced is understood.

The highest or most absolute subjective Truth does not change. Eternal Words never pass. All the evidence is internal, like happiness, a constant state, intimately connected with a new kind of life, fed by its eternal nature. No wonder, then, that Jesus spoke in "antithetical parallelism (piping and dancing versus singing a lament and mourning)."[16] How else to make the distinction clear than to juxtapose and contrast the simple essence of Being from existence in all its contrariety? Bible scholar John P. Meier states that "ancient Semitic thought, much more than our Western tradition of Aristotelian logic, delighted in paradoxical statements that held opposites in tension."[17] But here we have, not opposites held in tension, but two distinct universes, two unequal and opposite ways of life. Sickness is given over to health, aloneness to encounter, sadness to communion. Unbelief is transformed to belief, and death is superseded by life in the Word.

Jesus' way of interpreting the Scriptures was "in the Spirit," like a prophet. James D. Smart says:

> The prophet, immersed in the tradition, could never become its prisoner. Rather he was schooled by it to listen for what God was saying to his people in a new and different day. What he heard made him a reinterpreter of the tradition.[18]

Of course, Spirit would cause reinterpretation, because its experience leaves the mind entirely changed. The mere fact of Spirit is transformative. A different Self interprets everything differently, and a different world is lived in differently.

Paul speaks of the confidence of the spiritual man:

> Such is the confidence that we have through Christ toward
> God. Not that we are competent of ourselves to claim anything as
> coming from us; our competence is from God, who has made us
> competent to be ministers of a new covenant, not in a written code
> but in the Spirit; for the written code kills, but the Spirit gives life
> (2 Cor. 3:4–6).

Paul does not claim this competence of himself, but rather through the
Spirit that grants new life, beyond any conception of human selfhood. Any
human and limited interpretation would end in existence, and ultimately in
Sheol, in nothingness. But the Spirit reestablishes original mind to the original freedom of life.

According to Stevan L. Davies, "Spirit," "Word," and "Son" are in
essence all "paradigms for the possession experience,"[19] for the state of
being *in the Spirit.* He comments that "John's gospel appears complex
because it uses a multiplicity of terms for exactly the same thing."[20] There
is one experience just as there is one Spirit. The Word lives as nothing else
truly lives. Embedded deeply in the heart, the mind, and the soul, it grants
life because it is truly alive.

Paul says to the Corinthians:

> and you show that you are a letter from Christ delivered by us,
> written not with ink but with the Spirit of the living God, not on
> tablets of stone but on tablets of human hearts (2 Cor. 3:3).

These words written in Spirit share the experience of which they speak.
They share Christ, they share the Son, they share the Spirit, and they share
the Living Word, just as they share Life itself.

6
Creation, the Fall, and the End of the World

For behold, I create new heavens and a new earth;
and the former things shall not be remembered or come into mind.
—Isa. 65:17

Creation and the Fall into Existence

The commonly held Judeo-Christian conception of creation begins with God creating the Earth, whereupon a stray intention (not God's) inserts itself, causing the true creation to fall from its original, pristine state. The Hebrew myths of the creation of the world are retold and revamped from more ancient poetic myths such as the Babylonian *Enuma Elish* and the Ugaritic Baal epic. The more ancient Sumerian and Babylonian myths have the chaotic world already preexistent, with the god's creation of the world being an ordering of this chaotic mass of matter in order to bring at least a portion of it under His guidance. Elements of these ancient myths remain in the later Hebrew myths.

In the beginning God created the heavens and the earth. The earth was without form and void, and darkness was upon the face of the deep; and the Spirit of God was moving over the face of the waters. And God said, "Let there be light"; and there was light. And God saw that the light was good . . . (Gen. 1:1–4).

According to mythologist S. H. Hooke, both of the Hebrew accounts of creation (found, roughly, in Genesis 1 and Genesis 2, referred to by scholars as the Jehovah-Elohim and Priestly accounts) "assume the existence of some kind of material world."[1] God brings life and order to the preexistent chaos; He does not create it *ex nihilo,* from nothing. In the myth, something existed, but this primordial clutter of dust and clay did not yet live because it had not been breathed into Being by God. In the myth, God scoops up some of this lifeless matter and:

then the Lord God formed man out of dust from the ground, and breathed into his nostrils the breath of life; and man became a living being. And the Lord God planted a garden in Eden, in the east; and there he put the man whom he had formed (Gen. 2:7–8).

While matter and the stuff of the body preexisted according to the ancient mythology, God breathed an oasis of Life and Spirit therein.

God spoke creation into being—as Being. He breathed His life into it, and it became a living soul, to live forever in unspoiled Paradise. This part of the myth should not be taken too literally; even in material terms, it is attempting to describe an original spiritual state of being. The Tree of Life at the center of the Garden stands as the representation of Being, of life unbounded by form. The perfection of the original Garden is inherent in the Spirit by which it was created or breathed into being. A complete spiritual universe was spoken into being by the Word, an effortless Garden watched over by the Tree of Life. Completeness was already inherent in the original creation, an ultimate reality coequal with Spirit. The original Garden is the Ground of Being, and God is always there.

Early church father Origen conceived of God's creation as being entirely spiritual, with the material world being at best a vehicle for escape from the chaotic world of dust and a return to the original spiritual state of mind and being. For Origen:

> Originally all spiritual beings, *logikoi,* were minds, equal to one another, all contemplating the Father through the Word.[2]

Thus for Origen, mind is the true creation of God because it is more like God than are bodies. Bodies are the product of a later fall from Grace, a basic misperception and misunderstanding shooting up to overgrow the true state of Being. Yet the fallen body provides an opportunity for remembrance of the Divine Breath of God, an opportunity:

> to ascend again to contemplation of God by working themselves free from their bodies and becoming minds, *nous,* again. As *nous,* the spiritual being can contemplate the Ideas and realize its kinship with this realm.[3]

For Origen, the story of the fall of creation is an allegory not only of the descent into physical existence, but also of reconciliation with the state of original Being and an ultimate return to the perfect reality of Spirit. Underlying this view is the assumption (shared with the New Testament) that all things ultimately return to the essence of what they are.

In the biblical account, the fall from creation begins immediately with the first man and woman, the very first human existents. The perfect creation was not long for this world. It was glimpsed by Adam and Eve only for a few fleeting moments, never to be seen again. From this first couple on, from the beginning of either linear or circular time, human existence somehow runs counter to the perfection of Being—hence the need to deal with guilt. The first man and woman had, influenced by the lying serpent, rebelled against God and therefore were cast out of the Garden and from the direct sight of God, into human and historical existence.

In the Genesis account, Adam and Eve had eaten of the fruit of the tree of the knowledge of good and evil, having abandoned the Tree of Life and the original Garden. They were thereupon sentenced to a life of toil, suffering, pervasive conflict, degeneration, and ultimately death. They were sentenced to human existence:

> In the sweat of your face you shall eat bread till you return to the ground, for out of it you were taken; you are dust, and to dust you shall return (Gen. 3:19).

Physical creation and the fall are so closely bound together that it seems likely that they are really two parts of one motion, scenes of the same basic act. Theologian Paul Tillich states of creation and the fall from being: "The meaning of the myth is that the very constitution of existence implies the transition from essence to existence."[4] Existence itself is the fallen state.

As newly separated creatures, Adam and Eve began to see separation, a restless outer world in sharp counterpoint to their long-lost spiritual world of peace and wholeness. Therefore, they began to see opposition in everything they looked upon, including themselves, therefore to feel a sense of alienation, as if they were mere isolated things among the multitudes of things, as if their separation from God had constituted their lonesome, individualized existence. Feeling naked and alone, in their dread they felt an estrangement from God, an inner emptiness that had a moment before been filled with communion and communication. As their physical eyes opened, their spiritual sight closed off to them. Their minds and their eyes were filled instead with conceptions and perceptions of good and evil, and nothing was left of Life-giving innocence. They began to think of themselves as lowly creatures of dust rather than high and abstract creations of Spirit.

> And they heard the sound of the Lord God walking in the garden in the cool of the day, and the man and his wife hid themselves from the presence of the Lord God among the trees of the garden (Gen. 3:8).

They hid themselves from "the presence of God" and from their true Self, a state of peace and love and unity of knowledge, and this initial fear of God was exacerbated by their attempts to hide. Fearing consequences for the guilt of alienation they felt inside, they consigned themselves to an existence of toil, suffering, guilt and fear, and ultimately death.

This, then, is the state of sin, closely aligned with the state of human existence. To partake instead as the first ones did from the tree bearing fruit of the knowledge of good and evil was to try to live by "a knowledge founded on self-consciousness."⁵ Philosopher William Barrett comments:

> But the sinfulness that man experiences in the Bible—as in the Psalms or the Book of Job—cannot be confined to a supposed compartment of the individual's being that has to do with his moral acts. This sinfulness pervades the whole being of man: it *is* indeed man's being, insofar as in his feebleness and finiteness as a creature he stands naked in the presence of God.⁶

Running from their Creator, Adam and Eve ran from themselves, and they and their descendents successfully eluded the memory of the true nature of creation. Confined to the prison they helped to forge outside the Garden, they learned to forget and so to disregard the true state of Being that remained as but a hidden memory within them. Estrangement's anguished cries could not long be held back by alien roles and even selves spun from nothing at all.

Some early Christian Gnostics held similar views. The world was no place for the human soul. Gnosticism in general affirmed a total opposition and antithesis of spirit and matter; the two were innately distinct and even opposed. In Gnostic accounts, original man fell from spiritual union and was shattered through ignorance of this spiritual union into myriad fragments. Some attribute the making of the world to a kind of demigod or demiurge, as opposed to the real God Who dwelt forever in the Highest. Gnostics generally believed in drawing sharp lines of distinction between the existence of multiple bodies and the unified spiritual creation of God. They can trace this view back to the New Testament, stressing Paul's distinction between creaturehood and the spiritual truth of creation, as for instance in his stating that:

> they exchanged the truth about God for a lie and worshiped and served the creature rather than the Creator, who is blessed for ever! (Rom. 1:25)

The Christian mystic Meister Eckhart extends this line of thought when he declares that "all that touches creatures or can be touched by them is far from God and alien from him."[7] The alienation is in the very idea of existence apart from God—in any form other than Spirit, Mind, or Being.

Speaking of Gnostic views, Elaine Pagels, a scholar of early Christianity, states, "According to Ptolemy, a follower of Valentinus, the story of Adam and Eve shows that humanity 'fell' into ordinary consciousness and lost contact with its divine origin."[8] This fall into ordinary consciousness is more significant than the fall into bodies. For, as Origen pointed out, bodies can be seen as vessels of salvation rather than simply as vehicles of the fall. Gnostics spoke of the body as a corpse and a tomb, but this is because the ordinary consciousness, seemingly trapped in a body, does not recognize its spiritual origin, not because of the mere existence of bodies. The things of existence can be means to salvation, tangible yet transcendent means to the original spiritual world; they can be seen with new eyes, filled with the light of new purpose.

Contemporary with these views is the Neoplatonist Philo's allegorical reading of the fall, in which the serpent basically draws humans' eyes down to the things of the world and away from the "sovereign mind" immersed in heavenly realities.[9] Scholar of Mysticism Bernard McGinn speaks of Philo's achievement as "the first in a long line of interpretations of the Eden story as a timeless message about the inner conflict and fall in every soul."[10] Philo saw the myth as personalizing itself in the individual so that its meaning was then derived from an internal significance springing from a logic that defied the world's conceptualizations and a vision that redefined human perception. When the conflict of good versus evil occurs within the individual, then that individual has reached that psychological state of urgency that Jesus emphasized in his teaching.

The conscious or unconscious sense of estrangement from God and from others is the root of the idea of sin, even when sin is viewed as a transgression of an external law. Paul indicates that simply to know of an external law is to be alienated from it. Paul Tillich states simply that "sin" is "the state of estrangement from that to which one belongs—God, one's self, one's world."[11] The breaking or forsaking of the universal law of God produces feelings of despair where previously happiness reigned supreme in the mind; the conscience continually whispers that we are not being true to ourselves. Sin is not so much the transgression, the breach itself, but the broken state that lies in its wake. Absence from God and from the deep sense of union in togetherness is its own consequence. It is hell on Earth, being utterly alone, destitute in loneliness, separate from all that lives. Meister Eckhart states that "to be cut off from God at all is the pain of hell."[12]

With the onset of estrangement and the fall from the Grace of Being was the effortless life gone, replaced with the need of effort to sustain a sense of life. For Jesus, the life provided by God is effortlessly given, effortlessly received. He says in Luke 12:27:

> Consider the lilies, how they grow; they neither toil nor spin;
> yet I tell you, even Solomon in all his glory was not arrayed like one
> of these.

Jesus here is representing the effortless life before the long, slow clutch of existence. He counsels a return to that impossibly simple state far removed from worry and constant anxiety about existence. The function of the temporal being in search of the spiritual, then, is to forsake the worry that held the human being to hard labor, struggle, and despair. One's true function becomes instead to forsake, counter-instinctively, the preoccupation with the means of existence including clothing and food, and, as Jesus concludes in Luke 12:31, "Instead seek the kingdom, and these things shall be yours as well."

This saying of Jesus stands in sharp rebuttal to the Genesis account of despair in the dirt and dearth of existence: "in toil you shall eat of it all the days of your life" (Gen. 3:17). The daily compulsion to sustain existence wends away from God, rather than toward Him. The existent hides, from peace mainly, from different strata of consciousness, from a different life, sustained entirely by the presence of God, and from whatever flows from that. Preoccupying existential struggle is contrary to the eternal effortlessness of Being.

The first man and woman's fall was a tumble into existence. The Primordial Spirit breathed by God deep into the mind caused humankind eventually to recall the godlikeness of their origin. In Gen. 1:26, God says,

"Let us make man in our image, after our likeness"; God, it seems, creates more of Himself. They were godlike in the beginning; there was no need to "know good and evil" to become gods. But the very first existents chose duality over union, death over life, time over eternity, hiding over openness, and struggle over Being. The forbidden idea carried the fruit of its own consequence. The mistaken idea was that existence could exist in any way apart from God; the consequence was likewise the aftermath of this idea: existence apart from God. The first existents reconceived themselves into aberrations from God by hiding out from Him in the material world; with each passing step into seclusion in the body they mistook more and more the loveliness of the Presence of God. Could they hide and remain imprisoned forever, or would the lifting of the weight of their torments through the lightness of Grace eventually impel them to remember the original creation?

The End of the World as a Return to the Beginning

The primordial light of Gen. 1:3 was not that of a material sun: "And God said, 'Let there be light'; and there was light." This earliest light is created days before the sun and moon in the biblical account (Gen. 1:14–19). This original light was the transparent light of Mind and Spirit, the original Creation from before the foundation of the world. Death had not yet been conceived of. Time and toil had no task yet of putting off mindfulness of eternity. All was instant awareness, holiness, grace, and beatitude, for the original light was a light of pure Spirit.

Will the end be like the beginning? Where else is one to return except to God, to whom leaving is impossible? Paul advocates that early Christians "deal with the world as though they had no dealings with it. For the form of this world is passing away" (1 Cor. 7:31). When the "form of this world" passes away, then what will be left but God and His Authentic Creation? What will come of time? What will come of us?

Early Christians looked not for a new phase of history but for the end of history. Theirs was an implicitly radical worldview. Yet the end of everything one knows, including the world, may be nothing more than a return to pre-beginnings. Returning to light was a simple matter, really, of emerging from hiding places to which all of humankind had, in its alienation, grown accustomed. That the early Christians expected absolute world-altering change is testimony to the self-transforming nature of their spiritual experience. James D. G. Dunn states that Jesus, in his parables and apocalyptic sayings, was able:

> to distinguish the *power* of the End kingdom from the consummation of the End itself. This could only be his consciousness of effective spiritual power—such power as he believed belonged only to the end time.[13]

The kingdom of God envisioned by Jesus entailed the end of one world for another.

The end of the world is not the end of everything; it occurs, in Revelation, at the end of the Bible, in "the New Jerusalem" and this state's concomitant "true Peace" (the literal meaning of "Jerusalem"). Early church father Clement says that it is a "return to that peace which was the mark that from the beginning was set before us."[14] The holy city is now an entirely spiritual state, ruled by one God. The believer is now privy to its regal vision and to its full experience of the Presence:

> After this I looked, and lo, in heaven an open door! At once I was in the Spirit, and lo, a throne stood in heaven, with one seated on the throne! (Rev. 4:1–2)

S. H. Hooke explains the connection between the myths of creation and the end of the world thusly:

> Just as the divine act of creation lies outside the horizon of history and can only be described in the language of myth, so the divine act that brings history to a close can only be described in the same terms.[15]

Outside of history, all that exists is a state of mind and soul and being. Northrop Frye states that for the early Christians:

> The Garden of Eden, the Promised Land, Jerusalem, and

Mount Zion are interchangeable synonyms for the home of the soul, and in Christian imagery they are all identical, in their "spiritual" form . . . with the kingdom of God spoken of by Jesus.[16]

The end is like the beginning. The New City picks up where the Original Garden left off.

Jesus refers to the spiritual refreshment he brings as "living water" (John 4:10), saying that:

> whoever drinks of the water that I shall give him will never thirst; the water that I shall give him will become in him a spring of water welling up to eternal life (John 4:14).

This recalls the river of the water of life in the Garden and in the New Jerusalem:

> Then he showed me the river of the water of life, bright as crystal, flowing from the throne of God and of the Lamb through the middle of the street of the city; also, on either side of the river, the tree of life with its twelve kinds of fruit, yielding its fruit each month; and the leaves of the tree were for the healing of the nations (Rev. 22:1–2).

This end-time vision recalls Genesis' conception of a river "flowing out of Eden to water the garden" (Gen. 2:10). We can see in this passage, too, that the "tree of life" has been restored, and that its presence blesses ultimately with leaves of healing and of reconciliation.

The ancient prophets also conceived of the end as akin to the beginning, with a retraction of the travails of existence:

> Violence shall no more be heard in your land, devastation or destruction within your borders; you shall call your walls Salvation, and your gates Praise. The sun shall be no more your light by day, nor for brightness shall the moon give light to you by night; but the Lord will be your everlasting light, and your God will be your glory. Your sun shall no more go down, nor your moon withdraw itself;

for the Lord will be your everlasting light, and your days of mourning shall be ended (Isa. 60:18–20).

Deathlessness is key in the vision of everlasting light. The nations will lose their borders, and the walls will be spiritual ones: "Salvation" and "Praise." The eternal light is the primordial light through which true creation is always seen.

Both the original Garden of Eden and the ultimate New Jerusalem are one and the same in the kingdom of God. Rather than being cast from the Garden, the first human existents cast the Garden from themselves (for, like the kingdom of God, it was within them). They cast the Garden from themselves by removing it from the realm of possible human experience, by relegating such experience to either preexistence or postexistence. Therefore did time become a means of putting off the daylight of Being for the lost evening, stuck either in the distant past or future.

What ends, then, is not the true creation but (in Frye's words) the "gigantic illusion"[17] overlying it. What's more, the lost tree and water of life, as they are at the beginning and are at the end, are now "restored to redeemed mankind."[18] There is an immediacy in the moment of the end of all things that are not porous to light. Paul comments on the redemptive nature of the New Jerusalem as the font of Creation: "But the Jerusalem above is free, and she is our mother" (Gal. 4:26). Paul further distinguishes between creation from dust and creation from Spirit:

> The first man was from the earth, a man of dust; the second man is from heaven. As was the man of dust, so are those who are of the dust; and as is the man of heaven, so are those who are of heaven. Just as we have borne the image of the man of dust, we shall also bear the image of the man of heaven. I tell you this, brethren: flesh and blood cannot inherit the kingdom of God, nor does the perishable inherit the imperishable (1 Cor. 15:47–50).

This is reminiscent of what God said to Moses: "man shall not see me and live" (Exod. 33:20), for this vision and revelation are reserved for the mortality that puts on immortality (1 Cor. 15:53). Paul is saying that only the Being that is from God and that is like God can know God. Only eternal eyes can see it; only timeless minds partake of it.

The false self contains a built-in resistance to Spirit. The body takes no notice of truth as it unwittingly contributes to the turbulent world. Only mind can truly know mind, only Spirit is able to know Spirit. And so the form of the world fades slowly from view as the Presence of God is reestablished in the mind as it is upon the throne of Ultimate Reality.

> Therefore are they before the throne of God, and serve him day and night within his temple; and he who sits upon the throne will shelter them with his presence. They shall hunger no more, neither thirst any more; the sun shall not strike them, nor any scorching heat. For the Lamb in the midst of the throne will be their shepherd; and he will guide them to springs of living water; and God will wipe away every tear from their eyes (Rev. 7:15–17).

The end state is blessed with grace as was the primeval Garden. Both are likened to a peaceful and natural world in which needs are cared for without toil, danger and destruction are nonexistent, and death and mourning are things of the past. Sadness and sorrow do not exist; they are gone as if they never were, in the light of the Presence.

People are sheltered "with his presence," that is, with experience of God, encounter with God, communion with God, union with God. Once again does the Divine Being walk morning and evening in the Garden, among His Creation of Light and Likeness. Isaiah envisions:

> In that day:
> "A pleasant vineyard, sing of it!
> I, the Lord, am its keeper; every moment I water it.
> Lest any one harm it, I guard it night and day;
> I have no wrath" (Isa. 27:2–4).

Far from a world of dust, this end state, this "pleasant vineyard" is eternal. When it is seen, it changes the world:

Then the eyes of the blind shall be opened, and the ears of the deaf unstopped; then shall the lame man leap like a hart, and the tongue of the dumb sing for joy. For waters shall break forth in the wilderness and streams in the desert; the burning sand shall become a pool, and the thirsty ground springs of water; the haunt of jackals shall become a swamp, the grass shall become reeds and rushes (Isa. 35:5–7).

Life is restored in the parched world and is renewed through an inrushing flood of Spirit.

The original creation and its reculmination in the New Jerusalem are restored to those who are "in the Spirit":

And in the Spirit he carried me away to a great, high mountain, and showed me the holy city Jerusalem coming down out of heaven from God, having the glory of God, its radiance like a most rare jewel, like a jasper, clear as crystal (Rev. 21:10–11).

Even resplendent words must fail, however, to gather fully the true sense of that which awaits the experience of *being* with God. For the end of time is experienced in a present beyond time. As it was in the beginning, the existent is subsumed by the All, and the individual, no longer fearful in concealment, is reopened to the Grace of Being.

The Second Coming and the Last Judgment

Existence can become the means by which Being is restored and remembered. Human existence infused with spiritual experience can find itself standing before the throne of God in blessed reconciliation. Paradoxically, Jesus in John 16:7 says that he must leave for the Spirit to enter the believers:

Nevertheless I tell you the truth: it is to your advantage that I go away, for if I do not go away, the Counselor will not come to you; but if I go, I will send him to you.

Here, Jesus' going away was, in effect, his coming again (for, according to Paul, "the Lord is the Spirit"). As an entity of Spirit, without the confines of physical existence, Jesus is going to be able to "send" the Holy Spirit. As we have seen, the Spirit functions to comfort, to counsel, and to lead to "all truth"—and in this way it extends Jesus' teaching.

In the Gospel of John, Jesus uses the beginning- and end-time imagery of living water to describe the experience of Spirit:

> Jesus stood up and proclaimed, "If any one thirst, let him come to me and drink. He who believes in me, as the scripture has said, 'Out of his heart shall flow rivers of living water.'" Now this he said about the Spirit, which those who believed in him were to receive; for as yet the Spirit had not been given, because Jesus was not yet glorified (John 7:37–39).

This is apocalyptic language. It implies the end of one world or way of life and the restoration of another. One cannot accept the Spirit and then go on as before.

What then of Jesus' apocalyptic language elsewhere, such as when he says, "For as lightning flashes and lights up the sky from one side to the other, so will the Son of man be" (Luke 17:24)? Does this too describe an experience, specifically of Spirit? Schuyler Brown, a historian of early Christianity, states that:

> Jesus' teaching is not an apocalyptic dogmatic. His parables are an imaginative redescription of reality based on his own profound experience of God.[19]

James D. G. Dunn also believes it more probable that Jesus' reality-changing message was rooted not in a literal sense of apocalypse, but rather "in his own _sense_ that something new and final was happening in him and through him."[20] That is, Jesus' apocalyptic language is the result of his profound, "new and final" transformative experience.

This coupling of Second Coming with experience seems to be what John is getting at. That Gospel speaks of an outpouring of Spirit following Jesus' "glorification." His leaving of the world causes those who receive this Spirit to live—in union with him and with the Father to Whom he returns:

> I will not leave you desolate; I will come to you. Yet a little while, and the world will see me no more, but you will see me; because I live, you will live also. In that day you will know that I am in my Father, and you in me, and I in you (John 14:18–20).

Here Jesus' coming is one with his leaving. He leaves one world only to reappear in another. His life is in his followers' transcendent experience of Spirit, and in this way is it within them. The joy of reconciliation that he brings is his and theirs to share; the joy of his own transcendent experience becomes a new life for believers.

The Spirit comes in Jesus' name (John 14:26) because it comes *as Jesus.* Scholar of religion Thomas J. J. Altizer states that, in the original Greek, the phrase "second coming" more aptly signifies "presence":

> The phrase which has come to be translated as "second com- ing" (pertaining to Christ) is more aptly defined as "further ema- nation." The Greek term, *parousia,* literally signifies "presence" more often than it denotes "coming" or "arriving." The misappli- cation seems to have been borrowed from the apocalyptic Judaism flourishing in the centuries immediately preceding and succeeding Jesus. These concepts were in turn influenced by Chaldean and Persian eschatology, which included beliefs in a final Judgment and the resurrection of the dead.[21]

And so, just as mythological imagery was used to describe the original pristine and crystal-clear spiritual creation, so is it employed now to describe the life-changing, self-transforming and therefore world-ending experience of Spirit ("presence").

In this way does the Gospel of John reinterpret and so equate the idea of a future second coming with an experience of immediate presence. To quote Altizer again:

> Eschatology as a time-perspective has dropped out with John

because he has so radically transposed eschatological occurrence into the present. The kingdom in John has lost its future and apocalyptic elements and has become a present and spiritual reality.[22]

Past and future, history and prophecy, have their end (or find their fulfillment) in the present moment of spiritual experience. Speaking of his presence, Jesus says, "For I tell you that many prophets and kings desired to see what you see, and did not see it" (Luke 10:24).

Therefore the "second coming"—*parousia* or "presence"—is continually occurring in the heart and mind of the individual who has a personal experience of the Universal. Jesus comes to the individual *as* the Spirit, so that the believer now lives "in" Jesus, and Jesus "in" the believer (John 14:20). In this understanding, the final and world-ending event, or *eschaton,* would be the acceptance of the Holy and Universal Will through Spirit, which reunites one with God and therefore restores the most real sense of original creation.

Therefore, the risen Christ is portrayed in the Book of Revelation as saying, "I am the Alpha and the Omega" (Rev. 1:8)—the first beginning and the very last end, the one who restores that which is beyond time, before time and after time has run its course. In saying that he is Alpha and Omega, he is declaring that he abides before our opinions and after our opinions have run their course, because the low-lying conceptual mind is barred from understanding and even from true praise. It means that the risen Christ stands outside the reality made out of the remnants of time.

What then of the Last Judgment? John says:

> And this is the judgment, that the light has come into the world, and men loved darkness rather than light, because their deeds were evil. For every one who does evil hates the light, and does not come to the light, lest his deeds should be exposed. But he who does what is true comes to the light, that it may be clearly seen that his deeds have been wrought in God (John 3:19–21).

Again there is an implicit hiding from God and from spiritual presence spoken of in this passage. The human being tends to act out of surface darkness and so hide not only from God but also from the Self; so feared is the light within. It is not allowed into awareness, for fear of having to go through the darkness to get there, and so the darkness is never bypassed but rather hidden in. The light is not frightening except to those who hide from it by hiding from themselves. How can the light be frightening when it is the essence of one's True Self?

Paul says similarly that the presence of the Lord:

> will bring to light the things now hidden in darkness and will disclose the purposes of the heart. Then every man will receive his commendation from God (1 Cor. 4:5).

Again there is here an association of judgment with the bringing to light of hidden intentions. Judgment, it seems, is not so much an unquenchable fire as an indomitable light that renders a person open to oneself and to the Spirit that searches the depths. The revelation is an internal one, not external to anyone. That which is consumed by the fire is only the surface darkness, and only so that the inner light might have its way and shine on. One stands with integrity before the light, or not at all; one stands with honesty before the light, or one seeks to hide from oneself (mainly). But before true honesty can come, first come dark and superficial chafflike intentions, burned quickly in the eternal fire of revelation, the light of truth and new purpose.

Note also that in Paul's passage above there is this saying: "Then every man will receive his commendation from God." The word is *commendation*, not condemnation. In other words, God is supportive of His family in their yearning to reach Him; He trusts them fully because He knows who they truly are.

There is in the Bible an association between judgment and light. The primordial, eternal light looks upon that which is eternal like itself. It sees the good, the true, the everlasting, and everything else it lets fall away from sight. Paul Tillich says:

> This is what "last judgment" means—to separate in us, as in everything, what has true and final being from what is merely transitory and empty of true being.[23]

Thus the "last judgment" is the distinction and differentiation in the mind and heart and depth between that which is eternal from that which is not. What remains when surface darkness is lit and the eternal alone is left? God and His Creation and the Relationship between them is all.

Everything but that which is seen through this light is destined for the ash heap of history. Nothing is eternal and worthy of God's world except this—His true Creation. As Jesus says, "Every plant which my heavenly Father has not planted will be rooted up" (Matt. 15:13). This really is good news, should believers truly bring or simply open their former intentions and judgments to light in order not to be defined by them. Even a split second examining the old darkness from within the light invites the inevitable flood of light.

Because the light of judgment looks upon what is eternal, to judge instead by surface appearances is therefore to deceive oneself; it is to judge with darkness. Therefore it is said: "Do not judge by appearances, but judge with right judgment" (John 7:24). Actions come from intention, and intention comes from the deepest sense of value, from congruency of thoughts and feelings. Right judgment follows from the light within; it does not follow the light in order to rest upon the surface of things. Even Jesus states that judgment according to the deeds of the surface is not his emphasis: "You judge according to the flesh, I judge no one" (John 8:15). If judgment were merely of the flesh, Jesus in his alignment with Spirit would not judge at all.

That is what Jesus asks his followers not to do: They are not to judge at all. They must not go down that road. Any judgment in the sense of condemnation of others will only return on the self. Thus Jesus says:

> Judge not, that you be not judged. For with the judgment you pronounce you will be judged, and the measure you give will be the measure you get (Matt. 7:1–2).

Not to judge by appearances is to change one's mind about the world—because the world is built around such conscious judgment. Exclusion is the basis for its ever-shifting foundation. Through judgment of others, human existents seek to hide from judgment on themselves, and from their sense that God seeks to condemn them. Yet this judgment of others carries with it a subconscious judgment of oneself. The darkness remains despite the urge to get rid of it by passing it along. Though subconscious, this judgment is very real in its effects. And so, in a truly vicious circle, one's resolve to condemn others comes back to haunt in the form of one's own guilty conscience and hardened heart.

This passage seems to indicate also that *in order to escape judgment, one has simply not to judge others.* It seems that if one proceeds along the lines of condemnation, mind full of surface judgments, decrees "of the flesh," then one is oneself convicted. The key to freedom is already in one's own hand. It is judgment that condemns, but only oneself. There is a different way of seeing the world than through eyes that focus on its faults, its wrongs, its misgivings. There is a different way to see one's brothers and sisters than through judgment that points out their sins, errors, and mistakes. Jesus asks in Luke 6:42:

> How can you say to your brother, "Brother, let me take out the speck that is in your eye," when you yourself do not see the log that is in your own eye?

It is hypocritical to judge, because judgment of others is a result of lack of self-understanding.

Judgment of others actually prevents knowledge of oneself. What the human tries to do through judgment is to hide from self-awareness. Judgment prevents the eye from seeing clearly; it obstructs one's vision. The self that is vastly defended against others seems mysterious even to itself; hidden in shadows, it believes its only hope is to lash out at what it does not know, but it makes itself believe it knows. Such is the power of belief, and yet its true power lies in the ability and capacity to overcome the propensity to judge.

True judgment then becomes a looking within rather than a looking without, a searching look into one's inner self rather than the turning of a critical and defensive eye upon the world of equals. Judgment, as we have seen, becomes for Jesus a means of light, a way of allowing light into the most darkened awareness, and therefore a means of vision, of seeing again.

Jesus said, "For judgment I came into this world, that those who do not see may see, and that those who see may become blind" (John 9:39).

John is proclaiming here that Jesus is the Revelator—the one who sees clearly because honestly, whose vision brings everything to light, and whose light is shared easily and naturally with all of life, which is one with him.

Even those who say, "We see," in this world are fraught with guilt (John 9:41). To judge a brother, therefore, even from religious intentions, is at once to blind oneself yet attempt to lead. Jesus told a parable: "Can a blind man lead a blind man? Will they not both fall into a pit?" (Luke 6:39). Guilt can induce blindness because there is an entire world it does not wish to see. Such honesty of self-appraisal as would enlighten and allow the inner world to expand into awareness is possible only through forgiveness. Jesus' revelation of the innocence of the world was manifested in his forgiveness of others. First implicitly and then in full flower of feeling, forgiveness of others and therefore of oneself is the way to the overarching vision of light. In other words:

> The human being is invited to "see" with a vision lent by God rather than to "see" according to fallen human nature, and to participate in the love of God—that point at which the kingdom, the *malkut shamain,* looms in the Creation.[24]

The Absolute remains a mystery for those (even religious authorities, as in John 9:41) who do not recognize the need to transcend relative viewpoints to find it. The mind conditioned to the underlying relativity and conditionality of judgment believes in and therefore convinces itself of the genuineness of differences, comparisons, distinctions, and conflict. This is the true consequence of judgment by appearances; it prevents enlightenment by having banished a vision of innocence. It therefore carries on a distortion of true Creation and true Self.

Therefore it is said that, "The Father judges no one, but has given all judgment to the Son" (John 5:22). Those who identify with the Son (through hearing and believing and finally sharing the Son's light) are therefore not subject to judgment, but have rather "passed from death to life":

Truly, truly, I say to you, he who hears my word and believes him who sent me, has eternal life; he does not come into judgment, but has passed from death to life (John 5:24).

Accordingly, with no awaiting judgment, but rather "eternal life" here and now, Paul can say:

Behold, *now* is the acceptable time; behold, *now* is the day of salvation (2 Cor. 6:2, my italics).

In Matthew, we have "the day of judgment" (12:36), the Book of Revelation speaks of the "hour" of judgment (14:7), but perhaps the "instant" of judgment is more fitting, due to the immediate effects of the Presence. Paul says:

Lo! I tell you a mystery. We shall not all sleep, but we shall all be changed, in a moment, in the twinkling of an eye, at the last trumpet (1 Cor. 15:51).

We have seen that the judgment is already occurring in John, wherein Jesus says:

Now is the judgment of this world, *now* shall the ruler of this world be cast out; and I, when I am lifted up from the earth, will draw *all* men to myself (John 12:31–32, my italics).

God is not the avenging judge that many make Him out to be. The Old Testament says that only "the godless in heart cherish anger" (Job 36:13). In John 12:32, Jesus says he will draw *all men* to himself. 1 Tim. 2:4 says that God "desires all men to be saved and to come to the knowledge of the truth." And of the God who said, "Let there be light," and there was light— which of His intentions does not come to perfect and immediate fruition? 2 Peter 3:9 has it that the Lord "is forbearing toward you, not wishing that any should perish, but that all should reach repentance." The eschatological moment, the moment at which the world stops for an instant and comes to light, is not put off or delayed by any decision on God's part. The end of the former world of former things and thoughts and intentions is put off into the future by the mind that is more and more intricately tying itself to the world, only to hide in guilt, trying to subsist on the fear for which it forages.

"Every knee shall bow," "every tongue confess" (Phil. 2:10) that the Lord has come, when the heart returns to the Presence with its intimate and immediate experience. "The living God" is "the Savior of all men, especially of those who believe" (1 Tim. 4:10), because those who believe can come to *know,* simply through experiencing their salvation. For "God is light and in him is no darkness at all" (1 John 1:5). The human being senses the restoration of a new covenant by which *all* are saved, restored to original Creation, original Creator remembered. *All* are saved when Truth enters the mind through the living Word.

Truth invites all souls; there is a Truth at work in everyone despite unbelief (for that can quickly be changed). Truth is the open invitation:

> The Spirit and the Bride say, "Come." And let him who hears say, "Come." And let him who is thirsty come, let him who desires take the water of life without price (Rev. 22:17).

To open oneself is to receive the open invitation to Spirit, who returns from and to God. The water of life flows freely because it is God's, in Whose Vision all are sanctified, guiltless, of perfect origin all the way through endlessness, and therefore *commended* to great joy. "There shall no more be anything accursed, but the throne of God and the Lamb shall be in it" (Rev. 22:3); the Presence of God within sanctifies and purifies everything. Judgment would only mar this vision.

Every instant calls one to deepest decision, new intention with new purpose. The world-ending moment reveals experience of another world. The Original Light radiates through the world, so that the fields are white, and the grain is kept, blessing the world and healing the world by its sacred Presence, until everything and everyone are united in it.

> For he has made known to us in all wisdom and insight the mystery of his will, according to his purpose which he set forth in Christ *as a plan for the fulness of time, to unite all things in him,* things in heaven and things on earth (Eph. 1:9–10, my italics).

Ultimate and universal reconciliation is the meaning of God's will; therefore is it the great and original purpose of humankind. "The mystery" is the rejoining, how it occurs beyond human understanding, and "all wisdom and insight" come from such rejoining. Time itself is new and ripe and full—beginning and end being one even now. Whereas prior to this moment, time had carried along its own worries and anxieties, now the stilling of these thoughts brings to mind an utterly different, utterly pure Presence, and a fullness in the soul belonging to Union. From the higher vantage point of the Creator, Creation is considered "good," not an intermixture of "good and evil." The Original Creation restored remains forever and evermore within the sacred ground and great sea and full air of all Creation. A single Tree of Life spreads out its healing leaves over the divided and the fragmented, and what once sought to live and hide in judgment is in fear no more.

7

The Law, the Cross, and Salvation

Come now, let us reason together, says the Lord:
though your sins are like scarlet,
they shall be as white as snow;
though they are red like crimson,
they shall become like wool.

—Isa. 1:18

Sin and Salvation

Ritual animal sacrifice was practiced in ancient times almost universally. This ritual offering to the gods was likely originally seen as a way of trying to curry favor with the gods, but the idea of sacrifice came eventually to be psychologized as a way of redeeming an individual's guilt before the sight of God. At times, the Hebrew prophets spoke against the practice of animal sacrifice, emphasizing instead the entirely internal, psychological, and emotional salvation of a clean heart:

A new heart I will give you, and a new spirit I will put within you; and I will take out of your flesh the heart of stone and give you a heart of flesh. And I will put my spirit within you, and cause you to walk in my statutes and be careful to observe my ordinances (Ezek. 36:26–27).

A change of heart and mind so drastic that it is spoken of as "new" is necessary for salvation. Simply to follow the law one must first be changed and made willing to forsake all past intentions and to follow God.

The law began as an ancient covenant or pact that God made with the Hebrew patriarchs (Abraham, Isaac, Jacob, and Moses) for land and progeny and for the community itself to become a shining light and example to the world. This sense of the psychological and spiritual nature of the covenant between God and His people, Israel (and by extension between God and the soul in general), was upheld by a deep and abiding sense of faith on the part of the people as a whole. Bible scholar Samuel Terrien states that it was the patriarchs' experience of *the divine presence* (and the sense of this in the people) that lay at the center of the religion of the covenant:

By contrast, the reality of the divine presence proved to be the constant element of distinctiveness throughout the centuries of biblical times.[1]

This Divine Presence that held the people, the community, and the religion together also holds the Bible together. Scholar of religion Robert F. Davidson reports on the view of theologian Rudolf Otto that:

Without the original datum of religious experience (the sense of numinous sanctity) morality could never have meant more than calculating self-interest or conventionally approved conduct.[2]

Religious experience contains its own morality, based on delighting in the Will of God, as we shall see. Terrien states that sacramental rites, celebrations, and ceremonies were a way for worshipers to "participate in the life and power of the Deity. The worshipers receive a new existence. They are re-created."[3] The experience, the Divine Presence, behind morality and ritual is both their transcendence and their original cause.

The great prophets proclaimed the need for internal transformation in order to achieve a sense of salvation. Jeremiah spoke of the new covenant as the internalization of the law:

> But this is the covenant which I will make with the house of Israel after those days, says the Lord; I will put my law within them, and I will write it upon their hearts; and I will be their God, and they shall be my people. And no longer shall each man teach his neighbor and each his brother, saying, "Know the Lord," for they shall all know me, from the least of them to the greatest, says the Lord. For I will forgive their iniquity, and I will remember their sin no more (Jer. 31:33–34).

God resides within His people through His having written His law in Spirit upon their hearts. He is close enough as to be inside them, a part of them as they are part of Him. Terrien states that "the rite and ideology of covenant are dependent upon the prior reality of presence."[4] It is this sense of Presence that underlies the law of Moses, just as it underlay the earlier covenant of Abraham, Isaac, and Jacob.

Temple rituals such as animal sacrifice were ways of attempting to relieve a kind of recurrent and deep psychological and ontological guilt that comes simply from being human. The rituals themselves recur on a regular basis because their ameliorative effect was only a temporary remedy for a sense that both community and individual existed in a state of sin, essentially separate from God. For a true sense and conviction of salvation, the prophets and sages of Judaism knew the inner workings of the heart to be of deepest significance for individual and community.

Some early Christians interpreted the crucifixion of Jesus as a sacrifice that was to alleviate guilt "once for all" (1 Pet. 3:18). In this view, Jesus was the only Son of God who was sacrificed by God in order to redeem believers in him (as representative of God) from sin. This seems to be the prevailing view of modern-day Christians. But is it the prevailing view in the New Testament? Matt. 8:17, for instance, sees Jesus' *healing* of the sick, not his death, as the fulfillment of the prophecy in Isa. 53:4: "Surely he has borne our griefs and carried our sorrows." Moreover, Jesus and the New Testament scribes speak most clearly of a *love* that saves—a universal and bonding emotion being the antidote for the poisonous impression of guilt. Here again we are in the realm of psychological experience, such inner experience being the crux of salvation.

According to the Bible in general, guilt is the product of humanity's inherent inability to follow the internal laws of God, beginning with the very first existents. As such, guilt is closely associated with human nature, just as sin is closely associated with separation from God (as we have seen in the last chapter). The human being, marked by separation from God, is by definition and by constitution guilty. Such guilt is felt or implicated wherever the relationship, the Divine Presence, the experience, is not. It is the guilt of simply existing (separate from God), or ontological guilt. Innately, the individual with divided consciousness carries the underpinnings of guilt, and a consequent fear of punishment and deep-seated urge to hide.

Salvation in the New Testament

Salvation in the New Testament is internal. It must reach the inner person, the individual's subjective world of thoughts and intentions, will, feelings, and internal experiences. It joins the individual with the Divine Presence through the shared Spirit. Until it is read in the heart where it has been inscribed by the Spirit, the law seems external to the self, to be followed or not followed. But when the law is in the heart, God is as near as one is to oneself.

Paul writes of forsaking his former reliance on the law in order to achieve salvation. He comes to believe that the law actually convicts of sin rather than saving from it—that is, it reinforces guilt and therefore overloads the conscience. After all, "sin is not counted where there is no law" (Rom. 5:13). The law convicts an individual by its mere existence. Therefore, the law is not an effective means to escape the residual guilt of existence. There must be another, more internal, transformative ground to verify spiritual progress.

Paul speaks of salvation through Jesus' having "broken down the dividing wall of hostility, by abolishing in his flesh the law of commandments and ordinances" (Eph. 2:14–15). But Jesus did not break down the walls of separation and therefore "abolish" the law merely through his crucifixion, or we would be returning to the cult of sacrifice. Rather, Jesus abolishes the law through his relationship with the unifying Spirit, "for through him we both have access in one Spirit to the Father" (Eph. 2:18). Jesus, through the Spirit, broke down the wall of "hostility" or separation that stands between individuals and God and one another. That is, the sense of separation with its consequent guilt and fear is overcome through the sense of unity effected by Jesus through the Holy Spirit. Being was created unbroken, to remain forever whole.

The law is fulfilled by its transcendence, which occurs in the heart and the mind, through the action of Spirit. True values emanate from the depths of the soul, only then to be reinforced by books and codes of law and external sources. Jesus and Paul repositioned the codified law to a humbler post, due to their experience of the effects of God's mercy. Thus we shall find that the experience of godly love is just cause for the abrogation of the law in Paul, and is the very fulfillment of the law for Jesus.

His experience of a sense of freedom and equality in the Spirit is essential to an understanding of Paul's views on salvation. He teaches that the Spirit within is the sure foundation for experiencing the essential equality of individual souls in Christ and therefore freedom from the law. Judgment becomes unnecessary. Theological doctrines and churchly rites will differ, perhaps necessarily, but the subjective experience of spiritual presence can be shared. The universal and unifying nature of the presence of God grants believers all the sense of salvation they need and require.

Experience of the Spirit (and its internal psychological fruits) is a way of following the law without following any law. For, as Paul says:

> the fruit of the Spirit is love, joy, peace, patience, kindness, goodness, faithfulness, gentleness, self-control; against such there is no law (Gal. 5:22–23).

Internal righteousness does not depend on law. Nor does it depend on the effects of Spirit so much as it depends on Spirit itself. Paul's sense of the new covenant or agreement of salvation is therefore found "not in a written code but in the Spirit; for the written code kills, but the Spirit gives life" (2 Cor. 3:6). The fact of feeling and experiencing "love, joy, peace, patience, kindness" means that the individual lives within a new sense of life which is already saved. The new covenant is, in this way, a cosmic agreement of the heart with Spirit.

Laws tend to multiply, to the extent that Jesus exclaims to the law-doting and law-loving scribes and Pharisees: "You blind guides, straining out a gnat and swallowing a camel!" (Matt. 23:24). In other words, if laws and bylaws become the focal point of salvation, then more significant things are neglected and remain undone. The psychological state that subsists on the need for laws causes them to multiply by its own fragmentation. Regulations may be applied to every aspect of human existence and behavior, except the transcendent instant of cosmic agreement with God, which requires not doing but being. Even if one were to perform the Herculean feat of strictly adhering to every jot and iota of the ever-multiplying law, would a sure sense of salvation follow? No, says Paul, for the external focus is the wrong focus. No, says Jesus, for salvation is internal to the individual.

Psychologist John A. Sanford states of Jesus' "higher morality":

> It would not be necessary to have a Law forbidding murder, adultery, stealing, coveting, and slander if there were not a part of our personality that might do exactly these things. The scribes and Pharisees seek to avert the danger of this "inner shadow" by following rules that prohibit these things. But the higher morality requires confronting the shadowy one within us who has made the rules necessary in the first place.[5]

The darkness of the fragmented heart can be overcome with light, the shadowy parts of the self shone away with light. While the mind is lit with Spirit, dark shadows and boundary lines are dissolved. Spirit transcends the law by transcending the world and its relative viewpoints and fleeting emotions, in favor of something more universal.

I have discussed that Jesus focuses on the thoughts and intentions, rather than the behavior, of a person. He states that anger is as wrong as killing, a lustful heart as misguided as committing adultery (Matt. 5:22, 28). The standard seems to be set higher than the human being can bear;

who can forgo anger in this world? But the Spirit is already here. Adherence to an external code could never be sufficient; something more deeply transforming is required for effective salvation.

Throughout the Sermon on the Mount in Matt. 5–7, Jesus restates the original commandments, but then carries them an extra step, so that they apply now to the internal world of the human being, where Jesus indicates that redemption exists. From the inmost heart of the individual, they take on the sheen of an abundantly new vision of the world, which radiates out from the center and stretches out in peaceable pathways available to everyone. This understanding of the internal immediacy of salvation echoes the Psalmist, who says: "Open thou mine eyes and I will behold wondrous things out of thy laws" (Ps. 119:18). The Beatitudes, too, are reflections and revelations of cosmic, internal, but universal laws of wondrous beauty.

Jesus read his Scriptures as if they applied to a transcendent spiritual Self; it is in this way that they became a living Word to him. Reinterpreting the Scriptures of ancient Judaism, Jesus proclaims the effectiveness of forgiveness and love toward salvation:

> You have heard that it was said, "You shall love your neighbor and hate your enemy." But I say to you, Love your enemies and pray for those who persecute you, so that you may be sons of your Father who is in heaven; for he makes his sun rise on the evil and on the good, and sends rain on the just and on the unjust (Matt. 5:43–45).

Jesus is proclaiming that God does not distinguish among persons—even on moral grounds—so neither does the soul distinguish among them. Judgment is unnecessary to Jesus. He seems to be saying that the concepts of good and bad are not for the separated consciousness to understand; simply to join as one with the Father in Spirit is the whole Truth.

The passage above indicates that *to love* is to be "sons" of God and therefore to be like God, Who loves indiscriminately and comprehensively. Even those who cross our boundaries, enemies, and those who do us wrong are yet to be loved, in Jesus' unifying vision. To the separated consciousness, which strives to uphold itself against others, defending itself to the bitter end, this kind of unifying love would seem impossible. Another Self, one that through its union with God in the Divine Presence of Spirit cannot be crossed or double-crossed and cannot sin or experience sin, must replace the wronged one. And so it is only by joining with the Mind and Heart of God through His Spirit, and being like Him, effortlessly and naturally "sons of your Father who is in heaven" (Matt. 5:45), that a human being may truly forgive, save and be saved.

In this way, Jesus sets an impossibly higher standard of righteousness than that of the religious authorities of his day. He stated, "For I tell you, unless your righteousness exceeds that of the scribes and Pharisees, you will never enter the kingdom of heaven" (Matt. 5:20). An example of this is found in Jesus, again reinterpreting the written code, saying:

> You have heard that it was said, "An eye for an eye and a tooth for a tooth." But I say to you, Do not resist one who is evil. But if any one strikes you on the right cheek, turn to him the other also (Matthew 5:38–39).

Is this an impossible standard, or simply one that can be reestablished in the mind through the mental paradox of giving up self to find it? The transcendent and universal forgiver, who believes that God sends His rain down upon all without distinction, is more than human in the sense that he no longer has a home in any worldview, and so now can afford to forgive with total impunity. Total forgiveness is the prerequisite for salvation, and joining the mind with God is required for totality of any kind. Spiritual experience, by rising above all thought of law and conviction of sin, does the saving. So does the spring of great love that leaps from the heart at one with God.

The Spirit unifies, as love unifies. Upon experience of total union, the Law becomes, not so much a set of commandments to follow, but instead a vision of a life because a state of life lived with God. The one commandment that includes them all is, according to Jesus, the commandment to love (both God and others):

> And one of them, a lawyer, asked him a question, to test him. "Teacher, which is the great commandment in the law?"
> And he said to him, "You shall love the Lord your God with all

your heart, and with all your soul, and with all your mind. This is the great and first commandment. And a second is like it, You shall love your neighbor as yourself. On these two commandments depend all the law and the prophets" (Matt. 22:35–40).

There is a totality in this "great and first commandment" of which Jesus speaks. Paul seems to know this great commandment of Jesus, agreeing:

> Owe no one anything, except to love one another; for he who loves his neighbor has fulfilled the law. The commandments, "You shall not commit adultery, You shall not kill, You shall not steal, You shall not covet," and any other commandment, are summed up in this sentence, "You shall love your neighbor as yourself." Love does no wrong to a neighbor; therefore, love is the fulfilling of the law (Rom. 13:8–10).

According to Paul, "love is the fulfilling of the law." He likewise states in Gal. 5:14: "For the whole law is fulfilled in one word, 'You shall love your neighbor as yourself.'" An experience, one emotion of the heart, fulfills the law. It will remain a mystery until it is felt, in all its transcendent glory. Every commandment, every universal law, is contained in this emotion. It was never so much the misdeed of the creature, but, rather, the inner drive of the heart and the will of the mind that was counted by the law. Jesus himself was accused of being "a glutton and a drunkard, a friend of tax collectors and sinners!" (Luke 7:34). His retort was that "wisdom is justified by all her children" (Luke 7:35). Because he consented to oneness with his spiritual brothers and sisters in order to love and be loved, he behaved as he pleased. The innermost intention, he would say, is everything; everything falls into place once heart and mind are joined in love.

Jesus' unrelenting but meta-behavioral morality stems not from written laws and commandments, but rather from the mind and heart of the individual. The proscription requires a new sense of Self, a Self that can love *with* and *like* God. Scrupulous behavior, the most exacting adherence to the law, would not be enough to quench the unyielding, demanding sense of sin and guilt. Schuyler Brown notes that:

Jesus' radical demand for a religion of the heart (Mark 7:20–3 par.) abrogates the external observance of the law as a way to God (cf. Matt. 5:21–2, 27). The only appropriate response to the divine mercy is the total and unconditional surrender of the whole person.[6]

The commandment is comprehensive, and that is to love "with all your heart, and with all your soul, and with all your mind" (Matt. 22:37). In this way, the soul is reordered and re-created, again to feel with God. This greatest commandment is the commandment of internal congruence and unified purpose. To love is to give of oneself fully, utterly, and completely, to stand in full honesty and authenticity before God and neighbor and especially self.

The First Letter of John reiterates and restates the great commandment of Jesus:

And this commandment we have from him, that he who loves God should love his brother also (1 John 4:21).

The relationship here between love of God and of brother is interesting. As I've already mentioned, there is no discrimination—no acknowledgment of essential difference—among beings in this kind of love. Love is given to all or not at all. Love of God and love of one's equals is made congruent here, until even the world for a moment seems whole, albeit changed. As the Love of God is given fully, so will the love of the soul be, and universally shared, to emerge as a new Self in God.

Once again, the heart filled with love fulfills the law. One can do no wrong to another if the heart is filled with the love of God through His Holy Spirit. No law is needed when one's being is determined by love. Values and justice arise naturally from the presence of Love, and the transcendent intention of the heart seeps into one's actions. Where Love is valued fully within the heart, there is salvation found, with the Spirit of God.

He sends His Spirit to purify, to sanctify the inner temple in the heart, and to certify all that is of God. A pure heart is what God desires, obviously, because He created it pure. The Law of Love is therefore followed with a delight akin to the joy the first couple experienced in the Garden of

Eden. "I delight to do thy will, O my God; thy law is within my heart" (Ps. 40:8). The law is inner delight if it is followed simply by following one's true being. Because it is the Godly way of being, the supernatural way of being, it is also the most natural way of being. It does not matter that conceptualizations based on externalizing tradition would hold otherwise. Whatever tradition takes away from nature, she must give back at the end.

From where then comes the notion that God seeks out transgressors of the law to punish? Because, according to the vision of totality, to hurt another is to hurt oneself. Like a cosmic law of the universe, a decision carries the seed of its own consequence. As the Psalmist said of those who stray from the Divine Will, "His mischief returns upon his own head, and on his own pate his violence descends" (Ps. 7:16). The conscience—no matter how hidden—knows when one tries to lead oneself blindly through any thicket of self-interest, and in the process forsake true being. "He who digs a pit will fall into it" (Eccles. 10:8). One's thoughts, the intention of one's heart, will be borne out in one's world, all without any overseeing by God, Whose thoughts are of a higher order altogether. It is to this Most High, Who sits in totality, beyond the range of the individual existent, that the believer goes in Spirit for salvation.

Paul restates this cosmic law when he says:

> Do not be deceived; God is not mocked, *for whatever a man sows, that he will also reap.* For he who sows to his own flesh will from the flesh reap corruption; but he who sows to the Spirit will from the Spirit reap eternal life (Gal. 6:7–8, my italics).

Jesus affirms the reciprocal relationship, saying:

> Judge not, that you be not judged. For with the judgment you pronounce you will be judged, and the measure you give will be the measure you get back (Matt. 7:1–2).

Paul determines that the act of judging is a way of suppressing and neglecting one's own mistaken intentions. "Therefore you have no excuse, O man, whoever you are, when you judge another; for in passing judgment upon him you condemn yourself, because you, the judge, are doing the very same things" (Rom. 2:1). Judgment therefore convicts, in a roundabout way, tragically circling back on the separated self, while love and forgiveness save, directly. Judgment trains one's thoughts on the lower order, and confines them to a lower order of self; otherwise such thoughts and selves could be, through totality, transcended.

It is not the law that keeps a heart from God; it is rather fear that does it. Yet the law, in Paul's understanding, a type of "slavery," can increase fear (Rom. 8:15). "For the law brings wrath, but where there is no law there is no transgression" (Rom. 4:15). The standard for morality is found in the emotional capacity of the individual, where the fundamental things are joined in the love of Christ. And so Paul can internalize the law, stating of those who had never heard the law:

> They show that what the law requires is written on their hearts, while their conscience also bears witness (Rom. 2:15).

Again, the Self knows when it is not genuinely and simply and truly being, and knows when it *is*. Hearts are the fundamental things, the essence of the being created by God, because within them is carried the law of God.

Sin is estrangement and apparent alienation from God, from oneself, and from the totality. Sin is the state and experience of being an alien or a stranger, the sense of having turned away from one's own world and from participation in something infinitely greater: the Divine Ground of Being from which all come and to which all go. Sin is the act of turning inward toward oneself alone, yet not going deep enough inside oneself to *know* that the essential equality of creation ensures unity, and that the experience and direct knowledge of this unity saves. To feel utterly alone in the world, to feel no true relationship and connection with anyone else—not even with God—though it might seem to have its compensations, is to be in hell.

For Paul, a sense of *righteousness* comes not through the external law, but, rather, through union with Christ through faith. He speaks of "not having a righteousness of my own, based on law, but that which is through faith in Christ" (Phil. 3:9).

To follow the law is to be on one's own. To be united with Christ and with God is to be *not alone*. In fact, it is to be united not only with believers, but also with everyone, without distinction. Thus have the walls of hostility and separation been broken down in Christ's abstract being. Righteousness comes from trust of God with the heart of one's being, not from self-directed effort.

Paul goes so far as to call the law "the dispensation of death, carved on letters of stone" (2 Cor. 3:7) and contrasts this with "the dispensation of the Spirit," which he says will "be attended with greater splendor" (3:8). Paul understands that the codified law serves to deny the Spirit and Divine Presence, and thus it is not effective for salvation. He draws the same contrast between "the dispensation of condemnation" and "the dispensation of righteousness" (3:9). Everything on Earth, including the law, is temporary, but the righteousness of the Spirit is eternal. Concludes Paul: "For if what faded away came with splendor, what is permanent must have much more splendor" (3:11).

With the coming of the Spirit, then, "a better hope is introduced, through which we draw near to God" (Heb. 7:19). For to experience the presence of God is no longer to feel estranged and alone. Therefore is this experience of the Divine Presence the fulfillment of the law, just as it originally sparked initiation of the covenant; it is, beginning to end, salvation itself.

The Inner Significance of the Cross

The crucifixion of Jesus represented to early Christians much more than the selfless act of the anointed one. Stevan L. Davies points to the significance of early Christians' *experience* of the crucifixion, saying, "the *importance* of his death and subsequent appearances derived from the *experience* of later Christians that they too had died and subsequently arisen to new lives as persons possessed by his spirit."[7] Through their spiritual experience of Jesus' crucifixion and resurrection, early Christians received a taste of his universality, and likened this experience to dying to themselves and rising again in transformation. Because of the union they had with him in the Spirit, Jesus' experience was their experience; his new life was their new life.

Paul spoke of "always carrying in the body the death of Jesus, so that the life of Jesus may also be manifested in our bodies" (2 Cor. 4:10). This kind of paradoxical intention was common enough in early Christianity: It is through inner emptiness and self-negation (even to the point of dying to oneself) that one obtains a sense of fullness. Paul also speaks of being dead to the law, but alive in God through his own experience of Jesus' crucifixion and resurrection:

> For I through the law died to the law, that I might live to God. I have been crucified with Christ; *it is no longer I who live, but Christ who lives in me;* and the life I now live in the flesh I live by faith in the Son of God, who loved me and gave himself for me (Gal. 2:19–20, my italics).

The power of the metaphor of dying to oneself and rising to another Self in Christ, following Jesus, parallels the power of early Christians' new experience. Paul speaks of this experience as a new life and a new identity, a new self, "the new life of the Spirit" (Rom. 7:6).

Peter equates the crucifixion with being "made alive in the spirit": "For Christ also died for sins once for all, the righteous for the unrighteous, that he might bring us to God, being put to death in the flesh but made alive in the spirit" (1 Pet. 3:18). Early Christians experienced the relinquishment of former life and self in exchange for a very different kind of being here and now, and for true righteousness. Paul indicates that the experience is an ongoing dual process, death and resurrection, a ceding or relinquishment of one life and righteousness for a new one. This process is exemplified in and preordained by the crucifixion and resurrection of Jesus.

Paul relates of this process of dying and rising:

> We were buried therefore with him by baptism into death, so that as Christ was raised from the dead by the glory of the Father, we might walk in newness of life (Rom. 6:3–4).

This formula promises new life in Christ as an experience of eternity, even within the time-driven world of existence. That which can and does experience the eternal is not the old self that loses itself among twisting and convoluted pathways; it must be the new Self which walks *"in newness of life."* To walk in newness of life requires the experience of a new Self. The world is new when it is renewed by the Self. Life itself is new when thinking and feeling, world and self, are new and newly one.

There is no need to interpret any of this as sacrifice:

> For thou hast no delight in sacrifice; were I to give a burnt offering, thou wouldst not be pleased. The sacrifice acceptable to God is a broken spirit; a broken and contrite heart, O God, thou wilt not despise (Ps. 51:16–17).

The heart yearning to look upon its own brokenness, and have it healed, has its rift filled with God. Jesus is the Christ in the sense that he is "the one who sacrifices what is *merely* 'Jesus' in him."[8] No longer himself; he was God's. He became a new creation—dying to what used to be himself—rising to something infinitely greater. Nothing is sacrificed in his new life, and what is gained is great beyond measure.

John Macquarrie states: "To accept the cross and resurrection of Christ is to surrender self-sufficiency and to live in dependence on and in communion with God."[9] This means that the believer lives not as oneself, nor for oneself, nor by any personal strength. One's will is not one's own, depths have been filled and borderlands have been crossed to reach the gathering in the light of a universal will. Within the garden, extending from the Tree of Life, there is a greater vine, to which is connected all of life. Every step one takes, therefore, in this life, is taken in another.

Long before his crucifixion, then, Jesus had given "his life as a ransom for many" (Matt. 20:28). He had relinquished his life to Spirit to live through and for him. More than *led* by the Spirit, he no longer lived in estrangement from God and God's creation. Nor did he live as an ego, nor could his mindfulness of others proceed along the lines of a life of self-interest. He did not walk alone, but rather walked in newness of life as Son of God—so close to God he could feel His power and the peace of His constant presence, like God, intimately knowing His holy will, and like God, caring deeply about the well-being of all creation, enough to want to immerse everything in this new sense of life. He lived and moved and had his being in the kingdom of God.

This is why Jesus' teachings are, according to Northrop Frye, "evocations of a world very different from the one we live in, so that we may find them impractical or too exaggerated to be guides to practice. They are not guides to practice directly, however, but parts of a vision of an 'innocent' world, and it is that vision which is the key to practice."[10] The vision of innocence leads to its re-creation, its revealing, simply by its being there. The experience of a new Self and world leads naturally, inevitably to salvation in the most personal and universal sense.

According to the prophet Jeremiah, God says that the new covenant He makes with His people is to bless them with knowledge of God and innate wisdom and with a sense of deep, saving forgiveness (Jer. 31:33–34). "For they shall all know me," says God in this vision (v. 34); "I will put my law within them, and I will write it upon their hearts" (v. 33). The new covenant of knowledge of Being comes, Jesus said, through forgiveness and relinquishment of existence itself. It is not commanded, but rather emanates naturally from where it has been written. Spirit rejuvenates the heart and reinstates Truth into the mind; it is being with God, transcendent, that makes it possible to live in His light. The prophets say that each will know the Lord intimately, and all will wonder at their complete and total forgiveness.

John 11:52 has it that Jesus died "not for the nation only, but to gather into one the children of God who are scattered abroad." There was an inherent sense of universality in the salvation others gathered from him. Through shared experience of the crucifixion, through the unity of their experience, early Christians felt redemption, the power of something new. The experience brought of course a different kind of consciousness than merely nationalistic, for any grouping that is not total invites a sense of separation that draws borders and boundaries. It even superseded the usual religious consciousness, itself beset by demarcations like fences. It was in truth a new life he experienced and brought to the totality. Jesus as the Christ, as one who had left behind what was merely human about him, was a unifying, abstract figure who left after him a depth of experiences ranging "through righteousness to eternal life" (Rom. 5:21), each of them transcending human designations and limitations.

Jesus says that God desires "mercy, not sacrifice" (Matt. 12:7). This is because it is forgiveness that saves the individual from the guilt of existing in separation. In forgiving the physically afflicted of their sin, in removing in himself the barriers that seemed to stand between God and soul, himself and another, Jesus healed them (see Matt. 9:5–8). Jesus forgave and saved others *prior to* his crucifixion. Matt. 9:8 indicates that all people share this capacity to forgive sins and therefore to heal: The crowds who witnessed him forgiving as God forgives "glorified God, who had given such authority *to men*" (my italics). They were astounded by the new life he lived and brought.

Jesus says that insofar as one forgives, one is forgiven:

> Judge not, and you will not be judged; condemn not, and you will not be condemned; forgive, and you will be forgiven (Luke 6:37).

The experience of forgiveness comes from the single-minded intention to forgive, or at least not to judge. This is the new standard—which before seemed impossibly distant and impossible for the individual—to which the individual is raised in him. Forgiveness, in its magnitude and universality, could not help but produce a new state of mind in the believer, complete with a sense of salvation and of being born anew. Forgiveness applied liberally, to everyone, would be nearly as perfect as the love of God.

Jesus says in John that love is redemptive:

> A new commandment I give to you, that you love one another; even as I have loved you, that you also love one another. By this all men will know you are my disciples, if you have love for one another (John 13:34–35).

The new commandment, in effect, is to *be* love. And again, "This is my commandment, that you love one another as I have loved you" (John 15:12). Love fulfills not only the law, but also the heart. Jesus is redemptive by living, by being, for in him, with him, and like him his followers walked by themselves, becoming love in "newness of life."

Therefore Paul says, "Let all that you do be done in love" (1 Cor. 16:14). The emotion of universal love grants new intention for the mind, new purpose for the heart, and new behavior in a new world. To Paul, faith is made effective through love (Gal. 5:6). Love stands behind the transformation and the salvation it effects.

John says, "He who loves his brother abides in the light, and in it there is no cause for stumbling" (1 John 2:10). No stain, no impurity, no cast of sin exists in the light of love. It shines away the past, like forgiveness, and with it guilt, and with that fear, and with that, the urge to hide in separation. The exposed roots and dried brush of existence are nothing compared to the elysian fields that spread themselves across the mind bathed and reborn in eternal light.

As such, it is the redeeming experience of the emotion that truly saves. There is a sense of real transcendence in total forgiveness and in universal love. To love is to enter another realm and be given a new sense of life. The way to forgive and to love in this world is to allow oneself and one's world to be transformed. To forgive and to love on Earth is to model all relationships on the one experienced with the Father in Heaven.

Jesus went to the cross with love as the foundation of his being. His actions were redemptive because his life was redemptive. Psychologically, his experience affected early Christians deeply enough to recast even their individual sense of identity. They felt they existed in a vastly new dimension of life with him after his resurrection, and they loved him for it.

You heard me say to you, "I go away, and I will come to you." If you loved me, you would have rejoiced, because I go to the Father; for the Father is greater than I (John 14:28).

He is saying here that to love him is to rejoice in his ascension to this realm. Again, love must be experienced for its transcendence to be known.

The crucifixion is integrally paired with the resurrection in the biblical texts, because for early believers they were two parts of one experience that led to a sense of new life. Just as the fall from Grace came from a sense of separate existence, so the return to Grace and Beatitude comes from a renewed sense of unified Being, knowing the new Self in Christ, loving the Christ in every mind. All interpretations of the crucifixion reveal their peculiar assumptions underlying the sense of the relationship between Jesus and God, and among Jesus, God, and ourselves. In the early Christian mystical view, relationship with God depended on the dying of one self to rise in another, to relate like Him. The sense of separation from God is overcome by forgiveness of others, leaving only love and the Self capable of it.

Early Christians understood the crucifixion to be an experience of dying to oneself, while at the same time rising with Jesus into a different kind of life. Jesus trusted God and so he trusted himself. He taught them that they could do the same. Changed by this vision, Jesus changed others by this vision, before, during, and after the crucifixion and resurrection. Rising to newness of life by dying to self begins internally, but is readily transferred into any waiting relationship. Jesus' teachings and healings flowed from his conviction born of experience and new identity that God forgives fully, completely, totally. Thus could his crucifixion and resurrection also be interpreted, from a kind of shared experience, as a kind of initiation into a new sense of the universality of salvation. Those who were swept up with him into Relationship found themselves able, like him, to forgive, as they walked together with him in newness of life and the light of a new world.

Salvation in Experience

For Paul and other early Christians, sin was a problem only if it was allowed to inhabit the mind. It was a fixture of the world only insofar as separated existence was a firm proposition in the mind. As Jesus said, "a divided household falls" (Luke 11:17). And it is there, in the mind, where forgiveness and transcendent experience resolve the problem of sin and separation. To be filled with the Spirit of the Love of God, and to have it transform world and self, is to be saved once and for all—utterly, at last. Paul says:

> There is therefore no condemnation for those who are in Christ Jesus. For the law of the Spirit of life in Christ Jesus has set me free from the law of sin and death (Rom. 8:1–2).

Those who allow themselves to be transformed by God become *a new creation:* "For neither circumcision counts for anything, nor uncircumcision, but a new creation" (Gal. 6:15). Liberated from everything but true creation, they are saved.

The law shifts into new focus when it is seen as a vision of holy perfection, a vision that sees the new Self as perfect fulfillment. The law of sin no longer condemns because the bond of the Spirit saves. No longer need a person seek justification under the traditional law according to the New Testament, for all true righteousness comes from the newness of life experienced in Spirit and love. The law is a vision, and the vision needs only to be called upon, asked for, and opened to, to be experienced. If able to give in this measure, universally, like God, a person will be filled beyond measure (Luke 6:38).

Following Jesus' experience, his earliest disciples felt they were being transformed in his image, into "a new creation," complete and perfect, and, in this way, rightly called "children of the Highest." As he was transformed, at baptism, into Son of God, so are they, becoming his words and entering his vision of the eternal. Jesus said:

> But love your enemies, and do good, and lend, expecting nothing in return; and your reward will be great, and you will be sons of the Most High; for he is kind to the ungrateful and the selfish. Be merciful, even as your Father is merciful (Luke 6:35–36).

Forgiveness grants them the character of God. Jesus says in Luke 6:40, "A disciple is not above his teacher, but every one when he is fully taught will be like his teacher." This is salvation, and it is universality. Jesus prays in John 17:24 that those who follow him "may be with me where I am." This is oneness.

Truly to forgive, to forget the entirety of the past, including oneself, is to join together in will, purpose, and effect. It is to enter and realize part of the kingdom of God. To join is to transcend individual selfhood and self-interest, even for a moment. Even if this gift from God is offered with a sometimes-troubled mind and the most trembling of hands, it cannot help but recall a portion of this newness of life and effect an immediate rethinking of the self.

Forgiveness allows for higher, broader vision and a new way of seeing. What was formerly separated, spinning off alone, is now gathered together. That which had been cast aside is now reaccepted, in the resultant state of love. That which seemed to belong to a distant past or future is near. Paul sums up the great command to forgive, coupling it with a sense of universal salvation:

> Why do you pass judgment on your brother? Or you, why do

you despise your brother? For we shall all stand before the judgment seat of God; for it is written, "As I live, says the Lord, every
knee shall bow to me, and every tongue shall give praise to God"
(Rom. 14:10–11).

All that lives must return to Him, its Source, Whose Presence is always
near. His Will is the reconciliation of everything true through the sharing of
His transcendent and unifying Spirit. For, as we have seen, the nature of
God is perfect love. How could He be anything other than Love? For "It
is God who justifies; who is to condemn?" (Rom. 8:33–34). Origen con-
cluded that God had "no wrath to be propitiated."[11] For early Christians,
perfect love in God and like God meant perfect forgiveness.

Everyone one forgives is accepted as part of oneself. If the breadth of forgiveness is universal, then salvation is universal, and the vista it reveals is just
as magnificent. Communion is the consequence of forgiveness, for through
this forgiveness a new world is shared, a kingdom ruled and graced by the sublime and constant Light of God. Here, all is interrelationship. The self is new
because it has expanded beyond any particular confines. The present is clean
when the past is forgiven and all but forgotten. The channels of intercommu-
nication are open, and, suddenly, universal Heaven is a thought away.

Righteousness is always instantly evident, once it is acknowledged as
universal and so inherent. True righteousness comes not from works of any
kind, but rather from faith perfected in love (Gal. 5:6). One's sense of
righteousness must transcend even that of religious standards if the
believer is to "enter the kingdom of heaven" (Matt. 5:20). Through forgiveness, believers are made perfect even as their heavenly Father is perfect
(Matt. 5:48). Likewise, the believer is made perfect and whole in Christ.
Such is salvation, resolving the internal problem of sin and separation,
removing from the mind the obstructing encapsulations and conceptualizations that keep it from oneness.

Salvation, like righteousness, is an experience given freely by God to
His Creation. With the experience of universal salvation, the notion is
removed that there could be anything real that is different from God's Will.
That is why laws become not so much commands as they are all at once a
vision of a new world. Union with God effects in the moment of its experience a certainty of the impossibility of separation from God and from life.

8

Emptiness and Fullness

For the Lord will comfort Zion;
he will comfort all her waste places,
and will make her wilderness like Eden,
her desert like the garden of the Lord;
joy and gladness will be found in her,
thanksgiving and the voice of song.

—Isa. 51:3

Empty But for God

Jesus and the Early Christians regarded God and ordinary consciousness as two opposite states of mind that produced dissimilar experiences. God and the former self could not be experienced at the same time. The process of changing from one to the other is also spoken of in the New Testament. It is spoken of as a process, similar to that seen in crucifixion and resurrection, of giving up oneself in order to live again. Because even a lesser change would be experienced as difficult, to so relinquish control is an act of the complete being requiring an extraordinary degree of faith, but the new experience in which one subsequently finds oneself grants greater and greater certainty.

Early Christians thought of it as rebirth after a kind of death to the old. Relinquish the old, partake of the New, is a continuing theme of Jesus' teaching. Deny one self to find another. "New wine must be put into fresh wineskins" (Luke 5:38) indicates that a transformation must occur before the newly reborn Self can be experienced. To forgive is to have forgotten the past, so that not a trace of its memory remains, and one is free to begin again. Jesus' teaching is new in the sense that it fosters a new sense of experience which, as it unfolds, and is contrasted to what was before, appears more and more as a new sense of Self. Early Christians felt reborn because their experience transformed their very identity.

Jesus turns the ideals of the world on their heads. He tells a parable about turning down the place of honor when invited to a marriage feast, saying:

> But when you are invited, go and sit in the lowest place, so that when your host comes he may say to you, "Friend, go up higher"; then you will be honored in the presence of all who sit at table with you. For everyone who exalts himself will be humbled, and he who humbles himself will be exalted (Luke 14:10–11).

More than keen advice, this is for Jesus the way to live in this world so as never not to remember the greatness of God. Paradoxically, this intention for the lowest place will result in a fulfillment that is more full than the former emptiness was empty.

This inversion of the world's values is apparent also in Jesus' proclamations to his followers that they become like children: "Truly, I say to you, unless you turn and become like children, you will never enter the kingdom of heaven" (Matt. 18:3). He identified with and encouraged identification with children (Mark 9:36–37) because of their humility and readiness to open to new ideas, and because they are "the least" among the social orders of the world:

> Whoever receives this child in my name receives me, and who-

ever receives me receives him who sent me; for he who is least among you all is the one who is great (Luke 9:48).

In another of his continuing themes, Jesus speaks of his abstract identification, and through his, the believer's own new identification, with the Universal. We might surmise from this that Jesus willed lowliness even as he took a higher place. Matthew 11:25 has him lauding the great simplicity of the things of God, saying, "I thank thee, Father, Lord of Heaven and earth that thou hast hidden these things from the wise and understanding and revealed them to babes." This would seem to suggest that Jesus favored an utterly simple mode of thought, so elemental as to be universal. If everything were to be experienced as new, then the thought of oneself in a new world must have occurred, with a new sense of what it means to be.

Jesus refuted some of the religious teachers of his day, because, believing they *knew* based on only their limiting perceptions, they taught neither the will nor world of God. He was concerned that those they taught came to know a deeper truth. As religious authorities are wont to do, they held up the laws and traditions of man rather than "the heart," neglecting the whole internal being of an individual. Such traditionalists instead based their teachings on a self-righteousness that does not save, a self-righteousness based only on mental conception, underneath which lies delusory intentions for self-glorification.

> The Pharisees, who were lovers of money, heard all this, and they scoffed at him. But he said to them, "You are those who justify yourselves before men, but God knows your hearts; for what is exalted among men is an abomination in the sight of God" (Luke 16:14–15).

There is a contrast between even the religion of man and God's world. God does not see as a human being sees, Jesus is saying. He sees from within, from the soul, for what could be more infinite than the internal Being of God? All God sees is Heaven; even the Earth is without stain of impurity.

To be immersed instead in the offerings of the world is to live with "the pride of life" (1 John 2:16). Life itself was something more, and more infinite, to Jesus, than what one can get by looking into darkness. *Life* had nothing at all to do with pride in worldly status or with anything that man sees; it had to do with self-honesty, honest self-appraisement down to the deepest levels, down to the core beliefs and values. Worldly desires and the things to which they lead seem then to pale, and fade; one's deepest desire does not lie there, and there one's truest Self does not abide.

And so one's way of living must be transformed. Jesus encourages *lostness,* as in lostness of self, saying: "the Son of Man came to seek and to save the lost" (Luke 19:10). He also encourages *lastness:* "If any one would be first, he must be last of all and servant of all" (Mark 9:35). And *leastness:* "for he who is least among you all is the one who is great" (Luke 9:48). There is one true desire of the heart, and its realization lies not in the world.

The Psalmist says of the ways of the world:

> Man cannot abide in his pomp, he is like the beasts that perish. This is the fate of those who have foolish confidence, the end of those who are pleased with their portion. Like sheep they are appointed for Sheol; death shall be their shepherd; straight to the grave they descend, and their form shall waste away; Sheol shall be their home (Ps. 49:12–14).

The cold and frosty ground will cover everything in this world, eventually. All of its aspirations must succumb to the dust from which they came. Tiredness eventually overtakes everything.

> All things are full of weariness; a man cannot utter it; the eye is not satisfied with seeing, nor the ear filled with hearing (Eccles. 1:8).

There is an inherent tiredness in all the things that roll toward their demise; the mind that hungers after these things and tries to pocket them will not escape this weariness. The mind that thus sleepwalks gives itself over to fatigue, ceases really trying, and dies therefore a symbolic death. Faith is needed to reinspire the mind, awaken and renew it, and so enliven it.

The way of life that flows naturally from the heart attuned to one true desire does not subsist for itself, bound as if by a centrifugal force for outer nothingness, stumbling in "the outer darkness" (Matt. 8:12), whatever form that darkness may seem to take. It is "the lost," those dispossessed by the world, and who feel it in their hearts, it is these lost who are ripe for salvation (Luke 15:3–7). Jesus said that he "came to seek and to save the lost" (Luke 19:10), those who feel they have no way, because they are more open to being found. He sat down at tables with people branded unsavory by regulators of the law because he was seeking them:

> Go and learn what this means, "I desire mercy, and not sacrifice." For I came not to call the righteous, but sinners (Matt. 9:13).

He was looking to sit with and to *be* with "sinners," and was little concerned with the self-righteous. The lost individual is more willing to risk a new experience, like forgiveness, and a new life, in a new world. Even those who adhere to the religions of the world and who believe they have everything may lose out on the newness of the depth of his message. And of course those who "are whole have no need of the physician" (Mark 2:17, AV); not feeling their inner emptiness and their need for salvation, they are far from salvation and headed for a fall.

In his Beatitudes, Jesus blesses "the poor in spirit," saying that "theirs is the kingdom of heaven" (Matt. 5:3), and blesses "those who mourn," saying they "shall be comforted" (5:4). He blesses "the meek" (5:5), "those who hunger and thirst for righteousness" (5:6), and "the merciful" (5:7). That is, Jesus, again reversing the values of the world, blesses those who hold no hope for the world, but who retain even a slight hope and a sliver of faith in another realm. For even the slightest hope can rise before them like a mountain of faith, not so much over time as with present or timeless streams of experience.

Jesus himself provides the example to follow:

> If any man would come after me, let him deny himself and take up his cross daily and follow me. For whoever would save his life will lose it; and whoever loses his life for my sake, he will save it. For what does it profit a man if he gains the whole world and loses or forfeits himself? (Luke 9:23–25)

Lose your life to find it, he says. Rescind your self, expecting another to rise to take its place. He is asking for a total departure from what was believed to be known, a thoroughgoing transformation. Jesus contrasts "the world" with the true Self ("his life," "himself"), indicating that a person must choose one or the other, old world or new Self, as between two divergent ways of living. To live in the world is not really to live; it is to tend toward death, to sow one's dreams in limitation. By contrast, what may at first seem like relinquishment and renunciation of self turns out to be an entirely new way of living.

Paul expresses another way that Jesus is an example to follow:

> Let each of you look not only to his own interests, but also to the interests of others. Have this mind among yourselves, which is yours in Christ Jesus, who, though he was in the form of God, did not count equality with God a thing to be grasped, but emptied himself, taking the form of a servant, being born in the likeness of men. And being found in human form he humbled himself and became obedient unto death, even death on a cross (Phil. 2:4–8).

Because *he* so humbled himself, *you* must look out for others, Paul is saying. Have his mind among yourselves, *the mind of Christ within you.* Paul expresses it another way: "For you know the grace of our Lord Jesus Christ, that though he was rich, yet for your sake he became poor, so that by his poverty you might become rich" (2 Cor. 8:9). Paul suggests that believers live within the paradox introduced by Jesus, whose humility is their glorification, "for when I am weak, then I am strong" (2 Cor. 12:10).

Jesus speaks another parable:

> Truly, truly, I say to you, unless a grain of wheat falls into the earth and dies, it remains alone; but if it dies, it bears much fruit. He who loves his life loses it, and he who hates his life in this world will keep it for eternal life. If anyone serves me, he must follow me; and where I am, there shall my servant be also; if any one serves me, the Father will honor him (John 12:24–26).

To become a servant willfully is to reverse the values of the world, even to the point of hating one's life in this world. Earthly status is at its core nothing but a delusion. Jesus' follower assumes a background vastly different than that wherein the former self once seemed to move like a speck. Found within the intricate, nearly hidden design is a deeper will so fundamental, elemental, and simple that only a child could see it, and think of it as reality.

Jesus encourages self-humbling in order to achieve a different kind of exaltation: "Truly, I say to you, whoever does not receive the kingdom of God like a child shall not enter it" (Luke 18:17). The child is excited and pleased to learn about the hidden reality, and does not reject out of hand that which does not fit with his or her frame of reference. The child is open enough to ask in the hope of receiving, having nothing to lose but everything to gain.

Jesus encourages relinquishment of everything including one's "life" (Luke 17:33) with the promise of an eternal inheritance (Mark 10:28–31). He left instructions for his spiritual disciples, saying:

> Preach as you go, saying, "The kingdom of heaven is at hand." Heal the sick, raise the dead, cleanse lepers, cast out demons. You received without paying, give without pay. Take no gold, nor silver, nor copper in your belts, no bag for your journey, nor two tunics, nor sandals, nor a staff; for the laborer deserves his food (Matt. 10:7–10).

The relinquishment of everything would of course be resignation of self, particularly outer-directed self, the self whose only orbit is the world it sees. But such relinquishment of self also takes on the form of a looking after one another (healing and raising). Nothing is needed for this "laboring" except the Spirit of God. The ones who walk beside the individual are those through whom "God will ransom my soul from the power of Sheol, for he will receive me" (Ps. 49:15). For there lives inside the heart and soul of the stranger beside and also within oneself the beatific vision of a new and different kind of life that in its total immediacy and present-ness can truly be called eternal.

There is work to be done to follow this process. The lowly servant of God is kept working (Luke 17:7–10); even his sitting down is work, is opening to reconciliation, but with surety of eternal wages. And there is work to be done on relationships:

> and if he sins against you seven times in the day, and turns to you seven times, and says, "I repent," you must forgive him (Luke 17:4).

It becomes a continual and automatic process—for one's relationships in this world are a present indication of one's relationship with God, just as the deeply cherished relationship with God is a model of what all relationships must be.

Jesus says that he has no home in this world: "Foxes have holes, and birds of the air have nests; but the Son of man has nowhere to lay his head" (Luke 9:58). He says he has no family, no land (Mark 10:29), yet he says that this relinquishment gives him a sense of having hundreds of brothers and sisters, hundreds of houses, miles of land (Mark 10:30–31). The more he loses, the more he seems to gain. He loses everything, yet he seems to pick it up again and utilize it toward a greater purpose to which he seems driven. He labors by eating and drinking with friends old and new, creating stories out of the native language, thinking and speaking universally. He has no home in this world, "nowhere to lay his head," but that does not mean that he does not truly live; he lives more abundantly unencumbered by the usual strictures, from which he seems entirely detached—an effect of the Spirit. He does not allow himself to find his satisfaction in this world, so that he can instead receive his glorification from God.

As such, Jesus lives a life of paradox, but his intention is resolutely one. He says, "Follow me," because he rises to a kind of transcendence of mind, away from common concern about any old thing, and instead into concerns of a deeper order.

> Take no thought for your life, what you shall eat, or what you shall drink; nor yet for your body, what you will put on. Is not the life more than meat, and the body than raiment? . . . But seek first the kingdom of God, and his righteousness; and all these things shall be added to you (Matt. 6:25, 33, KJV).

Therefore, "Do not labor for the food which perishes, but for the food which endures to eternal life" (John 6:27). Anxiously seeking the things of this world makes one lose track of the sense of wholeness that comes, paradoxically, by lostness. "Take no thought for your life" and no thought for your body, and the kingdom of God will instead take thought of you. There is a lightness in living so simply, without regard for the illusions that seem to sparkle, but which cause one to remain of the past. Leaving everything behind, not desiring any of it for itself, but instead for what it offers toward salvation, one may yet use anything for the good of all:

> And I tell you, make friends for yourselves by means of unrighteous mammon, so that when it fails they may receive you into the eternal habitations (Luke 16:9).

"Riches," material wealth, except for this making of friends and psychologically deep search for the eternal habitations, is said by Jesus to be a deterrent to the experience of the kingdom of God (Mark 10:23). Only one of these worlds is of the light; the other is darkness, but darkness has potential to be lit. Nothing is of any value whatsoever except insofar as it helps lead ultimately to the kingdom of God. This kingdom of God is a greater sense of life as infinitely open, "for all things are possible with God" (10:27). As we have seen, the kingdom of God is the true value of the whole being, and so to live within it is salvation. It is the last thing that will ever be sought on Earth; the rest is completion.

Jesus states flatly: "He who finds his life will lose it, and he who loses his life for my sake will find it" (Matt. 10:39). That is, giving up everything else for the one goal every soul knows deep inside, the soul will uncover *a new life,* its own life, untethered to the limitations and hiding places of the past, but united with the present in infinite experience. The world dictates nothing to the soul, for the soul is more original than the world.

Jesus told the man who had followed all the commandments, "You lack one thing; go, sell what you have, and give to the poor, and you will have treasure in heaven; and come, follow me" (Mark 10:21). Simple advice really: Live the opposite of the way you live now. Such emptiness, the effect of resignation, is followed by a sense of "treasure in heaven." It is implied that giving everything to the poor makes for a different kind of life, a life

led by Spirit rather than by the things of the world. The giving up of everything is a way to receive an infinitely different everything, and a new sense
of life to "see" it. At the least, the poor will be gladdened, and this will glad-
den the heart due to interconnection. A life of giving fully to the point of
denying oneself is a life of complete receiving and restoration, a way to
enter the "eternal habitations."

Recalling the sense of toil introduced by the fall in the Garden, Jesus
says: "Come to me, all who labor and are heavy laden, and I will give you
rest" (Matt. 11:28). He saves through instruction—instruction in coming
to *think* like him, elementally but abstractly. This is the "labor" he calls his
hearers to, to change one's mind so as to experience his peace. He continues: "Take my yoke upon you, and learn from me; for I am gentle and lowly
in heart, and you will find rest for your souls. For my yoke is easy, and my
burden is light" (11:29–30). Crossing over the borderline between existence and Being, the believer's mind and will is joined or yoked to his. To
relinquish the bonds of individual existence is to lessen distractions to the
heart's knowledge, the simplest ties, and so to simplify delightfully the way
of living, to delight simply in being. Joining him in this, he says, "you will
find rest for your souls."

Early Christians believed in an eternity that rises from within the mind
when mental effort has ceased, and everything is let come and go, including Spirit and the deepest, most satisfying emotions, in every moment. "So
you have sorrow now, but I will see you again and your hearts will rejoice,
and no one will take your joy from you" (John 16:22). His followers must
let go even of everything they think Jesus is. The loneliness of losing him in
conceptualization is but prelude to the joy of simple union and togetherness with him, just as the loss of his physical presence increased his spiritual presence. The purpose of denying themselves is to deny all human
existence, including the bodily Jesus, and thus to allow the mind to rise to
a new level of Being.

When two ways of being clash in the mind, only one is followed. The
Christ Mind leads through the world, working on it as it passes by, not for
a later Heaven, but for the kingdom of God in the now. When temporal
sorrows meet eternal joys, the sorrows are first to go, eternal life last to stay.
When all that is not of God is seen as fading in the eternal light of His
Presence, and everyone takes a place at the heavenly banquet, then the

world is no longer distraction, but reinforcement, and a new Self is free to see everything as it truly might be and, in fact, is.

Jesus advocates this mental renunciation of values in order to instill a sense of peace and happiness:

> I have said this to you, that in me you may have peace. In the world you have tribulation; but be of good cheer, I have overcome the world (John 16:33).

He calls his disciples to raise their minds with his, and overcome any alien sense of self in order instead to share an eternal sense of peace. When, in the instant of spiritual experience, self is gone and world is gone, when no self-referential conception of God remains, then God is free to reveal Himself as He is, and to reveal in His most holy light that which He truly creates. Unless one is lost and truly open to truth, one will worship a god much like oneself. This would hinder salvation by defeating its purpose: to transcend all that inhibits transcendence, and so to experience the full flower of union.

There is a bit of effort in the process, but it is only the mental effort of asking from lostness, thereby undermining the pride of understanding. "Ask, and it will be given you; seek, and you will find; knock, and it will be opened to you" (Matt. 7:7). It is also the heart's effort, secretly seeking an open door, that leads beyond any but the ultimate Self. Finding the desired change of mind comes after a period of seeking; Heaven's gates unlock and its spiritual doors swing wide with but the internal act, thought and feeling, of knocking. To have asked from lostness and a true passion to know is truly to have asked.

Living Emptiness

Job speaks plainly with his alleged comforters: "How then will you comfort me with empty nothings? There is nothing left of your answers but falsehood" (Job 21:34). Eternal Comfort must come from a much, much deeper place than "empty nothings"; Job has come to the realization that the values of the world are inside out. Perhaps it was the moment he faced mortality, that eternal moment of resignation and responding to a call at the same time. Death is hardly necessary, asserts Jesus, who himself thought beyond death, because the very conception of death has been swept away with the former self. You will not *taste* death, Jesus says (Matt. 16:28), because you will be partaking of life instead.

The world of transitory things and human plans is as nothing to the one who overcomes:

> Behold, they are all a delusion; their works are nothing; their molten images are empty wind (Isa. 41:29).

That leaves no room for content, nor for comfort in material things. Things that come from nothing are ultimately nothing. A void of emptiness remains inside the most solid things on Earth, and that emptiness has everything to do with the Self that will never be satisfied with anything but truth. Masses of souls, deluded that they live outside themselves, are deeply fearful of openness, and so they would rather see and respond to nothing. The power of self-delusion is potent, yet it is never as real as the real creation.

It is dissatisfaction with everything except the kingdom that causes one to rise to it. There is a core of nothing at the center of this world that tries to pull everything to it. "Mammon"—the divided world based on money and possessions and physical and political power—is nothing, though one might delude oneself into thinking it is everything. Certainly, it is not eternal, but rather forever changing. And this lesser kingdom that so preoccupies the world can prevent one from entering the kingdom of heaven or even from knowing about it. That is why Jesus said:

> But woe to you, scribes and Pharisees, hypocrites! Because you shut the kingdom of heaven against men; for you neither enter yourselves, nor allow those who would enter to go in (Matt. 23:13).

The kingdom of heaven is the realm of mind high enough not to be dragged down into the world's hollow core and practices.

There is no separation, or lack of any kind, when fear is gone and only union remains. Even the world of nations must be rethought when "All the nations are as nothing before him, they are accounted by him as less than nothing and emptiness" (Isa. 40:17).

> There is neither Jew nor Greek, there is neither slave nor free, there is neither male nor female; for you are all one in Christ Jesus (Gal. 3:28).

This kind of deconceptualization brings to mind a new idea of being. All who roam the Earth stand as one together in the experience of oneness and of love beyond self-interest. The universal has become personal, and the personal has become more deeply personal. Distinctions cannot keep soul apart, only distinct and separate interests can do that. Unity will be realized when a personal experience of Spirit convinces each person of oneness with all.

But to have this encounter, true encounter, a genuine Self or two must be present. False images know nothing of relationship. "They shall call it No Kingdom There, and all its princes shall be nothing" (Isa. 34:12). The self lost in confusion is not the self that is truly lost. The self that is truly lost has no help in this world: "Whom have I in heaven but thee? And there is nothing upon earth that I desire besides thee" (Ps. 73:25). It is helpless for a second, but it does not remain hopeless. Shining naturally from the heart is its true desire: to *be* with God, truly to relate and more truly to be.

The old way of seeing has run its course:

> What has been is what will be, and what has been done is what will be done; and there is nothing new under the sun (Eccles. 1:9).

The past loops back into the future, so that it seems there is no stepping-off point from circular time. All the turmoil that one has suffered in interminable hours chained to the repetitions of existence comes to nothing; one's toil is "vanity and a striving after wind" (Eccles. 2:11).

> I have labored in vain, I have spent my strength for nothing and for vanity; yet surely my right is with the Lord, and my recompense with my God (Isa. 49:4).

Here we have the paradoxical inner process of this transformation of mind, the resignation of a former way of seeing so that another may take its place. The realization that this world leads to emptiness, as if it hangs on nothing, can spark its corollary realization, that there is something real behind it. Even in the midst of emptiness, there is something more. "But God will ransom my soul from the power of Sheol, for he will receive me" (Ps. 49:15).

There is no cause for pride in the world:

> For even if one is perfect among the sons of men, yet without the wisdom that comes from thee he will be regarded as nothing (Wisdom 9:6).

Realization of the core of nothingness at the center of this world makes the self that roams it seem like "a dreadful, self-kindled fire," with all those immersed in their own separate ways being subject to delusion and to horrible illusions:

> Nothing was shining through to them except a dreadful, self-kindled fire, and in terror they deemed the things which they saw to be worse than that unseen appearance (Wisdom 17:6).

The thought of nothingness is terror, fear of the dreadful core. The hollow core of the world is protected by icy rings of fear, but it attracts those who encircle it and they are immediately trapped, paralyzed in their fear, frozen in outer darkness by their adherence to the ice-cold things they touch and survey.

Yet "at the moment of his rescue he wakes up, and wonders that his fear came to nothing" (Sirach 40:7). Fear was just part and parcel of the mass delusion; it was not in the illusions themselves, but in their perceiver. There is great individual responsibility in the great escape from emptiness and meaninglessness. When the empty self has absconded in spiritual union, so has the fear that characterized it. And where no fear is possible, there is love, for "There is no fear in love, but perfect love casts out fear" (1 John 4:18).

The cold-to-the-bone nothingness of empty space is not the same as true emptiness, for true emptiness is warm in its solitude, ecstatic in its relationship. To empty the self in relationship, to forgive, is to give another an opportunity to *be,* thereby to rise into Being with them.

And Simon answered, "Master, we toiled all night and took nothing! But at your word I will let down the nets" (Luke 5:5).

Toil is hardship if it comes to nothing. But to lower the nets in an effortless way, borne aloft by the Presence that holds one in hope, is to overcome barriers to faith and its realization. "Put out into the deep and let down your nets for a catch" (Luke 5:4). All the effort required is simply to ask and to open and get out of the way. The nets may break—the mind will need new categories to understand it—but the catch will be an instance of newness of life. "Do not be afraid; henceforth you will be catching men," says Jesus in Luke 5:10, ever desirous that the world follow him in his sav-ing function.

Who has not sensed the emptiness of all things? Death sleeps at the center of the things of the world. Nothing escapes its tired pull. Whenever existence is seriously considered, it seems indeed that:

Man that is born of woman is of few days, and full of trouble. He comes forth like a flower and withers; he flees like a shadow, and continues not (Job 14:1–2).

And it is not only death that makes it so. Death is only a symbol for the overall emptiness and fleetingness of seemingly everything.

Philosophers have sensed the hollow core of the world:

Both habit and diversion, so long as they work, conceal from man "his nothingness, his forlorn-ness, his inadequacy, his impo-tence and his emptiness." Religion is the only possible cure for this desperate malady that is nothing other than our ordinary mortal existence itself.[1]

Individuals turn to the religious and the spiritual because they are lit-erally yet subconsciously seeking the reality of a higher realm, having come face to face with nothingness. Religion raises the possibility of rising above the world to escape the gravity of the void, high enough and long enough to reorient to the entire thing as a whole. The Heart of God floods the void, so that what remains feels like life and only life, beyond all sense of death and destruction.

For Paul himself, a little suffering was small price to pay for the magnificence of the glory he was called into. Yet he speaks of a kind of "godly grief" that is not all negative in that it serves to lead a person beyond habits and thoughts full of self, and enables one to detach from the emptiness of the world without suffering:

> As it is, I rejoice, not because you were grieved, but because you were grieved into repenting; for you felt a godly grief, so that you suffered no loss through us. For godly grief produces a repentance that leads to salvation and brings no regret, but worldly grief produces death (2 Cor. 7:9–10).

There is a kind of embracing of the hurt here and, in that moment, its healing. Repentance "that leads to salvation . . . brings no regret"; it is simply a form of reinterpretation, not only of things in the world, but of things in the individual. All that is really required is a change of mind about all things, which can come about through a mere moment of spiritual experience.

It is better to let one's interpretation of the world be handled by something closer to the original state of Being, at the deepest level of existence. Therefore does Job interpret all the hardship that has befallen him as part of the Divine Mercy that fills the Universe:

> Behold, God does all these things, twice, three times, with a man, to bring back his soul from the Pit, that he may see the light of life (Job 33:29–30).

Even in the midst of chaos there are traces of a higher order, glimpses into an overarching plan, and the revelation that brings sweet transcendence. The plans of an individual may be dashed at any time, but the laws of the universe are operational in every instant. To know the universal laws is to know oneself, as God knows. But the way to such knowledge leads through abandonment of self, resignation as plan maker, map interpreter, and even voyager.

This leaving behind of self and home in search of a greater can feel at times like the "dark night of the soul." This phrase was used by mystic father Saint John of the Cross for the anguished period of denial of the graceful Presence after initial exultation in it, and a seemingly endless waiting with hope that it might come again. In Exodus, this process is represented as a wandering through the desert for at least a generation, seeking the threshold of the Promised Land, which is the end of struggle and the resumption of Being.

There is a way to practice even through this dark night that leaves oneself far in the background, yet at the same time at the fore:

> But love your enemies, and do good, expecting nothing in return; and your reward will be great, and you will be sons of the Most High; for he is kind to the ungrateful and the selfish (Luke 6:35).

The background is, in the realm of Spirit, actually foreground. Everyone is included in it; not one is lost. The past no longer matters; it has been judged illusion, forgiven, and allowed to recede and retract itself back into its original empty space. The future is now, and it is full, even if it seems to take a long time to come to final realization.

All are accounted for in the present. And all needs are put to rest. "'When I sent you out with no purse or bag or sandals, did you lack anything?' They said, 'Nothing'" (Luke 22:35). They were too caught in the glory of the Lord to sense any lack. There was no longer any ensnaring feeling in themselves, for they were sharing everything, even themselves, until their joy was complete. Boundaries erased, barriers collapsed, there is no shadow before the world of light. Fear recedes and with it the need to absorb the cares of the world, so that instead a greater care might be assimilated:

> Thou dost show me the path of life; in thy presence there is fulness of joy, in thy right hand are pleasures for evermore (Ps. 16:11).

To cast one's cares on Him is to "let steadfastness have its full effect, that you may be perfect and complete, lacking in nothing" (James 1:4). What is given up is the desultory and delusory nature of the former life, the gravitation toward death, the emptiness of a stony heart, the "vanity" and the "striving after wind" (Eccles. 1:14). "And the world passes away, and the lust of it; but he who does the will of God abides for ever" (1 John 2:17).

When it is known how much one has received, having been given life, then do thoughts rise from the depths of the soul, tending toward greatness of being and a sense of completion: "And from his fulness have we all received, grace upon grace" (John 1:16). And in this reception of internal fullness is a new vision of the world in fullness: "The earth is the Lord's and the fulness thereof, the world and those who dwell therein" (Ps. 24:1). Can there exist a scrap of nothingness in the light of such vision? Emptiness and darkness in this vision are nothing but a gentle eve of transformation by which the lowly and the low rise to greatness.

Paul had his "thorn . . . in the flesh," which he felt held him "from being too elated by the abundance of revelations" (2 Cor. 12:7). He suffered his own personal dark night. Three times, he says, he prayed to God that this affliction should leave him (12:8), but he was told: "My grace is sufficient for you, for my power is made perfect in weakness" (12:9). So Paul concludes: "I will all the more gladly boast of my weaknesses, that the power of Christ may rest upon me" (12:9).

Yet Paul's is a religion of *fullness*. Paul says to his audience in Rome that he "shall come in the fulness of the blessing of Christ" (Rom. 15:29). That is, he shall come with a mind full of the glory of his Origin, knowing "the love of Christ which surpasses knowledge" so that his helpers "may be filled with all the fulness of God" (Eph. 3:19). In this, he is following his revelation from Jesus Christ, "for in him all the fulness of God was pleased to dwell" (Col. 1:19).

And the great purpose behind this taking of the background to follow one's leading is to "attain to the unity of the faith and of the knowledge of the Son of God, to mature manhood, to the measure of the stature of the fulness of Christ" (Eph. 4:13). For God has "a plan for the fulness of time, to unite all things in him, things in heaven and things on earth" (Eph. 1:10). That is, the purpose behind stepping back in faith is to experience unity, and through that, Sonship, even to full identification with "the fulness of Christ," and to "the fulness of him who fills all in all" (Eph. 1:23).

There is in this humbling of oneself a real exaltation in the depths, as a new Self rises up and with it a new realm of Being. For an individual to consent to forgo the accustomed self in an even exchange of selves is "to put aside his or her conscious ego structure so that access to the unconscious is made possible" and "to facilitate him or her in making use of already present unconscious potential."[2] The being who slips beneath the self rises to remembrance of a more original Self created in eternity, reexperienced in Spirit.

One's True Value

Anything possessed by a person, including thoughts and beliefs, must come to nothing before the eternal longing for the eternal in the heart. Jesus is spoken of as feeling like a "distressed and troubled" soul (Mark 14:33) when he prayed in the Garden of Gethsemane that he accept the cup before him, representing his life, though his heart was "very sorrowful, even to death" (14:34). It would seem that he—even he—suffered in this, but it was part of his service to the larger whole. It was part of his crossing over the valley of separation for the Most High.

Saint Stephen, before being stoned to death at the hands of those who thought he was disavowing the tradition by expressing the newness and vitality of what he felt through the Spirit, had an experience of the Glory of the Lord:

> But he, full of the Holy Spirit, gazed into heaven and saw the glory of God, and Jesus standing at the right hand of God; and he said, "Behold, I see the heavens opened, and the Son of man standing at the right hand of God" (Acts 7:55–56).

Samuel Terrien notes: "The theology of the glory, with its spiritual delight, explained the courage of Stephen before the imminence of his death."[3] Stephen had a revelation of fullness and a vision of glory as he slipped into heaven *before* his physical departure.

Deep in the heart, buried by ontological guilt and layer upon layer of defense against this guilt, lies the urge for something less distressing than existence. It can come out in nearly any worldly situation. But looking into the face of temporality, of mortality and of looming death, and renouncing all of it activates the sense of Ultimate Being. The depth of sorrow does not emanate from anywhere nearly as foundational as the depths of God. Existence need not be suffered through; it contains enough suffering already. It is good simply to remember this, and therefore hold out a grain of Being, a seed of full flowering in the glorious transcendence of God.

And so the Psalmist harbors hope and optimism in the face of his downcastness:

> Why are you cast down, O my soul, and why are you disqui-eted within me? Hope in God; for I shall again praise him, my help and my God (Ps. 42:11).

From the depths of his soul, he cries out for a brand-new life. He might as well be crying out for the removal of his thoughts and his values, and their replacement by higher thoughts and deeper values. The process begins with hope, walks with faith, and finally comes to rest in a childlike dependence on the Divine. The Psalmist (33:20–22) also prays:

> Our soul waits for the Lord; he is our help and shield. Yea, our heart is glad in him, because we trust in his holy name. Let thy steadfast love, O Lord, be upon us, even as we hope in thee.

James 5:8 states: "You also be patient. Establish your hearts, for the coming of the Lord is at hand." His presence will be realized; believers will realize themselves within the presence of the Lord. Ps. 13:5 says, "But I have trusted in thy steadfast love; my heart shall rejoice in thy salvation." His love is a certainty beyond the things of the world.

God will be *known,* truly known, though his mind seems unfathomable to the human mind. But the mind is indeed searchable, as long as it comes from Him. This requires a sense of holiness, simple innocence, and pure-ness of heart, as if God had "cast all my sins behind thy back" (Isa. 38:17). Another psalm (31:22) has it, "I had said in my alarm, 'I am cut off from thy sight.' But you heard my supplications, when I cried to thee for help."

That which is impossible for humans has been achieved by God through His Spirit.

Confidence and certainty in the true Self begin and end with trust in God, and trust in God looks at first like resignation of the false self. The full grain comes unexpectedly, sometimes after a period of high expectation, sometimes without explanation. One is destined finally to put all one's hopes in it, in order that the request for it be made continually. It is drawn to an open being through emptiness of self. It comes when mind and heart are most able to receive. The foreground is revealed in fullness when the background is chosen. Walking through the wilderness of inner emptiness reveals a portal through which one reattains the Fullness of the Original Garden.

Eternity is the suspension of time and its sorrows. Freedom from struggle, worry, and depression lies just behind resignation of self. Through the emptiness of the surface shines a light sublime, like the fullness of the present. Hope remains, though existence seems most hopeless, though the mind struggles with an unlike reality, though separation from everything and everyone is felt most acutely.

Paul gives a humble example of this new mind-set, saying "if any one thinks he is something, when he is nothing, he deceives himself" (Gal. 6:3). A person would deceive himself by not realizing that which makes him something, his union with God through Christ. He would deceive himself into thinking he was something other than he truly is. And so, paradoxical intention is in order, an intent on nothingness and a consequent sense that everything is good:

> For everything created by God is good, and nothing is to be rejected if it is received with thanksgiving (1 Tim. 4:4).

To receive these heavenly things, even on Earth, the mind must first be set on "the things that are above" (Col. 3:1). To do that, one must detach and dissociate oneself from the things and the thoughts that return to dust. Empty of all things except those of the Spirit, the heart is able to set itself upon a new transcendent realm. With the help of the Spirit who searches all things, even the Mind and Heart of God, the truest longing of the heart and the priceless desire of the soul will be revealed to the new Self. The Spirit is as eager to communicate the kingdom as God was to communicate Spirit.

The mind in alignment with Spirit is emptied of the self-serving pride of the world. Therefore, says Paul, "Do nothing from selfishness or conceit, but in humility count others better than yourselves" (Phil. 2:3). Consciousness is drained of the stagnant premises on which it attempts to construct its life. The heart is drained of eddying wishes, so that "having nothing," it may yet possess everything (2 Cor. 6:10). That which once seemed automatic is no longer automatic, and the new, more natural process has been reinstated. The direct intuition of the Son of God, not the tortured logic of the lower self, lights the way.

Simplicity in living is a product of Grace. John the Baptist presented a vision of a simple world of equal living:

> And the multitudes asked him, "What then shall we do?" And he answered them, "He who has two coats, let him share with one who has none; and he who has food, let him do likewise." Tax collectors also came to be baptized, and said to him, "Teacher, what shall we do?" And he said to them, "Collect no more than is appointed you." Soldiers also asked him, "And we, what shall we do?" And he said to them, "Rob no one by violence or by false accusation, and be content with your wages" (Luke 3:10–14).

Do what you do, expecting neither more nor less. Life is worth more than wages. The poor are themselves treasures to the rich in heart. In fact, Jesus indicates that it is the least on earth who will see Heaven first. Living among the poor and the wayward and lost, as Jesus did, seeking out association with them, became a way for him of fulfilling the will of God. It became a way of fulfilling himself by giving of himself in gladness.

"He must increase, but I must decrease," says John the Baptist of Jesus in John 3:30. While the former self is let go, the Christ is seen standing fully revealed in light, for His enlightened vision sees all the way through to the true and authentic Self, the Self that is already whole within the glory of the presence. In the presence of truth and its light, falsity cannot abide. What is left is simply "fulness of life in him" (Col. 2:10).

And so we return to the original theme: God is not known by the ordinary conscious self.

Further, I say that if the soul is to know God, it must forget itself and lose [consciousness of] itself, for as long as it is self-aware and self-conscious, it will not see or be conscious of God.[4]

To receive the superconsciousness with which to be known by God: First, one must ask. And then one must let go of the asking, in order to receive. And then one must let go of the receiving, so that one might give more, thereby to receive more.

Early Christians were advised to give themselves to the Ground of Being by giving themselves to the whole of Being (just as Jesus had). To trust like this is to call for the moment when individual effort must cease. To love Him with all one's strength is to realize one's rest in God:

For thus says the Lord God, the Holy One of Israel, "In returning and rest you shall be saved; in quietness and in trust shall be your strength" (Isa. 30:15).

Sit in stillness of mind and the solitude of prayer and let Him move you, as He would. He returns the world to those who turn it over to Him.

Let not yours be the outward adorning with braiding of hair, decoration of gold, and wearing of fine clothing, but let it be the hidden person of the heart with the imperishable jewel of a gentle and quiet spirit, which in God's sight is very precious (1 Pet. 3:3–4).

They are told to do what they can for those they could see, helpfulness being key here and a means to Divine Closeness, that they might reflect the great will and giving nature of their Father in Heaven. And their Heaven was seen from this Earth.

Give to him who begs from you, and do not refuse him who would borrow from you (Matt. 5:42).

The important things are not those that can be gotten from one another, but rather those things that can be received while they are given.

This kind of receiving takes nothing away from either self or other, but it blesses everyone. To open the receptive faculty is to have the lenses purified, so that it can be seen why, as the Golden Rule states, what is done to another is done to oneself. For there is an interconnection and a kind of equilibrium between and among all that lives, and that is what gives life fullness.

> Truly, I say to you, as you did it to one of the least of these my brethren, you did it to me (Matt. 25:40).

The sense of interconnection, the relationship of all things, of all beings, is known whenever the unknowing self is transcended. And with this there is surety:

> By this we shall know that we are of the truth, and reassure our hearts before him, whenever our hearts condemn us; for God is greater than our hearts, for he knows everything. Beloved, if our hearts do not condemn us, we have confidence before God (1 John 3:19–21).

Paul says of the effortlessness of faith: "So it depends not upon man's will or exertion, but upon God's mercy" (Rom. 9:16). Self was a relationship, which went unrealized while the lonely self dreamed of living in the spaces between. The fullness of Self as relationship will awaken naturally, of its own accord; the Self finds itself within the multitude with whom it once departed in exodus, only to return and reach the threshold of the Promised Land.

9
Prayer as Experience

These I will bring to my holy mountain,
and make them joyful in my house of prayer;
. . . my house shall be called a house of prayer for all peoples.
—Isa. 56:7

Silent Prayer

Jesus says that in prayer, not many words are needed:

> And in praying do not heap up empty phrases as the Gentiles
> do; for they think that they will be heard for their many words. Do
> not be like them, for your Father knows what you need before you
> ask him (Matt. 6:7–8).

Of course, the Creator would know what His Creation needs. If His
Creation somehow fell out of trust with Him, it would need faith in something
higher and more real. If it could forget the world for just a moment,

then it would be saved from all thought of limitation and returned to itself. That is, it would be saved from the sense that its harsh illusions cannot be escaped, by a return to intimacy with and knowledge of God, imparted through the initial trust. "May grace and peace be multiplied to you in the knowledge of God and of Jesus our Lord" (2 Pet. 1:2).

Therefore in deepest prayer, silence will do. The world ceases its activity as the self is hushed—not defeated, not conquered, but hushed—and the inner chamber comes alive again with praise and thanksgiving. The body will do what it does, its senses perform their routine tasks, but way down deep within the graced being there is a most secret stillness that changes everything. Breathing is a simple task because involuntary. Being oneself in authenticity is simple as can be. Thought can become effortless, taking its true place, subsumed in the mind and heart that gave it life. Surface anxieties remain on the surface, while the deeper mind reaches within itself for the grace of the most silent prayer.

When Jesus first visited the house of his friends Martha and Mary, Mary "sat at the Lord's feet and listened to his teaching" (Luke 10:39):

> But Martha was distracted with much serving; and she went to him and said, "Lord, do you not care that my sister has left me to serve alone? Tell her then to help me." But the Lord answered her, "Martha, Martha, you are anxious and troubled about many things; one thing is needful. Mary has chosen the good portion, which shall not be taken from her" (Luke 10:40–42).

"Mary has chosen the good portion"; that is, she has chosen silent contemplation of the eternal, a silence of mind and heart that is fully aware, a silence as great as that which permeated the initial, original creation. She opened her ears to listen, and this allowed her inner being not only to hear, but also to become the lesson of God.

A mind ensnared by the thicket of the world, drawn to its promise but snagged by its thorns, a mind that cannot find wings to rise above the tangle, will, of course, be troubled by it. But to set the mind on higher things, and to uncover the things that do not fade and do not rust, grants the grace of salvation and immense security to the mind. Mind and heart are integrated in the Spirit to know that "one thing is needful." A moment in prayerful silence, a moment in the sacred presence of the original light, a moment out of time can be their resting-place in infinity. "Contemplation and vision have no limits,"[1] says the philosopher Plotinus.

Contemplation begets singleness yet breadth of focus. It is the experience of contemplation that brings a sense of the reality of union with all things by virtue of the will of God. If He wants all souls to be one in Him, then this is how they will relate, eternally. There is a conviction of harmony in contemplation that the conceptual mind does not understand, yet certainty is there. When Paul prays that his fellow believers may be "filled with the knowledge of his will, in all spiritual wisdom and understanding" (Col. 1:9), he is praying that their understanding be a *spiritual* one. Knowledge in a divine sense is spiritual, that is, experiential. It is in no way separate from the person who knows. In the still silence of prayer, the person becomes the knowledge of God. God is fully known through experience, His depths self-understood through something more original inside the mind than conceptual understanding.

Silence of self breeds fullness of experience. Spirit is free to reveal its gentle presence in an awareness so deep it seems unconscious. It reveals a deep sense of comfort and care, and delivers a deep sense of ease. The restfulness of silent prayer is more than relaxation; the knowledge to which it leads is complete; the subject and object of this knowledge are one. Conceptual understandings must remain partial before it; it is made up of not even two parts. Though utterly still and silent, Spirit is dynamic in mind, replacing the self with grace and being.

The one who prays becomes part of a realm of heavenly beauty when silent in God:

> And as he was praying, the appearance of his countenance was altered, and his raiment became dazzling white (Luke 9:29).

When the human sits in prayer before God, the human is transformed. The former self, like the former world, is real only in a secondary and contingent sense; it is not real in and of itself, and therefore should not be spoken of as real at all. All the world is changed when God is revealed in His Glory through the holiness found in the inmost chamber of Self.

Prayer is the entryway to the inner sanctuary of God. It leaves room for spiritual experience, leaves time and space for God to fill. Stillness allows for presence, as emptiness allows for fullness, and at the same time there is an abdication of self-directed ego, while the Lord arrives in glory with the leaves of healing. One experience is the emptying out of the other. They may alternate over time and then overlap, until the reality of one is borne out.

Prayer is the means of reentering creation, yet it stands as harbinger of the end. It is the Temple of Holiness, the Fountain of Goodness, the Sanctuary of Being, just by being golden stillness in the clearing. The highest forms of prayer are the deepest: nonconceptual, wordless, selfless. They lead the mind into abstraction to leave it there, beyond all things, and let it receive and become its communication with God. Selflessness is itself prayer, an opening into Divine Presence. God reveals Himself in the depth of our Being, when the self that can only exist has for a moment absconded. Prayer is not an act of self, but rather a Divine Act that is accomplished by a momentary resignation of self. Prayer stills the body, empties the mind of all doings, drains the heart of pride and similar self-directed feelings, and therefore enables God to do, to feel, simply to breathe. If division is recalled, it will be seen, but to sit in forgiveness of the past, for truth, is to welcome truth with open arms.

Secret Prayer

Prayer grants access to the inner sanctuary, a refuge from a world that strives to capture the attention and not let go. Jesus visited his private sanctuary often; many times he is portrayed as going off to pray alone:

> And in the morning, a great while before day, he rose and went
> out to a lonely place, and there he prayed (Mark 1:35).

Also, "And after he had taken leave of them, he went up on the mountain to pray" (Mark 6:46). And at his most trying moment, his anguished existential crisis in the Garden of Gethsemane just before his crucifixion, Jesus needed not so much the comfort of his disciples as the comfort of his Father: he told them, "Sit here, while I go yonder and pray" (Matt. 26:36).

Jesus advocates private and deeply personal practice of the presence of God. Prayer is deepest when it is a matter between the soul and God. He advises how to pray and how not to pray:

And when you pray, you must not be like the hypocrites, for they love to stand and pray in the synagogues and at the street corners, that they may be seen by men. Truly, I say to you, they have received their reward. *But when you pray, go into your room and shut the door and pray to your Father who is in secret; and your Father who sees in secret will reward you* (Matt. 6:5–6, my italics).

Prayer is done beyond any ordinary sense of doing, from inside, in secret, where the kingdom resides. The practice of religion is so personal as to be private. It does not matter how one is "seen by men"; what matters is the "reward" from "your Father who sees in secret" (Matt. 6:1). Prayer allows the world to dissipate, and the subtle light of Heaven (the "reward") to settle in. Prayer surpasses the self and world that seemed so real before prayer was initiated.

To pray in secret where the Father sees, one must first get oneself alone: "go into your room and shut the door." Jesus advocates individual spirituality. Even a consensus in a worldly sense may serve as a means for exclusion. To join on the surface is not really to join. But agreement in the Spirit occurs when one is alone, but very aware. It is only through such initial solitude that agreement can be had with *everyone,* because it depends on no one's participation but one's own. Yet the world will be seen as one from within it.

Sitting in selflessness before God and His angels, that which was hidden by the boundaries of individual self begins more and more to fill awareness. To shut one's door to the world, as if to leave it behind, is to return and find one's home has changed. The Community of Being has been hidden, but it is aching to be found. So it is found. It is found in a "pre-conceptual experience of God . . . so subtle and delicate as to be almost imperceptible."[2] And so it starts small, nearly insignificant, in a deep inner chamber, but it grows to encompass the Earth.

Jesus couples effective prayer with a sense of forgiveness:

And whenever you stand praying, forgive, if you have anything against anyone; so that your Father who is in heaven may forgive you your trespasses (Mark 11:25).

The practice of forgiveness is essential to prayer because to hold onto scraps of past chaos is a distraction to the present experience of the Spirit of a unified creation. Forgiveness is a way of leaving behind the broken world and the disjointed thought and feeling system that holds it in place. Forgiveness lets go of guilt and fear, as by-products of judgment, and strengthens instead the holy bonds that hold life in oneness. As such, forgiveness opens the way to highest prayer, union with God, through a sense of harmony with those around us.

Forgiveness is implicit agreement. Any two who put differences aside, even for an instant, no matter how difficult initially, have joined in a way that they could not have understood before. Prayer rises naturally from such holy concord:

> Again I say to you, if two of you agree on earth about anything they ask, it will be done for them by my Father in heaven. For where two or three are gathered in my name, there I am in the midst of them (Matt. 18:19–20).

There is power and presence in the deep agreement of souls, even among two or three. If the two are Father and Son, then the third is the Spirit. But any mutuality in this world, any fundamental joining, any concurrence of being, is holy means *and* response in prayer. Such prayer can rise as high as Heaven itself.

Jesus therefore includes mutual forgiveness in his Exemplary Prayer (commonly called the Lord's Prayer):

> Pray then like this:
> Our Father who art in heaven,
> Hallowed be thy name.
> Thy kingdom come,
> Thy will be done,
> On earth as it is in heaven.
> Give us this day our daily bread;
> And forgive us our debts,
> As we also have forgiven our debtors;
> And lead us not into temptation,
> But deliver us from evil (Matt. 6:9–13).

He immediately follows with the explanation: "For if you forgive men their trespasses, your heavenly Father also will forgive you" (6:14). Forgiveness draws one close to God, prayer joins Him in secret universality, and in the secret world of spiritual depth, the one who prays and the prayer itself become one in God.

Ps. 46:10 offers the ultimate proscription for prayer: "Be still, and know that I am God." All is done in this simple exchange. There is great peace in allowing this to be done, as if one were following a universal will. Jesus emphasized the inwardness and forgiveness required to reach this fundamental knowledge of God. With the apocryphal 1 Clement X.3, then, "Let us consider how near he is to us."[3]

So near as to be inside. "Jesus prays to God and the Bible speaks of God being *in* Christ."[4] He prays within himself, not to himself, but in a place so secret it is secret even from himself. The limitations of selfhood dissolve, in preparation for the change. His will *is* done, on earth as it is in heaven, for His will *is* Heaven. The Son returns to God, and sits with Him in peace and utter familiarity.

Prayer is the way to peace, to stillness in a world ever-turning. In John 14:27, Jesus says he comes to bring a different kind of peace:

> Peace I leave with you; my peace I give to you; not as the world gives do I give to you. Let not your hearts be troubled, neither let them be afraid.

The troubles of the world are not yours, says Jesus. Even troubles must bow and genuflect before the Being in you. What is most truly *yours* is the peace of God, eternal and worthy of trust. This is reminiscent of Isa. 26:3:

> Thou dost keep him in perfect peace, whose mind is stayed on thee, because he trusts in thee.

The silence of prayer is indicative of the perfect peace of the mind "stayed on" God in perfect trust.

Prayer is the proper way to worship God because through such practice of private prayer, according to Jesus, the outer man will "sound no trumpet before" himself and will not seek to "be praised by men" (Matt. 6:2). Praise will be directed where it should forever be, and is. The exaltation and glorification of God shine away the illusions of the comparing and contrasting mind. "Thou hast put more joy in my heart than they have when their grain and wine abound" (Ps. 4:7). There is a new, calmer happiness than that which depends on the forms and doings of existence. Going inside, that which once called from without is undone. Yet so much more is done. The new light from within thaws the icy rings of fear so that they dissipate into a warm mist of a summer morning. Setting out to learn by private practice how to access the Spirit is to be provided undeniable presence and help.

Sitting therefore in godliness:

> Therefore let every one who is godly offer prayer to thee; at a time of distress, in the rush of great waters, they shall not reach him (Ps. 32:6).

Though each remains alone, a community of individuals prays together in Spirit. The Psalmist expresses that it is good to pray at all times, subconsciously and even unconsciously, to keep one's mind "stayed on" Him without ceasing:

> By day the Lord commands his steadfast love; and at night his song is with me, a prayer to the God of my life (Ps. 42:8).

Early Christians saw prayer as inducing joy in both ailing and rejoicing alike:

> Is any one among you suffering? Let him pray.
> Is any cheerful? Let him sing praise.
> Is any among you sick? . . .
> The prayer of faith will save the sick man,
> And the Lord will raise him up;
> And if he has committed sins,
> He will be forgiven (James 5:13–14, 15).

Jesus suggested that a life in prayer is lived more effectively: "And whatever you ask in prayer, you will receive, if you have faith" (Matt. 21:22). What is there to ask for except more of the Spirit of Completion? Secret prayer is deeply personal, between the soul and God, as the individual yields to the deepest yearning of the heart, and so it is universal. Jesus tells believers to "bless those who curse you, pray for those who abuse you" (Luke 6:28), because in this way one is carried further along the road to universality.

Effective Prayer

What is the opposite of heaping up "empty phrases" in a semblance of prayer (Matt. 6:7)? Jesus speaks of the tremendous power of prayer:

> Truly, I say to you, whoever says to this mountain, "Be taken up and cast into the sea," and does not doubt in his heart, but believes that what he says will come to pass, it will be done for him. Therefore I tell you, whatever you ask in prayer, believe that you are receiving, and it will be yours (Mark 11:23–24).

The power of prayer comes from belief bordering on conviction, a certainty that can arise only from experience. Prayer, for Jesus, is spiritual effectiveness. Prayer without doubt is able to move mountains (Mark 11:22). Mountains are obstacles placed in the way of universality by a misguided belief in the supremacy of the physical senses. Mountains are temptations not to forgive, temptations to see this world as everything, thereby forgetting the ultimate reality and oneness of the kingdom of God.

1 John 5:14–15 comments on the sense of confidence thus obtained:

> And this is the confidence which we have in him, that if we ask anything according to his will he hears us. And if we know that he hears us in whatever we ask, we know that we have obtained the requests made of him.

Whatever is asked "according to his will he hears us." That is to say, "Fear not, little flock, for it is your Father's good pleasure to give you the kingdom" (Luke 12:32). Union and ultimate reconciliation—His Will— begin in experience and are found fully matured in the subtle, effective moment of prayer. His Will is already done; prayer allows for this realization.

Jesus emphasizes that confidence is essential to effective prayer: "Therefore I tell you, whatever you ask in prayer, believe that you have received it, and it will be yours" (Mark 11:24). Faith in God, coming from the heart at one with Him, is full of confidence. This is not a faith that wavers in its belief. The confidence of faith comes from prayer in Spirit granting inner conviction and penetrating insight into the Will of God.

Jesus urges his followers to ask in his name in order to share his effectiveness in asking. The disciples are told, "Hitherto you have asked nothing in my name; ask, and you shall receive, that your joy may be full" (John 16:24). To ask in Jesus' name is to ask *as* Jesus, in the power of his ever-available identity. It is to ask in the Divine Presence in which he prayed and was transformed. To pray as Jesus is to share the power of his Spirit, that he shared with the One. If there is at all a question in this asking, it is a transformative one, because the response is transformation. But there is no question in full confidence; there is simply openness in simplest request, with no lessening of confidence.

And so, in prayer, as in faith, there is at once both asking and confidence, or confidence in asking. There is simultaneous openness and certainty. The Will of God is everywhere the soul is, in simple truth, fully accomplished, ready to be seen, ready to join. It is ready to be taken inside oneself and lived. The simple process again is:

> Ask, and it will be given you; seek, and you will find; knock, and it will be opened to you (Luke 11:9).

The problem is that one will not ask what the Will of God is if one thinks one knows. Human nature seems closed off to the deeper consideration of consolation. And so a confident openness is called for, or an open confidence—for all is still done within the secret room in silence.

Unifying Prayer

There is a way to:

> Rejoice always, pray constantly, give thanks in all circumstances; for this is the will of God in Christ Jesus for you (1 Thess. 5:16–18).

"Do not quench the Spirit" (1 Thess. 5:19), says Paul, but let it live, let it pray for you in groans too deep for words, from within the inner world imbued with all the transcendent colors of the Peace of God. Furthermore, "Pray at all times in the Spirit" (Eph. 6:18). Individuals can do this together, no matter how far apart they may seem in existence, through "the unity of the Spirit in the bond of peace" (Eph. 4:3).

Silent and secret prayer is union with God. To pray silently in one's inner chamber is to commune with the God of the far-reaching light. Thanks to silent inner prayer, the deeper will finds its eternal likeness in God. Eyes shut, self hushed to the world outside, the Grace of God rises to the fore of the mind. "Have faith in God" (Mark 11:22), says Jesus, for though His realm is subtle, almost imperceptible, it is very real. No one need fear that in the end anything of any true value or substance will be lost, for what is found instead is worth immeasurably more. Faith in its strength becomes conviction through the Spirit within, and so, "you, beloved, build yourselves up on your most holy faith; pray in the Holy Spirit" (Jude 1:20).

Though prayer is conducted in private, it will soar beyond the individual. Though it is secret, it is full of the living idea of oneness. Meister Eckhart says:

> It must be done by means of forgetting and losing self-consciousness. It is in the stillness, in the silence, that the word of God is to be heard . . . for when one is aware of nothing, that word is imparted to him and clearly revealed.[5]

It is through emptiness, through being aware, first of nothing, then of everything, that certainty comes. Psychologist Arthur J. Deikman writes: "any element of mental life can disappear while awareness itself remains."[6] Awareness remains "behind" the thoughts and images that sometimes seem to crowd it out.[7] Revealing the thoughts and images to be as nothing by slipping behind them, one finds oneself in eternal awareness.

Set words or rituals may therefore hinder the experience of contemplative prayer, just as tradition can hide (or "make void") the true word of God (Matt. 15:6). Saint Teresa of Avila believed that techniques are not only unnecessary, they may become hindrances.

The best way to pray, said St. Teresa, is for the prayer to flow simply from the heart like rain falling from heaven. No effort, no technique intervenes between the one who prays and the prayer that he prays.[8]

Nothing "intervenes between the one who prays and the prayer that he prays." Not only does her prayer rise up to the heavens, then, but so does she.

Prayer unifies thought and action, intention and reward. And because it reconciles or unifies the human being to God, not to mention asks with full confidence, one may express one's prayer like this:

Nevertheless I am continually with thee; thou dost hold my right hand. Thou dost guide me with thy counsel, and afterward thou wilt receive me to glory. Whom have I in heaven but thee? And there is nothing upon earth that I desire besides thee. My flesh and my heart may fail, but God is the rock of my heart and my portion for ever (Ps. 73:23–26).

This is the prayer that faith prays constantly. This is what even a few moments in prayer, on a daily basis, can convince the mind of. And this is the blessing that it gives:

The grace of the Lord Jesus Christ and the love of God and the fellowship of the Holy Spirit be with you all (2 Cor. 13:14).

Paul again prays in the spirit of perfect blessing:

For this reason I bow my knees before the Father from whom every family on heaven and earth is named, that according to the riches of his glory he may grant you be strengthened with might through his Spirit in the inner man, and that Christ may dwell in your hearts through faith; that you, being rooted and grounded in love, may have the power to comprehend with all the saints what is the breadth and length and height and depth, and to know the love of Christ which surpasses knowledge, that you may be filled with all the fulness of God (Eph. 3:14–19).

10

A New Identity in the Spirit

Fear not, for I am with you;
I will bring your offspring from the east,
and from the west I will gather you;
I will say to the north, Give up,
and to the south, Do not withhold;
bring my sons from afar,
and my daughters from the end of the earth,
every one who is called by my name,
whom I created for my glory,
whom I formed and made.

—Isa. 43:5–7

True Self

The Christian religion at its depths is not intended to be added to a person; it is meant to transform a person, from the inner being. The self-concept is too limited to comprehend God, or to experience the faith that Jesus emphasized. When *I* seek to believe in God, then *I* am still present, and so the Grace of God cannot reveal Itself and my true Self to me. *I,* whatever I've been doing, have been working on fashioning a self out of scraps of whole cloth, out of nothing, but deep inside I know this manufactured self can know nothing of the higher world nor of the higher Self forgotten in the mists of eternity. In fact, the lesser self stands in the way of the higher.

When I am afraid, who is the "I" that is afraid? Is it the same "I" who is, at other times, at peace or overjoyed? Let us suppose for a moment that when I am afraid, "I" am the emotion of fear; in effect, I am what I feel. The self that feels and *is* fear, is obviously different from the self that feels and is peace, expansion, happiness, love. Such different gardens of emotion are as different as any two opposing selves could be.

Truly to practice Christianity, the individual is to put away the false self, like Paul "gave up childish ways" (1 Cor. 13:11), yet, paradoxically, to find an "I" more childlike in total acceptance of the expansive Self. It is to give up control, in a very fundamental way. It is to cede one's point of origin and therefore oneself to the original moment of creation. To practice Christianity is no longer to see oneself or anyone else "from a human point of view" (2 Cor. 5:16), but, rather, to become and to see "a new creation" (2 Cor. 5:17):

> From now on, therefore, we regard no one from a human
> point of view; even though we once regarded Christ from a human
> point of view, we regard him thus no longer. Therefore if any one
> is in Christ, he is a new creation; the old has passed away, behold,
> the new has come (2 Cor. 5:17–18).

To see Christ from a higher vantage point is to see all things, all persons, including oneself, from that same vantage point.

There are many indications of the unveiling of this higher Self, this new creation and identity, in the New Testament. Believers began to see themselves as "sons of God" and "the children of God." They declared that they were God's offspring, designating an inseparable connection with Him, and a new heavenly identity. Paul indicates that the essential nature of one's existence will have been changed:

Just as we have borne the image of the man of dust, we shall also bear the image of the man of heaven (1 Cor. 15:49).

The Self established by God is fundamentally and essentially different from the self drawn out of dust. The self of dust obscures clear vision of the Self of Heaven. These two selves are distinct ways of being: with not only different behaviors, but also and more fundamentally having different thoughts and different feelings. The distinction comes ultimately from their different experience. To experience God is also to experience a new Self in union with God, while to hold to the fabrication of the fleshly mind is to invest one's hopes in the evanescent.

It is in this sense that:

So far as man is fallen away from his true self, he is fallen away from the being which the Creator has given him. He is, therefore, denying God and rebelling against God, whose command is life. . . .[1]

The fall from Heaven was a rebellion of will, motivation, and purpose. That is to say, it was a rebellion of self. It came from the mad guilt- and fear-inducing desire to fashion a self apart from God, which attempts to perpetuate itself through guile, fear, and guilt. Though it is but a thought or a step away, it seems a world away from the Garden in which God set His Creation.

The assertion in the Old Testament that humans were created in the image and likeness of God is intended to glorify the soul. With the fall into existence, humans were beset with an inability to fathom or comprehend themselves in eternal relation to others, let alone with God. Yet because humans were originally created in the image and likeness of God, they possess the new nature deep within themselves, safely tucked away as Spirit and Love, for these are the simplest descriptions of God given in the New Testament: "God is spirit" (John 4:24); "God is love" (1 John 4:8). God too is glorified when one becomes *oneself* in Spirit and in Love.

To be Christian is to find oneself first by giving up thought of oneself and letting it go, after which finding God may prove as simple as letting God find the soul. First to be left behind in this process is, of course, all prior claim to self-knowledge. One would have to humble oneself (or be humbled) to that extent. Presuppositions about oneself and the world, tempting as they may be to perpetuate, only stand in the way. To experience Divine Being, one has to begin to see from a more than human point of view.

One self experiences aloneness, the other closeness. One suffers the pangs of separation, the other the ecstasy of togetherness. One exists in constant comparison and competition, the other in essential sameness. One self, though it is but a concept of self, seems desperate for outside adoration, the other rests in the peace and fullness of the sustaining love of God. One self is nurtured by self-interest to the point where it cares only for itself, the other cherishes giving and forgiving for its glimpse into a universal sense of identity and a higher vantage point from which to view the world.

Jesus speaks of this new Self:

> But I say to you, Love your enemies and pray for those who persecute you, *so that you may be sons of your Father who is in heaven;* for he makes his sun rise on the evil and on the good, and sends rain on the just and on the unjust (Matt. 5:44–45, my italics).

There is a way of seeing things from far beyond the juncture of self and self-interest. But if the fleeting self is not the final arbiter of one's feelings, thoughts, and actions, then what is? If there is a deeper value, it abides in a deeper Self. All that is internally and eternally true flows from the heart of a transcendent Self revealed by Spirit in order truly to forgive and to love.

Jesus points out in the previous passage that love and forgiveness provide a new sense of identity as *"sons of your Father who is in heaven."* As we have seen, to be a son suggests likeness, it suggests affinity, it confirms eternal relationship. Who but the Family of God could abide in the Household of God? Who but Beings of God can love with perfection?

Sonship also designates *knowledge:* knowledge of God concomitant with a new Self-knowledge. Jesus speaks of such nonconceptual knowledge when he says that:

no one knows who the Son is except the Father, or who the
Father is except the Son and any one to whom the Son chooses to
reveal him (Luke 10:22).

Son and Father *are* the relationship they share. They know one another
through one another, not through intellectual knowledge, which of neces-
sity stands apart from what it knows. They *know* one another in a way that
the separated beings of existence cannot know.

Theologian Jacques Guillet speaks of the experiential bond between
Son and Father in the previous passage as being marked by "their reciprocal gaze":

The Son, on the contrary, is wholly present here; he is not
defined by his action or his passion, but by what he is, by the bond
that unites him with the Father, by their reciprocal gaze.[2]

The Son is defined by what he is, and what he *is* is indefinable, except
that God knows him and he knows God. They share an experiential knowledge. Like God, His Son is Spirit, and like God, His Son is Love. It is only
through union with God in Spirit and in Love, therefore, that this new Self
can be known. Their reciprocal gaze is the gaze of being one in Spirit and
Love.

The Son is defined by what he is, as is God. When asked by Moses
who He is, God replies: "I AM WHO I AM" (Exod. 3:14). God is Being-
in-itself, indefinable in relation to the lower order, because complete, perfect as it is. There are no words to describe it, yet it need not be described,
only experienced. The Gospel of John has Jesus use the same formulation
to express his own inner being, saying: "Truly, truly, I say to you, before
Abraham was, I am" (John 8:58). Jesus here identifies with God and with
his own eternal Self in union with God. He speaks through his experience
of God: "I know him" (John 8:55). He knows God in intimate relationship:
"no one knows who the Son is except the Father, or who the Father is
except the Son" (Luke 10:22). It is as a Son that Jesus knows his God the
Father of Life and is known by Him.

As Son of God, part of the Being of God, one with God, Jesus has *life
in himself:* he is *who he is,* complete, eternal in relation to his Father:

> For as the Father has life in himself, so he has granted the Son also to have life in himself (John 5:26).

This is a different family, order, and class of Being than is known by the continual comparisons and contingencies of physical existence. Life on Earth depends on the things of the Earth to sustain it; God sustains Himself, He has life in Himself, and so does the Son of God, being of God. They subsist on Spirit and Love; their joy is constant. Depending only on one another, they share with all life a different kind of Life. They are together the family of Being.

John comments that Jesus opened the way for the Sonship of others:

> But to all who received him, who believed in his name, he gave power to become children of God; who were born, not of blood nor of the will of the flesh nor of the will of man, but of God (John 1:12–13).

This "power to become children of God" is more than an ability, more even than a capacity; it is an actuality, known only to God. This experience of power changes not only the present, but also past and future; it affects one's present state of being to such an extent that one's moment of conception, one's point of origin, as well as one's eternal destination, are changed. Obviously, we are dealing with a very different sense of *Being* and a new reality here.

This experience of a new Self in God was prevalent among early Christians. Stevan L. Davies argues that:

> the identity of possessed persons as "sons" twenty years after Jesus' death arose from the fact that those persons were modeling themselves on Jesus who, when possessed, was possessed by the Spirit labeled "the Son."[3]

For early Christians, to become a Son of God—to take on this new identity—was to follow in Jesus' example and share his experience of the Spirit. When the Spirit was experienced, as it was at Jesus' baptism, it came with a new sense of identity as a Child of God.

Becoming Sons or Children of God was central to Paul's teaching:

> For the creation waits with eager longing for the revealing of
> the sons of God . . . because the creation itself will be set free from
> its bondage to decay and obtain the glorious liberty of the children
> of God (Rom. 8:19, 21).

To be revealed as a Child of God was to know Eternity, an eternal relationship within. His Children are free because of their transcendence, their
experience of themselves in God. All of this is granted by "the Spirit"
(Rom. 8:23); it is the fruit of spiritual experience. Paul says: "It is the Spirit
himself bearing witness with our spirit that we are children of God" (Rom.
8:16). The revelation of the Spirit speaking to our own spirit grants a new
identity of the "I" as spirit.

For John, seeing God "as he is" renders the experiencer "like him":

> *See what love the Father has given us, that we should be called*
> *children of God;* and so we are. The reason why the world does not
> know us is that it did not know him. Beloved, we are God's chil-
> dren now; it does not yet appear what we shall be, but we know
> that *when he appears we shall be like him, for we shall see him as he*
> *is.* And every one who thus hopes in him purifies himself as he is
> pure (1 John 3:1–3, my italics).

Faith in God as the Source of all reality and identity leads through
experience and revelation to *knowledge* of God as Source of Life (knowing
God "as he is"). Knowledge is inherent in Sonship, that is, in new identity
and relationship. The believer becomes as pure as God is pure.

Likewise, for Paul, the contemplation of Christ's glory transforms the
believer into that which is contemplated:

> And we all, with unveiled face, reflecting the glory of the Lord,
> are being changed into his likeness from one degree of glory to
> another; for this comes from the Lord who is the Spirit (2 Cor.
> 3:18).

How gradual this transition is will vary from person to person—but not to the soul, which is in constant relationship. Yet it is clear that Paul sees the Christian experience as being for the purpose of transforming the individual into the likeness of God, thus granting a new sense of identity in relationship.

Elsewhere Paul states that believers themselves become people "of heaven"—no longer of "dust"—just as Jesus was "of heaven" (1 Cor. 15:48–49). He speaks of the transformation that believers will have once they have: "put on the new nature, which is being renewed in knowledge after the image of its creator" (Col. 3:10). Stating that "our commonwealth is in heaven," Paul indicates that the believer/experiencer will take on new identity in "glorious" spiritual being (Phil. 3:20–21). There is a transformation here that results in a new being: It is a transformation of identity, a change of the entire being into the likeness of God, a "new nature."

As stated, this change of identity is so complete and thoroughgoing that it changes even one's point of origin. To experience oneself as Son or Child of God is to have been "born of the Spirit," for "that which is born of the flesh is flesh, and that which is born of the Spirit is spirit" (John 3:6). To know oneself as a Child of God is to know one's Creator as Spirit knows Spirit. It is to know oneself, like God knows Himself. To be a Child of God is to know one's Self as Spirit, through God as Spirit.

To be Children of God is to be born of God (John 1:13). To be born of God is to be fully accepted by God—in effect, forgiven everything—in reality, never judged. To be forgiven everything is to "obtain the glorious liberty of the children of God" (Rom. 8:21); it is to be "justified"—and to be justified is to be "glorified" (Rom. 8:30). And to be glorified is to know oneself as joined with God in Spirit.

These Children or Sons of God appear in time to grow and mature:

> until we all attain to the unity of the faith and knowledge of
> the Son of God, to mature manhood, to the measure of the stature
> of the fulness of Christ (Eph. 4:13).

It is to the high and spiritual station of "the fulness of Christ" that the believer, now a Son, is led. When faith is unified with knowledge, faith has become knowledge; hope and expectation have become reality. In this fullness does faith come to be grounded in knowledge of oneself as Son or Creation of God. Paul again speaks of Christ being formed in the believer: "My little children, with whom I am again in travail until Christ be formed in you!" (Gal. 4:19). Christ comes to the individual and remains with one and in one. Does it not follow that Christ therefore would take over the old identity of the believer? When Christ has come to be "formed in" the believer, then the believer has been changed, or perhaps more accurately, the believer has absconded, leaving a truer commonwealth in Heaven. This is the "mystery hidden for ages and generations but now made manifest" (Col. 1:26) to those who believe in:

the glory of this mystery, which is *Christ in you,* the hope of glory (Col. 1:27, my italics).

The "glory of this mystery" reveals itself to be a new identity in Christ and in Sonship to God. The believer is reborn in the Spirit; that is, the believer receives a new identity closer at once to God and to the true Self. Glory is thus more than a hope to one who expects the truth to unfold from within. Paul followed Jesus in seeing Christhood as being a universal experience and identity, not reserved for Jesus alone.

Paul states that the "new nature" of the believer is "created after the likeness of God in true righteousness and holiness" (Eph. 4:24). When knowledge such as this is revealed to one's experience, then the day of salvation has arrived, the day of creation has returned as a day of resurrection. "Behold, now is the acceptable time; Behold, now is the day of salvation" (2 Cor. 6:2). It is as if it has always been, and could never not be. It is as if all of this were entirely predetermined: "He destined us in love to be his sons through Jesus Christ" (Eph. 1:5). Believers became convinced they were preestablished from before the foundation of the world in the very love of God for His Creation. God knew us before we came to know ourselves.

Peter speaks of this transformation of the Christian as being "born anew . . . to an inheritance which is imperishable, undefiled, and unfading, kept in heaven for you" (1 Peter 1:3, 4). Again, the believer takes on the new experience of a new identity in God. This transformation allows believers to "become *partakers of the divine nature*" (2 Peter 1:4, my italics).

That is, the divine nature is universal; it exists to be experienced and joined in. Since "God is spirit" (John 4:24), those who know themselves as God's (or "of God") know themselves as the Spirit leads them. As such, according to Jesus, "they cannot die any more, because they are equal to the angels and are sons of God, being sons of the resurrection" (Luke 20:36). They have overcome death and the other tragic flaws of the world through the abiding eternal joy of the Spirit into which they themselves are transformed.

Paul again affirms that Sonship follows from experience of the Spirit:

> *For all who are led by the Spirit of God are sons of God.* For you did not receive the spirit of slavery to fall back into fear, but you have received the spirit of sonship. When we cry, "Abba! Father!" it is the Spirit himself bearing witness with our spirit that we are children of God (Rom. 8:14–16, my italics).

Once again, this new identity as children of God is obtained, experienced, and lived through highest spiritual experience: "the Spirit himself bearing witness with our spirit." Furthermore, "He who believes in the Son of God has the testimony in himself" (1 John 5:10). Experience of the Son confirms identity as the Son; that is how he "has the testimony in himself." From belief there comes conviction, for belief is itself a form of experience, and from new experience comes the certainty of the "new nature." Those who have assumed God's nature are those who "do" or manifest in themselves God's Will for reconciliation and return.

True Relationship

The will of God is eternal, always in effect, always effective. The universal will of God for scattered humankind is reconciliation, "and not for the nation only, but to gather into one the children of God who are scattered abroad" (John 11:52). And so Paul emphasizes unity in his letters, saying for instance that "we, though many, are one body in Christ, and individually members one of another" (Rom. 12:5). Like Sonship, Christ is a unifying force and experience for early Christians.

Paul states that the fullness and revelation of the mystery are "Christ in us" (e.g., Col. 3:11). What is "Christ in us" except the true Self, in true interrelationship with all that lives? What is the Self ultimately, in the day of salvation, except its relationship to others? God created it, but He did not make it to be alone. Only the true Self ascends to Heaven, for, having come from Heaven, it retains within itself full memory of its Origin.

The slowly crafted separate self, on the other hand, seems to define itself according to its notions of contrast and difference with others and everything. Otherwise it is absolutely nothing:

> It is possible that *there is no such self* as westerners have been taught to imagine themselves possessing. Possibly, the self cannot be conceived in a positive way, as some sort of thing inside my body or my personality. The image used by William James may make the maximal claim for the self; it is a sort of *resistance* against culture, society, the world.[4]

The ordinary conceptualized and therefore limited self is itself a resistance against relationship. Does the worldly self exist outside the world, the self-concept outside the mind? Does the conceptualized self exist outside its own thoughts? The self is constricted by its own thoughts about itself and the world, and, in this way is the self defined by its relationship with the world, whether or not that relationship truly exists anywhere but in the mind.

Early Christians believed that there is one true kind of Relationship, patterned after the Self in eternal relation to God. It is the bond of the Spirit, and it is not in any way influenced by the world or by any "human point of view." It is the irrevocable Relationship of Spiritual Child to Spiritual Parent, set in a context that does not fade. This relationship is known only by a rethinking of self, allowing for temporary emptiness, then ever-present direct emanation from God.

One must be *of the truth* to hear his voice: "Every one who is of the truth hears my voice" (John 18:37). This means one becomes again as originally created, which means one finds oneself "in the Spirit," thereby becoming what one always was. Truth, like the true Self, like true relationship, exists from the beginning. Relationship with the Creator is inherent in the very point of origin, in the fact and reality of creation. Early

Christians believed in the closeness of God because they experienced themselves in relation to Him.

In John, Jesus tells his disciples that they have been with him "from the beginning" (John 15:27). The Prologue of John has it that the Father had known Jesus from the beginning (John 1:2). Yet the incarnation of the Word into a tent of flesh is not Jesus' alone. Paul says that God:

> *chose us in him before the foundation of the world,* that we should be holy and blameless before him. He destined us in love to be his sons through Jesus Christ, according to the purpose of his will (Eph. 1:4–5, my italics).

That is to say:

> The goal of spiritual life in all its forms is that the individual should disappear gracefully into his or her intrinsic nature, which is the Divine Nature. This blending of the separate person into Divine Radiance is accomplished effortlessly if we experience each other to be parts of one Mystical Body, as Paul suggests. Then our sense of separate individuality is attenuated without destroying our special function in the whole.[5]

Paul not only speaks of being "in Christ," but says, "we have the mind of Christ" (1 Cor. 2:16). He speaks of believers being "united in the same mind" (1 Cor. 1:10). He says that believers:

> should seek God, in the hope that they might feel after him and find him. Yet he is not far from each one of us, for "In him we live and move and have our being"; as even some of your poets have said, "For we are indeed his offspring" (Acts 17:27–28).

To share the mind of Christ is not to think different thoughts—it is to think differently, to think in a different way, and so to have a wholly different sense of Being. The object of Christ-minded thought is in the subject. The subject is the object, but something needs to change for subject to notice. The mind must recall its being in God, and the fact that God has made His Heavenly Home inside the soul. Paul says that "the glory of the celestial is one" (1 Cor. 15:40); that is, it is universal, everywhere.

This sharing of the mind of Christ, this higher identification with Being, does not emerge out of nowhere. This original identification has been hidden within the soul since the superimposition of a chaotic and scattershot will over the original creation. The entire relationship of the soul and God is hidden in every ray of original love that binds them together eternally. The world of separate existents is only superimposed on the original loving creation; still, nothing is more fundamental or more real than the Heaven of True Relationship.

Paul says that in seeking God, believers "feel after" God. That is, they are irrevocably drawn to the love, the peace, the safety in His spiritual arms, the security that was with them from the beginning. What they strive for from deep within their spiritual will is to find a bond of eternal love, a bond that does not grow old and die. Salvation is found in the surrender of one's "very autonomy, even if obedient to God."[6] What is this but a spiritual reconciliation with one's neighbors, friends, and enemies? As Jesus says to any who would pray and give praise to God: "leave your gift there before the altar and go; first be reconciled to your brother, and then come and offer your gift" (Matt. 5:24). The gift that is given to God is the very sense of self.

Jesus says, "Blessed are the peacemakers, for they shall be called sons of God" (Matt. 5:9). Wisdom 5:5 asks: "Why has he been numbered among the sons of God? And why is his lot among the saints?" Because the peacemakers make their peace through the bond of Spirit; they are those who are "eager to maintain the unity of the Spirit in the bond of peace" (Eph. 4:3). Conflict gone, innocence rules the mind. The bond of Spirit is the bond of relationship; through the eternal bond of Spirit, early Christians discovered their true relationship to God and to one another. Having found peace within themselves, they extended it simply by being this new sense of Self as one in interrelationship.

Early father Origen, we have seen, wrote that God created minds, minds that were one with Him as their Source and with one another. Early father Clement of Alexandria said that "man . . . is *of celestial birth,* being a plant of heavenly origin."[7] Biographer Robert Payne says of Clement that "throughout his work the theme of man's celestial birth is continually repeated. This belief was shared by the Christians and the attendants at the Orphic mysteries."[8] Being of celestial birth, humankind is very close to God, and has a celestial destination.

Sonship is the divine knowledge of having been created together, as one. John speaks of the "children of God" as being united and bonded with the Father through love:

> See what love the Father has given us, that we should be called children of God; and so we are. The reason why the world does not know us is that it did not know him (1 John 3:1).

Early Christians were transformed in their knowledge of true Selfhood. To know oneself is to know as one. To know the object in the subject is to be in eternal relationship.

The New Testament emphasizes that loving others is a way of loving God. It is to love what is infinite in a being, and eternal, "for they cannot die any more, because they are equal to the angels and are sons of God, being sons of the resurrection" (Luke 20:36). This is how Jesus sees, and this is how he taught that his disciples should see. He had said, "A disciple is not above his teacher, but every one when he is fully taught will be like his teacher" (Luke 6:40). They would find their own abstract sense of Being with him. He had seen them and related to them in the light by which all is seen and to which it is related. Thus had he enlightened them.

Unity and Universality

In Matt. 5:44–45 and its parallel Luke 6:35 ("and your reward will be great, and you will be sons of the Most High"), the experience of Sonship is preceded by an intention to forgive *everyone. All* are given to be Children of God. Human judgments are less than meaningless in the light of His tender Care "for he is kind to the ungrateful and the selfish" (Luke 6:35), Creator and Sustainer of all that lives.

The great mystery here is that the individual wholeness of the believer is now part of a greater wholeness, a greater community of being. That an experience could be at once so personal and yet so profoundly universal makes it entirely different from ordinary individual consciousness. Through the sense of interconnection brought by this experience of Spirit, it is realized that, in Paul's words, "none of us lives to himself, and none of us dies to himself" (Rom. 14:7). Life is integrated; we are one body, says Paul, one mind, one Spirit in Christ.

That is, the Sonship is one as God is one. Individuals are parts of it though they carry the Whole within themselves. Paul says, "Christ is all, and in all" (Col. 3:11). The Christhood of all is unifying, equalizing, extensively glorifying. It means that "it is no longer I who live, but Christ who lives in me" (Gal. 2:20). The human identity has been surrendered and the mind transformed; it has been *raised* with Christ and *to* Christ. With the relinquishment of the limited self comes a Self that is so expansive in its experience that it is all-encompassing and all-embracing, one with God.

In regard to comprehensive interconnection, Christ's call in John 15:4 is "Abide in me, and I in you." He prays for the oneness of believers as he is one with God:

> *that they may all be one;* even as you, Father, are in me, and I in you, that they also may be in us, so that the world may believe that you have sent me. The glory which you have given me I have given to them, that they may be one even as we are one, I in them and them in me, that they may become perfectly one, so that the world may know that you have sent me and have loved them even as you have loved me (John 17:21–23, my italics).[9]

For even though bodies might split off in different directions, relationship rendered one in love cannot end. Love is the single purpose. Perfect oneness exists in perfect love and is eternal; salvation and glory flow from this new identity, which knows others as itself.

The way of the Christian is not to be about Christ, but to be *in* Christ. Paul asks that believers "complete my joy by being of the same mind, having the same love, being in full accord and of one mind" (Phil. 2:2). This is accomplished not through human conceptualization, perception, emotion, or opinion, but, rather, through higher mind, the universal mind through which all are one in the Spirit. It is the Spirit that raises the mind to the unity of Christhood, beyond polarity and particularity, beyond individual and surface differences, allowing the mind to comprehend from within the fundamental and essential oneness of everything in God.

Paul seems to juxtapose "falsehood" or delusion against unity when he says, "Therefore, putting away falsehood, let every one speak the truth with his neighbor, for we are members one of another" (Eph. 4:25). As opposed to the former delusion of separateness, the new identity in Spirit is fused with unity and relationship: "Now you are the body of Christ and individually members of it" (1 Cor. 12:27). Whatever it is that makes one capable of such unifying relationship with others does so despite the apparent multiplicity of bodies on the surface. Unity comes from equality in Christ:

> There is neither Jew nor Greek, there is neither slave nor free, there is neither male nor female; *for you are all one in Christ Jesus* (Gal. 3:28, my italics).

For "all were made to drink of one Spirit" (1 Cor. 12:13). Sharing one Spirit meant that they experienced themselves as one. That is, believers were "raised with Christ" (Col. 3:1) into a new and holy identity at one with God and with all that lives. All that lives is suffused with a new and subtle universality. If the Self is new, then the World is new, as both partake of the inbreaking light of the original Spirit of Creation.

Paul states that, "in Christ shall all be made alive" (1 Cor. 15:22). Is this a return to the original creation, wherein all were "made alive" in pre-beginnings, or chosen (created willfully) before the foundation of the world? Christ is "the Alpha and the Omega, the first and the last, the beginning and the end" (Rev. 22:13). Does this mean that Christ is "all in all"? What better description of eternal spiritual creation?

Oneness is the truth that sets creation free. "So if the Son makes you free, you will be free indeed" (John 8:36). It releases *everyone* to the vastness of God and to inner vastness. "There shall be one flock then, one shepherd" (John 10:16). This experience of union may have been achieved only in moments, but its effects went far beyond those individual moments, for in the timeless moment one feels not alone, but joined together as one in mind and heart and strength and Spirit. All share the experience and identity inherent in being in Christ and being together the Sons or Children of God. In the Presence of God, all thoughts and feelings, intentions and experiences, are directed to all of Being; God is abstract Communicator of Being. The Christ mind is abstract in its oneness and its comprehensiveness.

And so the early Christians thought themselves to be, under the influence of Christ and of the Spirit of God, *one*. That which once seemed to hold them apart was perceived no more. The invisible bonds that held them together were then visible. If this experience lasts for but an instant in time, its effects are transformative and enduring. The experience confers knowledge and understanding of the Community of Being: "If one member suffers, all suffer together; if one member is honored, all rejoice together" (1 Cor. 12:26). This is no command for a new behavior; it is a deeply emotional and psychological truth.

Love creates harmony. Paul speaks of "love, which binds everything together in perfect harmony" (Col. 3:14). Love unites believers with one another and with God:

> God is love, and he who abides in love abides in God and God abides in him (1 John 4:16).

God can be feared only by those who would hide from themselves, and from the love sown within. As 1 John continues: "fear has to do with punishment, and he who fears is not perfected in love" (1 John 4:18). To identify with the separate self manifest in flesh is to experience God and one's peers as far away. But to identify with the Sonship of Christ in love and Spirit and mind is to be so near as to be "in God" as God is "in him." "In that day you will know that I am in my Father, and you in me, and I in you" (John 14:20), essential elements in the Mind and Heart of God.

Self-absorption is a way of rejecting this experience of union. That is why the grasping, acquisitive self must be transcended in order to experience oneness. It is self-definition that was mistaken, the boundaries never drawn large enough. To separate oneself from God is to become *less* than God; this goes against the universal will, which is unity. Humankind has defined itself too severely and constricted itself too tightly. It has constructed barriers above and below and on every side, but still it feels undefended. It has narrowed its focus and contracted its awareness by excluding all that does not seem to belong to its frightened, isolated self.

Thus self-blinded, it tries to accustom itself to tangents and imperfection, which cause it to wander into a downward-spiraling, ever-darkening dream of delusion.

Once separated from the whole, the self finds itself at odds with the whole. Now it will struggle, now feel sorrow, as it seeks to retain its distinct identity against the whole. Salvation depends on its being overcome, transcended altogether, as any kind of self-indulgence might be overcome. What is left after the false self is given up for lost, is only the truth.

Paul says of being in the Spirit that "if we are beside ourselves," it is because "the love of Christ controls us" and so we live no longer for ourselves (2 Cor. 5:13, 14, 15). The comprehensive Self contained everything the self-limiting self did not think belonged to itself alone. Paul goes on to reveal the reason why "we regard no one from a human point of view" (2 Cor. 5:16) and are therefore forever to be known as "a new creation":

> Therefore if any one is in Christ, he is a new creation; the old has passed away, behold, the new has come. All this is from God, who through Christ reconciled us to himself and gave us the ministry of reconciliation; that is, in Christ God was reconciling the world to himself, not counting their trespasses against them, and entrusting to us the message of reconciliation (2 Cor. 5:17–19).

Sin is no more; a new identity has come. Life did not begin in nothingness, and it does not end there. Is "the image and likeness of God" anything less than perfect and eternal? The "blameless and innocent, children of God . . . shine as lights in the world" (Phil. 2:15); they reflect in truth the original light of creation.

Conclusion

Ascension

Seek the Lord while he may be found,
call upon him while he is near;
let the wicked forsake his way,
and the unrighteous man his thoughts;
let him return to the Lord, that he may have mercy on him,
and to our God, for he will abundantly pardon.
For my thoughts are not your thoughts,
neither are your ways my ways, says the Lord.
For as the heavens are higher than the earth,
so are my ways higher than your ways
and my thoughts than your thoughts.

—Isa. 55:6–9

Sons of Light

Spiritual experience is a great potential for transcendence in all individuals. When it comes, it comes with a new sense of identity. Paul writes that creation waits for the revealing of "the glorious liberty of the children of God":

> For the creation waits with eager longing for the revealing of the sons of God; for the creation was subjected to futility, not of its own will but by the will that subjected it in hope; because the creation itself will be set free from its bondage to decay and obtain the glorious liberty of the children of God (Rom. 8:19–21).

To say that creation waits for the revealing of the Children of God is to say that creation waits for the truth of itself and longs to return to its original light. What is the "bondage to decay" except physical existence itself, characterized by suffering, deterioration, and, finally, death? The converse of such futility, then, is salvation: to "obtain the glorious liberty of the children of God." The children of God in Paul's expansive definition are His children because they share one Spirit with Him. God creates by sharing Himself; true creation is recalled by a like sharing.

Paul writes that the revelation of the sons of God was predestined by God, which means that it is part of an original and ultimate purpose, and that it is as certain as God:

> We know that everything works for good with those who love God, who are called according to his purpose. For those whom he foreknew he also predestined to be conformed to the image of his Son, in order that he might be the first-born among many brethren. And those whom he predestined he also called; and those whom he called he also justified; and those whom he justified he also glorified (Rom. 8:28–30).

The original creation was "predestined" by God to be "conformed to the image of his Son." Before the foundation of the world, a great purpose was instilled deep within the first light of original creation, in the Children of God. This seemingly secret and hidden purpose was eternal Self-awareness before the onset of individual and broken consciousness. Great purpose is given with life: to heed the call of God that comes from above or below consciousness, and to reply affirmatively to glorification. Jesus prays to the Father that his followers:

> may be with me where I am, to behold the glory which thou hast given me in thy love for me before the foundation of the world (John 17:24).

The Spirit of God works through the individual, but always for the good of all. Therefore Paul knows that "everything works for good with those who love God, who are called according to his purpose." He knows because he has seen, whether by vision or by revelation. And we have seen that for Paul the grand and mighty purpose granted by God was reconciliation: the reunification of all being—so that they might through His Spirit be recast in the likeness of the original creation. And since "the Lord is the Spirit" (2 Cor. 3:17):

> All this is from God, who through Christ reconciled us to himself and gave us the ministry of reconciliation (2 Cor. 5:18).

All who are called by Him, therefore, are called to reconciliation. That is the essence of the Christian message. The separated children of God are called to reunion. The call comes to all because all were predestined—as a natural fact of the Creation of Love. They are more than human, having become in the Lord who is the Spirit a new creation.

The House of God is open to all, because it is the very idea of freedom. His children are His House. For what is a house ultimately except the love that abides there? That which God implanted in His children from before the beginning is an eternal bond of love; He created out of his surplus of love. It was that which made them what they forever are, and gave them their original purpose. He predestined them always to remember this love, from their heart, from the very depth of their being.

And so, as His House is Heaven, His children are also His House on Earth:

> For we are the temple of the living God; as God said, "I will live in them and move among them, and will be their God, and they shall be my people" (2 Cor. 6:16).

God lives in His children. He has never left them. Even though they forget, and run to hide from the fearful image they've made of Him, His love is steadfast, and does not forget them. When, as predetermined, they return to His House, they are met as the prodigal son was met, with open arms warm with love: "But while he was yet at a distance, his father saw him and had compassion, and ran and embraced him and kissed him" (Luke 15:20). In the story, the father says to his servants: "let us make merry; for this my son was dead, and is alive again; he was lost, and is found" (Luke 15:24).

Can anything that lives remember the original moment of creation, of awareness? The Living Word dwells in pre-beginnings eternally and entirely, as does the Spirit, yet through them is everything reborn. Might the soul remember a time before limitation when harmony reigned, when joy in the presence of God reigned supreme instead of fear? No matter, for whether or not one yet remembers, from the great depth within:

> Without having seen him you love him; though you do not now see him you believe in him and rejoice with unutterable and exalted joy (1 Pet. 1:8).

The heart is predestined to love as He loves; this was its eternal function from its divine and holy Origin. And so Paul writes of the earliest Christians' spiritual experience:

> we look not to the things that are seen but to the things that are unseen; for the things that are seen are transient, but the things that are unseen are eternal (2 Cor. 4:18).

Paul states that this ability to know the inner world and Self comes because "we walk by faith, not by sight" (2 Cor. 5:7).

The light from this revelation has been dimmed by the systems built around this central truth of Christianity. Systems we build for ourselves, but experience such as that spoken by the Spirit is given to the soul. Can the human being stop building, stop worrying and planning, categorizing and excluding, long enough for the instant it would take to receive this light and new understanding?

Love is the unifying force, yet it does nothing but call out and draw together, for the heart near its truth responds in kind. This causes the soul to rejoice, recalling and envisioning "how good and pleasant it is when brothers dwell in unity!" (Ps. 133:1). To love is to be like God: "Therefore be imitators of God, as beloved children. And walk in love, as Christ loved us . . ." (Eph. 5:1–2). To love is to be Children of God. Love is that which loosens the strictures and bindings human beings impose on themselves by looking outside themselves for answers, picking over laws and regulatory minutiae, secretly sabotaging themselves and maintaining their fear while attempting to alleviate this by judging appearances with ever-shifting basis. The new, transformative power of Spirit would lift them into a complete, unconditional, and liberating love. It would lift the believer, now in Spirit, into God.

The experience of likeness to God may be given inside church doors or outside in a garden. It may happen among others or alone in apparent isolation. But it is always a communication between God and soul, generally as quick as light. Everyday cares may keep it on the threshold for a while, but a deeper sense of faith carries it through transmogrifying darkness to the shrine of pure awareness beside two crystalline streams. When the inmost holy Sanctuary is shined through with God, and the church doors stand open, then the entire world has been charged with supreme radiance.

No conformity of belief is required to rest in the love of God. No community is needed except the true fellowship that comes from Heaven and the original equality of creation. There is no need to separate oneself out from the world, in anything except one's mind, so that the heart may draw ever nearer to the world as a whole and care for each and every one there according to his or her deepest need.

The original creation remains one with God, having been created by Him to be with Him who is eternal. God is one. But having been created by Him to share His Being and to be like Him, His creation can rightly be called an extension of Him. Though they have their own being, His children are one with Him, neither born of separate personality nor partaking of different interest, as are parents and children in this world. Jesus says, "The glory which thou hast given me I have given to them, that they may be one even as we are one" (John 17:22). In effect, Jesus imparted his experience of Sonship to those who would be one with him in God, in an apparent effort to hasten reconciliation.

Speaking of internal relationships, Paul asks: "Do you not realize that Jesus Christ is in you?" (2 Cor. 13:5). Such was the power of faith. Jesus Christ inhabited the most fundamental part of them, gave them whatever they needed by revealing the Presence within them, made them feel as one with others through this Presence until boundaries had vanished, and finally caused them to understand it all as a return to God. To encounter Jesus Christ in the Spirit was to encounter not a human being; simply the fact that he was making encounter with them, bodilessly in his postresurrection appearances, shows this. Jesus was no mere historical persona to them, though he was that as well; after his ascension into Heaven, he was perhaps even more alive in those who followed him. Certainly, he made them feel more alive, resurrected, reborn. Passages such as the following show him to be lifting his disciples beyond limitation:

> Abide in me, and I in you. . . . I am the vine, you are the branches. He who abides in me, and I in him, he it is that bears much fruit, for apart from me you can do nothing (John 15:4, 5).

Jesus was the one who had lifted them to God, through the Spirit at work in him, so why would they not be one with him if they shared the same Spirit? They retained at least some of their own thoughts, but he stood at the center of them, and at times their thoughts tended naturally (or preternaturally) to revolve around him, even when he seemed abstracted in transfigurative experience, or in postresurrection appearance, or in ascension into glory. Telling them they would be his "witnesses," telling them they would "receive power when the Holy Spirit has come upon" them (Acts 1:8), the resurrected Jesus ascended into heaven before them:

> And when he had said this, as they were looking on, he was lifted up, and a cloud took him out of their sight. And while they were gazing into heaven as he went, behold, two men stood by them in white robes, and said, "Men of Galilee, why do you stand looking into heaven? This Jesus, who was taken up from you into

heaven, will come in the same way as you saw him go into heaven"
(Acts 1:9–11).

They had known Jesus to be always pointing away from himself,
toward God, so that they could know what he knew, and share his peace.
His thoughts revolved around God, and once theirs rose to his, he would
appear again before them.

And so the body is to be used as a vessel for "transcendent power":
"But we have this treasure in earthen vessels, to show that the transcendent
power belongs to God and not to us" (2 Cor. 4:7). There is a drift away
from self and there is a resumption in transcendence of the original Self,
born with the light, breathed with Spirit, in the earliest eternal moments of
creation. This is how believers knew themselves to be "sons of light" (John
12:36). "For with thee is the fountain of life; in thy light do we see light"
(Ps. 36:9). They saw the original creation, knew that it was good, and, in a
sense, knew it as themselves.

They had been infused with the light of Being. They had, with Christ,
"put on the new nature, created after the likeness of God in true righteousness and holiness" (Eph. 4:24). The light of the Son shone from within
them, and they came to know themselves to be one with this light. "For you
are all sons of light and sons of the day; we are not of the night or of darkness" (1 Thess. 5:5). "For we cannot do anything against the truth, but only
for the truth" (2 Cor. 13:8). To experience the soaring Truth inherent in the
inner being is to be thoroughly transformed; it is this that is accomplished
by prayer in the inmost chamber.

Those in the light had therefore already "put on the new nature, which
is being renewed in knowledge after the image of its creator" (Col. 3:10).
Just the fact that this "new nature" is shared is new; the old nature had
defined itself according to shadowy differences and limitations and could not
experience this most fundamental, most human, yet more than human, sense
of joining in sharing. Paul said, "when they measure themselves by one
another, and compare themselves with one another, they are without understanding" (2 Cor. 10:12). There are obviously no true distinctions among
beings when "Christ is all, and in all" (Col, 3:11). They are universal, and
that universality is what makes "Christ in you, the hope of glory" (Col.
1:27).

It is the sons of light who recall the pre-beginnings. God said to Job:

> Where were you when I laid the foundation of the earth? Tell
> me, if you have understanding. . . . On what were its bases sunk,
> or who laid its cornerstone, when the morning stars sang together,
> and all the sons of God shouted for joy? (Job 38:4, 6–7)

To recall creation is to experience its universality, its inner truth. Early Christians had the sense that "in Christ Jesus you are all sons of God, through faith" (Gal. 3:26). Like God, they were filled with God. They spoke of "the fulness of him who fills all in all" (Eph. 1:23), meaning he who had ascended to his original nature.

It was the universal nature of this psychological sense of the nearness of God that drove Paul, and that guided him to see the application in all things. It was the universal nature of his experience of the internal Spirit that impelled Paul to want to share it universally. Paul spoke of it as once having been a "mystery hidden," but now "made manifest" in them, revealing the saving "glory of this mystery":

> I became a minister according to the divine office which was
> given to me for you, to make the word of God fully known, the
> mystery hidden for ages and generations but now made manifest
> to his saints. To them God chose to make known how great among
> the Gentiles are the riches of the glory of this mystery, which is
> Christ in you, the hope of glory (Col. 1:25–27).

Paul sees in "Christ in you" the fulfillment of ancient Judaism's tendency, especially in the Prophets, toward universalism. Ancient Israel was to shine like a beacon in the world, to reveal the way back to God. Paul and his contemporaries were imparting an ancient mystery that could "make the word of God fully known," which means that the "glory" of this Presence of God fulfilled the Prophets and the Scriptures as well as themselves.

The subtle light of the risen man stirred a slumbering capacity and power within the early Christians. A living idea was renewed in the mind. Jesus' kingdom of God appeared in their midst. It might not have been experienced the same way had he remained physically with them because their feelings and thoughts would have tended toward the outer perimeter, away from his inner axis of Being. And so, because he has risen to God, he shares his abstract Self and the resultant experience from the heavenly places. For, "No one can receive anything except what is given him from heaven" (John 3:27). Anything less would have been fundamentally unsatisfying.

The original mystery of Christianity pertains to the original mystery of the creation:

> Great indeed, we confess, is the mystery of our religion: He was manifested in the flesh, vindicated in the Spirit, seen by angels, preached among the nations, believed on in the world, taken up in glory (1 Tim. 3:16).

Jesus Christ was the light by which one could see the eternal, the living word by which one could hear. He was the one "vindicated in the Spirit, seen by angels" because he was not of any lower world; he represented and manifested for them a higher world that bound together and released together all those who hoped by his glory.

> So we do not lose heart. Though our outer nature is wasting away, our inner nature is being renewed every day. For this slight momentary affliction is preparing for us an eternal weight of glory beyond all comparison, because we look not to the things that are seen but to the things that are unseen; for the things that are seen are transient, but the things that are unseen are eternal (2 Cor. 4:16–18).

The things that are unseen are in actuality more real, because eternal. All the suffering inherent in existence is no match, not even a counterweight. It is in this vein that Paul says, "Let us cast off the works of darkness and put on the armor of light" (Rom. 13:12). The inner nature is being renewed each day as the mind becomes reaccustomed to the subtle eternal light that shines through it.

Saint Peter quotes a psalm of David:

I saw the Lord always before me, for he is at my right hand that I may not be shaken; therefore my heart was glad, and my tongue rejoiced; moreover my flesh will dwell in hope. For you will not abandon my soul to Hades, nor let your Holy One see corruption. You made known to me the ways of life; you will make me full of gladness with your presence (Acts 2:25–28).[1]

Experience leads; the gladness of His Presence always with them, it leads to "the ways of life." These ways are not really new; though they seemed new to early believers, these ways of life were part of their original creation and their true identity. They are the ways of life of a new world, rising entirely from within. The Ascended One from his lofty heights draws believers through the Spirit into his light, the light of Heaven.

Simon Peter and the other disciples did not recognize the postresurrection Jesus, except through the power they received through him, as for instance in his directing them to catch a net-straining quantity of fish where before they had caught none (John 21:11). Yet, "none of the disciples dared ask him, 'Who are you?' They knew it was the Lord" (21:12). They knew who he was through being made "full of gladness" with his Presence. "And the disciples were filled with joy and with the Holy Spirit" (Acts 13:52). Neither did they recognize him as in resurrected form he walked with them on the road to Emmaus while he reinterpreted the Scriptures for them (Luke 24:13–27). In truth, he had already ascended to his new, true Being.

The question of how much divinity there is in the mind when the mind is in the Spirit is less a philosophical question than an experiential one. It has to do with all that humanity is from within. Philosophy is murky about such nontheoretical matters, but experience thrills to the very question, because it is itself Divine Response. God is known through His Presence; the Lord of Heaven need not be speculated upon, and neither need our true inner being. True knowledge does not hang on words and concepts, but even these can reveal the guide lights of heaven gently illuminating the straight and direct path within ourselves. God is known directly, and in this knowledge is direct realization of Self as well.

And so it is that "None of us lives to himself, and none of us dies to himself" (Rom. 14:7); that is how it is within the Community of Being, our commonwealth in Heaven (Phil. 3:20).

> So let no one boast of men. For all things are yours, . . . and you are Christ's; and Christ is God's (1 Cor. 3:21, 23).

One does not exist without the other. They are in eternal relationship. And so the practice of the presence is a simple resetting of intention, until another will claims that intention as its own:

> If then you have been raised with Christ, seek the things that are above, where Christ is, seated at the right hand of God. Set your mind on things that are above, not on things that are on earth (Col. 3:1–2).

That is, "Have this mind among yourselves, which is yours in Christ Jesus" (Phil. 2:5). What does the abstracted mind think except thoughts of God and the spiritual creation? Having suffused oneself with Heaven, by a simple agreement of will, the one joined with Christ is graced with the gifts of Heaven:

> Every good endowment and every perfect gift is from above, coming down from the Father of lights with whom there is no variation or shadow due to change (James 1:17).

"The Father of lights" sends perfect gifts of original light that shine directly into the mind, and so have the power to draw the heart's return. Joined in Christ, the Sons of Light were "taken up to heaven" (Mark 16:19), there to be "imitators of God, as beloved children" (Eph. 5:1).

Heaven

The kingdom of God is inside the individual but it is not confined to physical existence. Once found inside, it begins to manifest in glory in everyone. It is truly spread out over all the Earth, if it is within all of our equals. Gently unfolding from within the mind, the kingdom allows for a new way of thinking, feeling, living, and relating—or simply being—in the world. Because it is the depth within each, it subsumes individuality in universality. Because it is the depth within everyone, every personal encounter within existence becomes a chance to encounter Presence in Heaven:

> Come, O blessed of my Father, inherit the kingdom prepared
> for you from the foundation of the world; for I was hungry and you
> gave me food, I was thirsty and you gave me drink, I was a stranger
> and you welcomed me, I was naked and you clothed me, I was sick
> and you visited me, I was in prison and you came to me (Matt.
> 25:34–36).

Jesus continues: "Truly, I say to you, as you did it to one of the least of these my brethren, you did it to me" (25:40). He exists in relation to them, those who are lost and who are judged by the world's standards to be least. They are more truly identified as one, through the Christ, with oneself; this can happen only from a deep place within. This universal experience cannot be contained; it abides within each being insofar as it is opened to. Each need only knock or ask, and each is revealed to be one with it, through it with others, through others with God.

Because of this universal experience and its universal emotion, the disciples sense the limitlessness of eternal Being upon them:

> We know that we have passed out of death into life, because
> we love the brethren. He who does not love abides in death (1
> John 3:14).

Death is the fallen fruit of separation, incomprehensible from within the experience of limitless Being and the Divine Love inherent in interrelationship. It is only from the viewpoint of the flesh, specifically the separated flesh, that death seems sure. But the vantage point of the eternal Spirit assures of truth and the reality of eternity. It saves—by assuring of deep, abiding holiness at the depth of all being. 1 John 3:9 has it:

> No one born of God commits sin; for God's nature abides in
> him, and he cannot sin because he is born of God.

And if sin is impossible in light of the original creation, then so is death, because the thought of death depends on separation from the Whole.

Sin is utter delusion; every aspect of it is a lie. What is this unnatural, irrational fear of God that keeps Him distant? It is similar in nature and purpose to fear of Self, the deep-seated terror of looking deeply within. But there is nothing to fear when "Thou hast set our iniquities before thee, our secret sins in the light of thy countenance" (Ps. 90:8).

> For it is impossible to restore again to repentance those who have once been enlightened, who have tasted the heavenly gift, and have become partakers of the Holy Spirit (Heb. 6:4).

Those who have been "enlightened" are those who have been raised by the Spirit. They have moved to a new level of Being. The light that shines from the countenance and presence of God reveals the way to ascension, rising again to God, knowing not of guilt, fear, and separation, neither ever really becoming something it is not.

> But the path of the righteous is like the light of dawn, which shines brighter and brighter until full day (Prov. 4:18).

The Psalmist prays for the light of God to lead his people to his spiritual house:

> Oh send out thy light and thy truth; let them lead me, let them bring me to thy holy hill and to thy dwelling! (Ps. 43:3)

The dwelling of God is the mystical house of God that is shared through the Spirit within. Praise rings out eternally where happiness fills the house and connects all its inhabitants. Can Heaven be far away if joy already exists within? "To thee I lift up my eyes, O thou who art enthroned in the heavens!" (Ps. 123:1). Lifting one's eyes to the heights within lights the way to the Peace of joining in happy and majestic Presence. Heaven is very close for those who share the same Spirit. One need only lift one's eyes to see it. Heaven is everywhere if it is inside everyone.

Paul states that "the kingdom of God is . . . righteousness and peace and joy in the Holy Spirit" (Rom. 14:17). He says that "the kingdom of God does not consist in talk but in power" (1 Cor. 4:20), and he says that the coming of the kingdom negates all worldly power (15:24). The kingdom of God is like Heaven in that both are entered by stepping out of one's former world. The kingdom is the threshold of another reality, known from within. Only "the imperishable" can "inherit the kingdom of God" (15:50); they are deathless in Spirit.

The Psalmist writes of the eternal relationship: "O give thanks to the God of heaven, For his steadfast love endures forever" (Ps. 136:26). Heaven is a state of unbroken and blameless relationship with God:

> No, in all these things we are more than conquerors through him who loved us. For I am sure that neither death, nor life, nor angels, nor principalities, nor things present, nor things to come, nor powers, nor height, nor depth, nor anything else in creation, will be able to separate us from the love of God in Christ Jesus our Lord (Rom. 8:37–39).

Believer and Creator, through Christ are joined in eternal, unbreakable love. And so: "There is therefore now no condemnation for those who are in Christ Jesus" (Rom. 8:1). Only the ounce of flesh can maintain the delusion of separation from God:

> But you are not in the flesh, you are in the Spirit, if in fact the Spirit of God dwells in you (Rom. 8:9).

One's sense of life and one's identity had to change to accommodate one's experience of Spirit, so real was it.

The news of this internal transformation by Spirit meant that the kingdom of God was being borne into the world by the human being who was allowing his or her mind to be used for the transcendent power of the Spirit. This is what it means to be "sent" by God. Paul asks: "And how can men preach unless they are sent? As it is written, 'How beautiful are the feet of those who preach good news!'" (Rom. 10:15). It is the Spirit who sends out and the Spirit who speaks, the Spirit who, replacing the Self, grants newness of life, sustaining forever, the Spirit within all who hear.

Yet he commanded the skies above, and opened the doors of heaven; and he rained down upon them manna to eat, and gave them the grain of heaven (Ps. 78:23–24).

Paul's spiritual experience had revealed to him the universality of the Son:

But when he who had set me apart before I was born, and had called me through his grace, was pleased to reveal his Son to me, in order that I might preach him among the Gentiles, I did not confer with flesh and blood . . . (Gal. 1:15–16).

Paul speaks of his experience as being entirely spiritual; he "did not confer with flesh and blood." It was Spirit that taught him "the deep things of God" (1 Cor. 2:10, AV). Paul's universal sense of Spirit led him to interpret the Old with the New:

I want you to know, brethren, that our fathers were all under the cloud, and all passed through the sea, and all were baptized into Moses in the cloud and in the sea, and all ate the same spiritual food and all drank the same spiritual drink. For they drank from the supernatural Rock which followed them, and the Rock was the Christ (1 Cor. 10:1–4).

The universal Spirit he experienced led him into his new purpose as a bearer of light:

For it is the God who said, "Let light shine out of darkness," who has shone in our hearts to give the light of the knowledge of the glory of God in the face of Christ (2 Cor. 4:6).

The spiritual worldview represented in this passage is reminiscent of Ps. 108:5: "Be exalted, O God, above the heavens! Let thy glory be all over the earth!"

The spiritual way of life is described by Meister Eckhart as the birth of the Son of God in the believer, so that, echoing Paul's experience that "in everything God works for good with those who love him, and are called according to his purpose" (Rom. 8:28):

> all who experience this birth [of the Son of God in us] . . . together with all around them, earthy as you please, are quickly turned toward it. Indeed, what was formerly a hindrance becomes now a help. Your face is turned so squarely toward it that, whatever you see or hear, you only get this birth out of it. Everything stands for God and you see only God in all the world.[2]

God re-creates the world through the believer. Those who dwell in the Spirit have no intention within them apart from God, because they are close to the heart of everyone and everything, which has no Being apart from Him. Their mind is transformed by the Presence of Spirit until it shines with divine likeness.

What can prepare an individual for the experience of Heaven? Only the Spirit, which knows what Heaven is. And so, Paul tells the Galatians: "Do not be deceived; God is not mocked, for whatever a man sows, that he will also reap" (6:7), for "he who sows to the Spirit will from the Spirit reap eternal life" (6:8). In the end, as in the beginning, "God will show your splendor everywhere under heaven" (Baruch 5:3); He does this to call all life back to Heaven to live as one with Him.

When the Spirit reveals one's union with God, where is God not seen? As the prophet says:

> Can a man hide himself in secret places so that I cannot see him? says the Lord. Do I not fill heaven and earth? says the Lord (Jer. 23:24).

This reminds us of:

> If I ascend to heaven, thou art there!
> If I make my bed in Sheol, thou art there! (Ps. 139:8)

Is it not more dangerous to one's self to retain self-imposed limitations and delusions, than to give them all up to the Father of Light? Who is so bound to despair that they would not escape it if they could? And so the believer in Spirit is entitled to:

> Receive what the Lord has entrusted to you and be joyful, giving thanks to him who has called you to heavenly kingdoms (2 Esd. 2:37).

Ps. 97:6 says that: "The heavens proclaim his righteousness; and all the peoples behold his glory." Universality of salvation is found in the universal sense within each individual.

That is why the least and the lost are not really least or lost. They shine like lights in Heaven. From the vantage point of Spirit, we are all the same. The one who is hungry is the one who is full, the one who thirsts is like the one who never thirsts again. The interval between those who mourn and weep becoming those who laugh is not one of time, it is one of internal transformation—a mere but mighty change of mind.

Jesus says in John 4:35–36:

> I tell you, lift up your eyes, and see how the fields are white for harvest. He who reaps receives wages, and gathers fruit for eternal life, so that sower and reaper may rejoice together.

Again there is here a call to a community of Being, of giving and receiving, of the eternal laws applied to Earth. These universal laws appear as "springs flowing with milk and honey, and seven mighty mountains on which roses and lilies grow; by these I will fill your children with joy" (2 Esd. 2:19). And so believers are delivered from "the dominion of darkness" and lifted upon the rays of Spirit to Heaven itself:

> He has delivered us from the dominion of darkness and transferred us to the kingdom of his beloved Son, in whom we have redemption, the forgiveness of sins (Col. 1:13–14).

In the Son is salvation; in this new identity as Son is the forgiveness of sins. Jesus' emphasis on forgiveness, even of one's enemies, is one of the most distinctive aspects of his teaching. And, as we have seen, he associates forgiveness with being forgiven and being revealed to be a Son of God.

Those who forgive are like those who are forgiven. Their understanding is light, and their transparency to God is light. This recalls Matt. 4:16 (quoting Isaiah):

> the people who sat in darkness have seen a great light, and for those who sat in the region and shadow of death light has dawned.

Paul prays for believers in the Spirit that:

> their hearts may be encouraged as they are knit together in love, to have all the riches of assured understanding and the knowledge of God's mystery, of Christ, in whom are hid all the treasures of wisdom and knowledge (Col. 2:2–3).

Once again, God is not known through conceptual intellect, but rather He is known through experience and encounter in love:

> If any one imagines that he knows something, he does not yet know as he ought to know. But if one loves God, one is known by him (1 Cor. 8:2–3).

When one is known by God, then one will know Him.

> Ascribe to the Lord, O heavenly beings,
> Ascribe to the Lord, O sons of God,
> Ascribe to the Lord glory and strength (Ps. 29:1).

Experience that is also encounter would, of course, be weighted greatly on the Heavenly part in the relationship. There is no effort required except an opening of oneself to the searching light of God, and to one's transformation through His Living Spirit. Here is the fulfillment of the prophet's saying:

> Arise, shine; for your light has come, and the glory of the Lord has risen upon you (Isa. 60:1).

Paul says that the believer will "bear the image of the man of heaven" (1 Cor. 15:49). He says, "Here indeed we groan, and long to put on our heavenly dwelling" (2 Cor. 5:2). Yet, through experience of Spirit, even now, "we know that if the earthly tent we live in is destroyed, we have a building from God, a house not made with hands, eternal in the heavens" (5:1). That is because Spirit brings experience of the eternal, and of course, "what is permanent must have much more splendor" (2 Cor. 3:11).

> Now the Lord is the Spirit, and where the Spirit of the Lord is, there is freedom. And we all, with unveiled face, reflecting the glory of the Lord, are being changed into his likeness from one degree of glory to another; for this comes from the Lord who is the Spirit (2 Cor. 3:17–18).

Understanding will take on the sheen of brilliant permanence. How but in the realm of the eternal "can you believe if I tell you heavenly things?" (John 3:12). Those who focus on lesser things, such as personal pride and status, when they "compare themselves with one another, they are without understanding" (2 Cor. 10:12). Yet such knowledge and experience of God through His Spirit are meant to reach out universally:

> For it is all for your sake, so that as grace extends to more and more people it may increase thanksgiving, to the glory of God (2 Cor. 4:15).

Grace is meant to increase upon the Earth, therefore to increase at once the understanding and gratitude of the Children of God. The Care of God is meant to extend to everyone, as it does in Heaven. Within such gratitude is found a familiar universal and eternal emotion, beatifically expressed by Paul:

> Love never ends; as for prophecies, they will pass away; as for tongues, they will cease; as for knowledge, it will pass away. For our knowledge is imperfect and our prophecy is imperfect; but when the perfect comes, the imperfect will pass away. When I was a child, I spoke like a child, I thought like a child, I reasoned like

a child; when I became a man, I gave up childish ways. For now we see through a mirror dimly, but then face to face. Now I know in part; then I shall understand fully, even as I have been fully understood. So faith, hope, love abide, these three; but the greatest of these is love (1 Cor. 13:8–13).

Because the Will of God is reconciliation, love is its fulfillment. "And above all these put on love, which binds everything together in perfect harmony" (Col. 3:14). Love, like Heaven, like Spiritual Presence, is neither definable nor describable in ordinary terms. Love unifies by its very presence, and it convinces the mind of the basic equality of Spirit. Spirit is Spirit, and where it goes it goes, and where it is seen it is seen. And where it is seen, within its light, there is no difference one from another. Filling the Earth, it lights the sky as it ascends all the way to God.

For thus said the Lord God, the Holy One of Israel, "In returning and rest you shall be saved; in quietness and in trust shall be your strength" (Isa. 30:15).

Endnotes

Introduction
1. Bernard McGinn, *The Foundations of Mysticism,* p. 65.
2. Jacob Needleman, *The Heart of Philosophy,* p. 85.

Chapter 1
1. Lex Hixon, *Coming Home,* p. 157.
2. John E. Smith, *Experience and God,* p. 27.
3. Robert F. Davidson, *Rudolf Otto's Interpretation of Religion,* p. 167.
4. Helmut Koester, "Gnomai Diaphoroi," in James M. Robinson and Helmut Koester, *Trajectories through Early Christianity,* p. 124.
5. Dana Gioia, "The Epistle of Paul the Apostle to the Philippians" in Alfred Corn, *Incarnation,* p. 182.
6. J. G. Davies, *The Early Christian Church,* p. 57f.
7. Joseph Wilson Trigg, *Origen,* p. 190.
8. Wilfred Cantwell Smith, *The Meaning and End of Religion,* pp. 42–43.
9. Ibid., p. 123.
10. Meister Eckhart in Raymond B. Blakney, *Meister Eckhart,* p. 129.
11. Andrew Louth, *The Origins of the Christian Mystical Tradition from Plato to Denys,* p. xv.
12. William James, *Varieties of Religious Experience,* p. 298.
13. John A. Sanford, *The Kingdom Within,* p. 10.

14. Arthur J. Deikman, *The Observing Self,* p. 49.
15. Ibid., p. 46.
16. Ibid., p. 48.
17. Frits Staal, *Exploring Mysticism,* p. 57.
18. Jacob Needleman, *The Heart of Philosophy,* p. 183.
19. Harvey D. Egan, *What Are They Saying about Mysticism?* p. 2.
20. Bernard McGinn, *The Foundations of Mysticism,* p. 17.
21. John E. Smith, p. 49.
22. Ibid., p. 49.
23. John A. Sanford, p. 73.
24. C. G. Jung, *Civilization in Transition,* p. 137.
25. Language modernized.

Chapter 2

1. C. H. Dodd, *The Parables of the Kingdom,* pp. 37–38.
2. John Bowker, quoted in John Shea, *An Experience Named Spirit,* p. 28.
3. James D. G. Dunn. *Jesus and the Spirit,* p. 38.
4. Ibid., p. 88.
5. James D. G. Dunn, *Unity and Diversity in the New Testament,* p. 186.
6. John E. Smith, *Experience and God,* p. 80.
7. Alexander J. McKelway, *The Systematic Theology of Paul Tillich,* p. 99.
8. Ibid.
9. Marcus J. Borg, *Meeting Jesus Again for the First Time,* p. 29.
10. Stevan L. Davies, *Jesus the Healer,* p. 97.
11. Ibid., p. 88.
12. John Dominic Crossan, *In Parables,* p. 52.
13. Ibid., p. 22; my italics.

Chapter 3

1. Paul Tillich, "The Eternal Now" in *The Eternal Now,* p. 128.
2. James D. G. Dunn, *Jesus' Call to Discipleship,* p. 19.
3. Ibid., p. 22.
4. Ibid., p. 24.
5. J. G. Davies, *The Early Christian Church,* p. 56.
6. John Dominic Crossan, *In Parables,* p. 70; my italics.
7. Henri de Lubac, *The Religion of Teilhard de Chardin,* p. 66.
8. Denis Edwards, *Human Experience of God,* p. 65.
9. 1Clement XI.17 in *The Lost Books of the Bible.*

Chapter 4

1. Albert Schweitzer, *The Mysticism of Paul the Apostle,* p. 168.
2. Stevan L. Davies, *Jesus the Healer,* p. 177.
3. Schweitzer, p. 167.

Chapter 5

1. James D. Smart, *The Past, Present, and Future of Biblical Theology,* p. 108.

2. Ibid.

3. Andrew Louth, *The Origins of the Christian Mystical Tradition from Plato to Denys,* p. 64.

4. Ibid.

5. Northrop Frye, *The Great Code,* p. 220.

6. Ibid.

7. Ibid.

8. John Macquarrie, *An Existentialist Theology,* p. 244.

9. Northrop Frye, p. 223.

10. Meister Eckhart in Edmund Colledge and Bernard McGinn, *Meister Eckhart,* p. 29.

11. C. F. D. Moule, *The Birth of the New Testament,* pp. 52–53.

12. John Macquarrie, p. 57.

13. James D. Smart, p. 91.

14. Ibid., p. 93.

15. John P. Meier, *A Marginal Jew,* p. 147.

16. Joachim Jeremias in Meier, p. 147.

17. John P. Meier, p. 176.

18. James D. Smart, p. 90.

19. Stevan L. Davies, *Jesus the Healer,* p. 198.

20. Ibid.

Chapter 6

1. S. H. Hooke, *Middle Eastern Mythology,* p. 109.

2. Andrew Louth, *The Origins of the Christian Mystical Tradition from Plato to Denys,* p. 61.

3. Ibid.

4. Paul Tillich, "From Essence to Existence (The Fall)," in Mark Kline Taylor, *Paul Tillich,* p. 197.

5. Northrop Frye, *The Great Code,* p. 110.

6. William Barrett, *Irrational Man,* pp. 71–72.

7. Meister Eckhart in Raymond B. Blakney, *Meister Eckhart,* p. 215.

8. Elaine Pagels, *Adam, Eve, and the Serpent,* p. 65.

9. Bernard McGinn, *The Foundations of Mysticism,* p. 38.

10. Ibid.

11. Paul Tillich, "Estrangement and Sin," in Mark Kline Taylor, p. 199.

12. Meister Eckhart in Raymond B. Blakney, p. 204.

13. James D. G. Dunn, *Jesus and the Spirit,* p. 48.

14. 1Clement IX.2b in *The Lost Books of the Bible.*

15. S. H. Hooke, p. 115.

16. Northrop Frye, p. 171.

17. Ibid., p. 112.

18. Ibid., p. 145.

19. Schuyler Brown, *The Origins of Christianity,* p. 62.

20. James D. G. Dunn, p. 43.

21. Thomas J. J. Altizer, *Oriental Mysticism and Biblical Eschatology*, p. 73.

22. Ibid., p. 83.

23. Paul Tillich, "Forgetting and Being Forgotten," in *The Eternal Now*, p. 35.

24. Gjertrud Schnackenberg, "Commenary of the Epistle of Paul the Apostle to the Colossians," in Alfred Corn, *Incarnation*, p. 206.

Chapter 7

1. Samuel Terrien, *The Elusive Presence*, p. 42.

2. Robert F. Davidson, *Rudolf Otto's Interpretation of Religion*, p. 202.

3. Samuel Terrien, p.16.

4. Ibid., p. 26.

5. John A. Sanford, *The Kingdom Within*, p. 35.

6. Schuyler Brown, *The Origins of Christianity*, p. 65.

7. Stevan L. Davies, *Jesus the Healer*, p. 183.

8. Alexander J. McKelway, *The Systematic Theology of Paul Tillich*, p. 86.

9. John Macquarrie, *An Existentialist Theology*, p. 193.

10. Northrop Frye, *The Great Code*, Frye, p. 220.

11. Joseph Wilson Trigg, *Origen*, p. 101.

Chapter 8

1. William Barrett, *Irrational Man*, pp. 112–113 (quoting Blaise Pascal).

2. Stevan L. Davies, *Jesus the Healer*, p. 129 (explaining the psychology of Milton Erickson).

3. Samuel Terrien, *The Elusive Presence*, p. 450.

4. Meister Eckhart in Raymond B. Blakney, *Meister Eckhart*, p. 131.

Chapter 9

1. *Enneads* 3.8.5, quoted in Bernard McGinn, *The Foundations of Mysticism*, p. 53.

2. Denis Edwards, *Human Experience of God*, p. 93.

3. *The Lost Books of the Bible*.

4. John E. Smith, *Experience and God*, p. 79.

5. Meister Eckhart in Raymond B. Blakney, *Meister Eckhart*, p. 107.

6. Arthur J. Deikman, *The Observing Self*, p. 10.

7. Ibid.

8. Margaret Lewis Furse, *Mysticism*, p. 192.

Chapter 10

1. John Macquarrie, *An Existentialist Theology*, p. 109.

2. Jacques Guillet, *The Consciousness of Jesus*, p. 201.

3. Stevan L. Davies, *Jesus the Healer*, p. 157.

4. Michael Novak, *The Experience of Nothingness*, p. 55; my italics.

5. Lex Hixon, *Coming Home*, p. 154.

6. R. Melvin Kaiser, "Introduction" in Stanley Romaine Hopper, *The Way of Transfiguration*, p. 7.

7. Clement of Alexandria, quoted in Robert Payne, *The Fathers of the Eastern Church,* p. 29; my italics.

8. Ibid.

9. Pronouns modernized.

Conclusion

1. Language modernized.

2. Meister Eckhart in Raymond B. Blakney, *Meister Eckhart,* p. 123.

Bibliography

All Bible quotations, unless otherwise noted, from *The Holy Bible: Revised Standard Version*. New York: William Collins & Sons/Division of Christian Education of the National Council of Churches of Christ in the United States of America, 1973.

Adams, James Luther, Wilhelm Pauck, and Roger Lincoln Shinn, eds. *The Thought of Paul Tillich*. San Francisco: Harper & Row, 1985.

Altizer, Thomas J. J. *Oriental Mysticism and Biblical Eschatology*. Philadelphia: Westminster Press, 1961.

Barrett, William. *Irrational Man: A Study in Existential Philosophy*. Garden City, N.Y.: Doubleday, 1958.

Blakney, Raymond B., trans. *Meister Eckhart: A Modern Translation*. New York: Harper & Bros., 1941.

Borg, Marcus J. *Meeting Jesus Again for the First Time*. San Francisco: HarperSanFrancisco, 1994.

Brown, D. Mackenzie, ed. *Ultimate Concern: Tillich in Dialogue*. New York: Harper & Row, 1965.

Brown, Schuyler. *The Origins of Christianity: A Historical Introduction to the New Testament*. New York: Oxford University Press, 1984.

Colledge, Edmund, and Bernard McGinn, trans. *Meister Eckhart: The Essential Sermons, Commentaries, Treatises, and Defense.* New York: Paulist Press, 1981.

Corn, Alfred, ed. *Incarnation: Contemporary Writers on the New Testament.* New York: Viking, 1990.

Crim, Keith, ed. *Abingdon Dictionary of Living Religions.* Nashville, Tenn.: Abingdon Press, 1981.

Crossan, John Dominic. *In Parables: The Challenge of the Historical Jesus.* San Francisco: Harper & Row, 1973.

———. *Jesus: A Revolutionary Biography.* HarperSanFrancisco/HarperCollins, 1994.

Davidson, Robert F. *Rudolf Otto's Interpretation of Religion.* Princeton, N.J.: Princeton University Press, 1947.

Davies, J. G. *The Early Christian Church.* New York: Holt, Rinehart & Winston, 1965.

Davies, Stevan L. *Jesus the Healer: Possession, Trance, and the Origins of Christianity.* New York: Continuum, 1995.

Deikman, Arthur J. *The Observing Self: Mysticism and Psychotherapy.* Boston: Beacon Press, 1982.

Dewar, Lindsay. *The Holy Spirit and Modern Thought: An Inquiry into the Historical, Theological, and Psychological Aspects of the Christian Doctrine of the Holy Spirit.* New York: Harper, 1960.

Dodd, C. H. *The Parables of the Kingdom.* New York: Scribner, 1961.

Dunn, James D. G. *Jesus and the Spirit.* Philadelphia: Westminster Press, 1975.

———. *Unity and Diversity in the New Testament.* Philadelphia: Westminster Press, 1977.

———. *Jesus' Call to Discipleship.* New York: Cambridge University Press, 1992.

Edwards, Denis. *Human Experience of God.* New York: Paulist Press, 1983.

Egan, Harvey D. *What Are They Saying about Mysticism?* New York: Paulist Press, 1982.

Frye, Northrop. *The Great Code: The Bible and Literature.* New York: Harcourt Brace Jovanovich, 1982.

Furse, Margaret Lewis. *Mysticism: Window on a World View.* Nashville, Tenn.: Abingdon Press, 1977.

Guillet, Jacques. *The Consciousness of Jesus.* Bonin, Edmond, trans. New York: Newman Press, 1972.

Halpern, Paul. *Time Journeys: A Search for Cosmic Destiny and Meaning.* New York: McGraw-Hill, 1990.

Harper's Bible Dictionary. Paul J. Achtemeier, ed. San Francisco: Harper & Row, 1985.

Hixon, Lex. *Coming Home: The Experience of Enlightenment in Sacred Traditions.* Garden City, NY: Anchor Press/Doubleday, 1978.

Hooke, S. H. *Middle Eastern Mythology.* New York: Penguin Books, 1963.

Hopper, Stanley Romaine. *The Way of Transfiguration: Religious Imagination as Theopoiesis.* Keiser, R. Melvin and Tony Stoneburner, eds. Louisville, Ky.: Westminster/John Knox Press, 1992.

James, William. *Varieties of Religious Experience: A Study in Human Nature.* New York: New American Library, 1958.

Jung, C. G. *Civilization in Transition, Collected Works of C. G. Jung,* Vol. 10. New York: Random House, 1964.

Koester, Helmut. "Gnomai Diaphoroi." In James M. Robinson and Helmut Koester, *Trajectories through Early Christianity.* Philadelphia: Fortress Press, 1971.

Krishnamurti, J. *The First and Last Freedom.* New York: Harper, 1954.

Kugel, James L., and Rowan A. Greer. *Early Biblical Interpretation.* Philadelphia: Westminster Press, 1986.

The Lost Books of the Bible. New York: Alpha House, 1926.

Louth, Andrew. *The Origins of the Christian Mystical Tradition from Plato to Denys.* New York: Oxford University Press, 1981.

Lubac, Henri de. *The Religion of Teilhard de Chardin.* Garden City, N.Y.: Image Books, 1968.

Macquarrie, John. *An Existentialist Theology: A Comparison of Heidegger and Bultmann.* New York: Harper & Row, 1965.

McGinn, Bernard. *The Foundations of Mysticism,* Vol. I of *The Presence of God: A History of Western Christian Mysticism.* New York: Crossroad, 1991.

McKelway, Alexander J. *The Systematic Theology of Paul Tillich.* Richmond, Va.: John Knox Press, 1964.

Meier, John P. *A Marginal Jew: Rethinking the Historical Jesus.* New York: Doubleday, 1994.

Moule, C. F. D. *The Birth of the New Testament.* San Francisco: Harper & Row, 1982.

Needleman, Jacob. *The Heart of Philosophy.* New York: Knopf, 1982.

Novak, Michael. *The Experience of Nothingness.* New York: Harper & Row, 1970.

Pagels, Elaine. *Adam, Eve, and the Serpent.* New York: Random House, 1988.

Payne, Robert. *The Fathers of the Eastern Church.* New York: Dorset Press, 1957.

Robinson, John A. T. *Twelve More New Testament Studies.* London: SCM Press, 1984.

Sanford, John A. *The Kingdom Within: The Inner Meaning of Jesus' Sayings.* San Francisco: Harper & Row, 1987.

Schweitzer, Albert. *The Mysticism of Paul the Apostle.* William Montgomery, trans. New York: Macmillan, [1931] 1955.

Shea, John. *An Experience Named Spirit.* Chicago: Thomas More Press, 1983.

Smart, James D. *The Past, Present, and Future of Biblical Theology.* Philadelphia: Westminster Press, 1979.

Smart, Ninian, and Steven Konstantine. *Christian Systematic Theology in a World Context.* London: Marshall Pickering/HarperCollins, 1991.

Smith, John E. *Experience and God.* New York: Oxford University Press, 1968.

Smith, Wilfred Cantwell. *The Meaning and End of Religion.* New York: Macmillan, 1962.

Staal, Frits. *Exploring Mysticism: A Methodological Essay.* Berkeley: University of California Press, 1975.

Taylor, Mark Kline. *Paul Tillich: Theologian of the Boundaries.* San Francisco: Collins, 1987.

Terrien, Samuel. *The Elusive Presence: Toward a New Biblical Theology.* San Francisco: Harper & Row, 1978.

Tillich, Paul. *The Courage to Be.* New Haven, Conn.: Yale University Press, 1952.

———. *The Dynamics of Faith.* New York: Harper & Row, 1957.

———. *The Eternal Now.* New York: Scribner, 1963.

Trigg, Joseph Wilson. *Origen: The Bible and Philosophy in the Third-Century Church.* Atlanta, Ga.: J. Knox, 1983.

Wilson, A. N. *Jesus.* New York: W. W. Norton, 1992.

Index

About the Author

Michael Roden graduated from Kent State University with a master's in community counseling and an undergraduate degree in psychology. His background in psychology and counseling and years of self-study provide him with an extraordinary understanding of the inner world and its mystical processes, and position him well to understand the spiritual psychology within the Scriptures.

Michael is familiar with Eastern and Western religions, having studied theological, philosophical, and literary scholarship for more than two decades. He has been writing and studying Scriptures and poetry for more than 25 years. Besides articles for metaphysical newspapers and periodicals, he has written two published books: *Jesus and Ourselves: An Understanding of Christianity* (1996) and *Songs of the Morning: Meditations for Healing and Self-Knowledge* (1997).

Michael works as a professional clinical counselor in Columbus, Ohio.

Hampton Roads Publishing Company

. . . for the evolving human spirit

HAMPTON ROADS PUBLISHING COMPANY publishes books on a variety of subjects, including metaphysics, spirituality, health, visionary fiction, and other related topics.

For a copy of our latest trade catalog, call toll-free, 800-766-8009, or send your name and address to:

HAMPTON ROADS PUBLISHING COMPANY, INC.
1125 STONEY RIDGE ROAD • CHARLOTTESVILLE, VA 22902
e-mail: hrpc@hrpub.com • www.hrpub.com